Study Guide to Accompany
Critical Thinking
Sixth Edition

by Brook Noel Moore
and Richard Parker

Nickolas Pappas
City College of New York

Mayfield Publishing Company
Mountain View, California
London • Toronto

Mayfield Publishing company
1280 Villa Street
Mountain View, California 94041

Cover illustration: © Terry Hoff, courtesy Freda Scott.

Text credits: P. 26 "State of the Sleaze," *New York Times*, January 28, 1997. Copyright © 1997 by the New York Times Co. Reprinted with permission. P. 51 "McCall Puts on His Partisan Hat," *New York Post*, February 10, 1997. Copyright © 1997 NYP Holdings, Inc. Reprinted with permission of the New York Post.

CONTENTS

PREFACE

HOW TO USE THIS STUDY GUIDE

This study guide accompanies the sixth edition of Moore and Parker's *Critical Thinking*. Each chapter in the study guide will take you through the corresponding chapter in *Critical Thinking* with a digest of that chapter's main ideas, further discussions of some points, and review questions and exercises.

This study guide is not a substitute for the textbook and should not be used as one. A work so brief can't contain all the explanations, examples, and exercises found in *Critical Thinking*. But the student who reads the book and then dutifully uses this guide to review and study its material should feel confident of mastering critical thinking.

Take a moment to get acquainted with the format of this guide. Every chapter contains the same elements, presented in the same order; once you see what they are and what they are there for, you will be able to find the specific help you are looking for more efficiently.

Introductory paragraph

The chapter begins with a few comments about the contents of the particular chapter and its place in the book.

CHAPTER SUMMARY

The Chapter Summary presents the complete content of the chapter in standard outline form. It condenses the discussions found in *Critical Thinking*, but includes all the principal claims of the chapter, explanations for them, and—where useful—examples.

KEY WORDS AND IDEAS

This section complements the glossary in *Critical Thinking*. It differs from the glossary in that the words are explained in the chapter they appear in, typically in somewhat different words than the glossary uses, so that the reader can see a concept from a different perspective.

REVIEW QUESTIONS

Once you have gone over the chapter outline and a reminder of its central vocabulary, you can use the Review Questions to make sure you have understood the chapter. These five or so questions touch on many of the main ideas in the chapter. These are not trick questions; nor are they meant to replace exercises. They often work best as the opposite of a test: Rather than wait until you have studied the material to answer the Review Questions, you might start there to see how much you have absorbed so far.

Sample answers come at the very end of the study guide's chapter, after the answers to all the exercises.

COMMONLY ASKED QUESTIONS

Here you will find questions that students often have after reading the book or working on its exercises.

Some of these are practical matters. For instance, the logic chapters will contain additional hints about how to make a proof work; the pseudoreasoning chapters look at fallacies that often get confused with one another, and suggest how to keep them distinct. One question in Chapter 1 concerns sensible tests for telling a matter of fact from a matter of pure opinion.

Other questions are conceptual worries about what the material means or implies. What do we do when all the experts in a field might be wrong (Chapter 3)? Does the wrongness of ad hominem arguments mean that we can't discount anyone's character flaws when deciding on moral issues (Chapter 6)? Why are there two kinds of logic, and what is the advantage of each (Chapter 10)?

Strictly speaking, you do not need these discussions in order to succeed at a critical-thinking course, unless some perplexity is getting in the way of your absorbing and using the material. The interested student can read these more philosophical sections with profit, while the uninterested one may skip them without harm.

TIPS ON APPLICATIONS

The study of critical thinking should be applicable to real-world situations as well as to the learning challenges of other courses. This section devotes some space to one issue per chapter that may arise in the course of applying the techniques and methods of critical thinking.

In this section, you can expect to find an example from daily life—television advertising, newspaper editorials, contemporary debates—that calls for critical thinking. The Tips on Applications section may suggest an exercise that brings critical thinking to bear on this example, or it may merely alert you to the role of reasoned discussion about it.

EXERCISES

Sample exercises from the book

Some of the book's exercises have answers in the back. Some of these in turn are treated in this section. You will first find the exercise stated, together with the book's answer, and then additional remarks about how to reach that answer, and what might make a given exercise more complex, or trickier, than it first appears. The purpose of reviewing these selected exercises is simply to help you if you feel lost when doing the homework.

Additional exercises

The exercises found in this section should remind you of the exercises in the book. Many students like to leave this section until they have finished the chapter, and then use it as a sample test.

Answers to additional exercises

Here you will find answers to **all** of the study guide's own exercises.

Answers to review questions

When turning to this last section, always bear in mind that it contains sample or model answers. You may well have written something different and still gotten the answer right. But if you find something in this final section that you did not include in your answer, check to make sure you have learned all the relevant material.

CHAPTER 1

WHAT IS CRITICAL THINKING?

Clear, reasoned thinking makes the best strategy for escaping human error and ignorance. The study of critical thinking is intended to help you make good decisions and form intelligent opinions by better evaluating the claims, facts, and beliefs you encounter. This chapter begins the process with a digest of what critical thinking is, which sorts of claims it takes as its subject matter, and how it differs from the unreflective possession of mere opinions. You can expect to find an emphasis in this chapter on fundamental vocabulary, and on the distinction between opinion alone and a reasonable opinion.

CHAPTER SUMMARY

I.   For all its undeniable potential, human thinking often falls into error. Critical thinking is a way of avoiding that error.

    A.   Many people adopt unfounded opinions on important issues. Although a free society grants the opportunity to think for oneself, it can't simply grant the ability to.

    B.   The ability to determine good **reasons** for opinions will develop with the study of critical thinking.

II.   Critical thinking is careful thinking about what we should do with a **claim.**

    A.   A claim is a sentence that has a truth value, that is, is either true or false. We may not know a claim's truth value; what matters is that it has one.

    B.   Although we may respond to a claim in a number of ways, critical thinking directs itself to the commonest response: assessing its likely truth or falsity.

        1.   When assessing a claim in this way, we may accept it, reject it, or suspend judgment.

            a.   Accepting a claim means believing it.

            b.   Rejecting a claim does not mean simply *not* believing it, but rather believing it to be false.

        2.   We accept or reject claims with varying degrees of confidence.

    C.   There is no simple way of deciding whether to accept a claim.

        1.   When done correctly, the process includes reading and listening carefully, spotting unstated assumptions, evaluating arguments, and assessing the claim's further implications.

2. Most learning entails grasping basic principles, looking at examples, and making guided attempts at doing something for oneself. So does the study of critical thinking.

III. Most frequently, the study of critical thinking is the study of arguments about **issues.**

    A. Any matter we try to assess can count as an issue.

        1. The issue may arise in a disagreement between two parties—for example, whether the county treasurer should invest public money in mutual funds.

        2. It may just as easily arise in one person's deliberations—for example, whether I should go out tonight to see this new band.

        3. Because an issue impels us to judge a claim (if possible) true or false, we can state most issues with the word "whether," followed by the claim being evaluated.

    B. People often confuse the issues they want to assess.

        1. Sometimes the confusion concerns the relative priority of issues, so that they are taken out of order.

        2. Confusion more typically causes a dispute when people address different issues in their disagreement.

        3. Thus a first rule when preparing to settle an issue is to determine and remain focused on what claim the issue is about.

    C. Once we have specified an issue, we may try to settle it with an **argument.**

        1. Along with observation and the consultation of reliable authorities, arguments are among the most important instruments of the critical thinker.

        2. An argument is an attempt to support a claim by giving reasons for believing it.

            a. The claim being argued for is the argument's **conclusion,** while the claims given as reasons for believing the conclusion are **premises.**

            b. One may, of course, support a claim without an argument. If you have me look through your magnifying glass so that I can read the fine print of a contract, you are supporting your claim that the contract cheats me; but there is no argument until the support takes verbal form (premises).

    D. We can also read arguments in order to clarify what an issue is.

        1. Arguments are intended to support a position on a given issue, so the conclusion being defended in an argument will be one side of the issue.

        2. Certain words help identify conclusions and premises: Conclusions are often preceded by "therefore," hence," "so," and so on, and such words as "since" and "because" may come before a premise.

IV. You may divide issues into **matters of fact** and **matters of pure opinion,** as long as you use those words correctly. The tools of critical thinking are particularly well suited to deliberating about the former.

    A. A **fact** is a true claim, whereas an **opinion** is something that someone believes to be true.

        1. Notice that these two concepts don't conflict. Just because something is an opinion does not stop it from possibly being true.

        2. Some opinions are indeed true, while others are false: Which they are is determined by careful inquiry, not just on account of their status as opinions.

    B. A claim describes a matter of fact (**factual matter**) when people agree on what methods would decide the truth of the claim.

        1. Even when no one yet knows whether a claim is true, it stands as a factual matter as long as clear methods exist for discovering that truth—even if the situation in which one could unearth the relevant facts must remain purely theoretical.

        2. Always bear in mind that a claim about a factual matter is not necessarily a fact itself, because it's not necessarily true; but if it's true, then it's a fact.

    C. A claim describes a matter of pure opinion when we have no way of settling it as we would settle a factual matter, that is, when the claim seems impervious to argument.

        1. Many (though not all) expressions of personal preference belong in this category.

        2. Whereas disagreement over a matter of fact means that at least one side is wrong, people may disagree on matters of pure opinion without either side being wrong.

    D. The distinction between matters of fact and matters of pure opinion is identical to the distinction between **objective claims** and **subjective claims.**

        1. The truth of an objective claim does not depend on our personal preferences and biases, while the truth of a subjective claim does.

        2. The controversy that certain claims arouse does not automatically make them subjective. "President Clinton's policies improved the economy" is controversial but a matter of fact (either true or false), whereas "President Clinton has an appealing personality" is a subjective claim.

    E. People have long debated whether one large class of claims should count as objective (matters of fact) or subjective (matters of pure opinion).

        1. This class includes most serious judgments of value, both ethical ("Lying is wrong") and aesthetic ("This is a good painting").

        2. But even if such judgments turn out to belong in the subjective realm, they resemble objective claims in the important sense that some opinions about them have better reasons behind them than others.

F. We must take care to treat matters of fact and matters of pure opinion differently.

   1. It is a waste of time trying to prove the truth of subjective claims for which no such proofs exist.

   2. It is even worse to treat objective claims as if they were subjective; for then we give up trying to reach the truth about important matters.

V. It is misleading to insist too strenuously, and in the wrong spirit, that all people are "entitled to their opinions."

   A. Human beings do deserve dignity, respect, and toleration: To this degree the view says something worth saying.

   B. The view goes wrong when it leaves people's opinions invulnerable to argument or criticism.

   1. Given the dangerous falsity of some opinions, too much tolerance will do more harm than good. (Am I entitled to the opinion that tar water will cure my baby's lung infection?)

   2. In the practice of conversation, such putative tolerance rules out serious inquiry into important issues: To insist that we are all entitled to our opinions is to give up trying to reach the truth about an issue.

KEY WORDS AND IDEAS

Argument. A set of claims intended to support or prove a conclusion. More specifically: a set of claims, one of which is the argument's conclusion, and the remainder of which are premises meant to show that conclusion's truth.

Although the word "argument" in ordinary English properly refers to heated disagreements between people, the critical-thinking sense of the word implies neither disagreement nor emotional heat.

Claim. A sentence that is either true or false, even if its truth is not known at present, and even if there is no way of deciding on its truth.

Conclusion. A claim in an argument, which the rest of the argument is intended to support.

Fact. A true claim.

Factual matter. Not the same thing as a fact; rather, a matter (1) whose truth can be settled by an agreed-on method for collecting evidence, and (2) the truth about which (whether it is now available or not) is a fact.

Issue. A claim whose truth is up for evaluation. Usually stated with the word "whether," an issue has at least two sides. This can mean that two or more people are engaged in a disagreement about the issue; but an issue can also arise for a single person who considers both sides of it.

Matter of fact. Factual matter.

Matter of pure opinion. A matter that is not factual, that is, a matter for which there is either no true answer, or no recognized way of determining that true answer, even theoretically. When two people disagree on a matter of pure opinion, neither one is wrong.

Objective claim. A claim about a matter of fact. An objective claim will be either true or false, and what makes it true or false is the state of the world, independent of people's fantasies or desires.

Opinion. Something that someone believes. It may be true or false, or a matter of pure opinion. Just because something is someone's opinion does not make it a matter of pure opinion.

Premise. A claim in an argument, intended to support the conclusion.

Reasons. Not just what someone says while upholding an opinion; nor the causes that brought someone to hold it (e.g., "I was brought up to believe . . ."). The reasons for an opinion are grounds that other people ought to find good reasons for holding the same opinion. In an argument, such reasons are called premises.

Subjective claim. A claim about a matter of pure opinion. The subjective claim gets its name from being really about the subject (i.e., the person) who asserts it. Thus Sabina's claim, "Leeks are disgusting," is in actuality not about leeks at all but about her feelings toward them.

REVIEW QUESTIONS

1. What is a claim, and how can we respond to it?
2. Explain the difference between a fact and a factual matter.
3. When is something an argument?
4. In what ways do people get confused about issues?
5. Explain the difference between an opinion and a matter of pure opinion.

COMMONLY ASKED QUESTIONS

Is there a clear way of distinguishing matters of pure opinion from factual matters?

If you want a simple criterion you can apply in every case to give you an uncontroversial answer, you should know that philosophers have tried to develop one for thousands of years and haven't yet come up with a standard that everyone agrees to. That is not to say that no one will ever develop such a criterion, only that none exists today—which is what this question is asking for.

However, there are good practical ways of drawing a distinction. First, reflect on what type of answer you expect to reach on the issue. If there is a fact down the line that resolves the issue, then you are addressing a factual matter. That is, if a claim, C, is a claim about a matter of fact, then either C is a fact or the contradiction of C is. Take the claim "The universe began with an explosion." If that claim is true, it is a fact that the universe began with an explosion. If the claim is false, it is a fact that the universe did not begin with an explosion. Either way you wind up with a fact; so the claim concerns a factual matter.

Put this point another way. There is no room in the universe for both a fact and the contradictory fact. When we disagree about a factual matter, at least one side is wrong. And that wrongness is itself a fact: To call people wrong for having believed the sun to go around the earth is to state a fact about their error.

In a second strategy for identifying factual matters, you can look at how the people involved in a disagreement defend their positions. You can ask: Do any arguments exist, either that might work or that you feel compelled to make, to settle the issue?

Some people put sugar in their coffee and others don't. Rarely do they have cause to sit down and discuss their practices. For this reason, the preference for sugar or no sugar usually counts as a matter of pure opinion. Now, suppose someone did feel inclined to argue against sweetening coffee, saying that the sugar harms your teeth, or that it contains empty calories. Now we have factual matters in the air: We have left the domain of pure opinion.

Somewhere along the way, you might respond that the benefits of not adding sugar don't make up for the effect on the taste of the coffee. Your co-conversationalist might urge you to try sugarless coffee for a week and see how you like it, but you could answer that you've tried it plenty of times already and the coffee just doesn't taste as good. It would be fruitless for the person to keep at the subject, insisting that coffee tastes better without the sugar. Your discussion has returned to judgments of taste that no observation or argument can settle: This has become again a matter of pure opinion.

Finally, prepare to err on the side of caution when drawing this distinction. It gets tempting to sweep all difficult, complex, and especially emotionally charged issues into the dustpan of pure opinion. Yielding to that temptation leads to errors about which issues belong where. If, on the other hand, you act from the prejudice that an issue concerns a matter of fact, only changing your mind when you feel forced to acknowledge that there's no way of reasoning about an opinion, you will make sounder judgments about which claims are which.

Aren't people ever entitled to their own opinions?

To be sure. Criticizing the overindulgent appeal to that principle does not mean that we need to hammer the disagreement out of anyone whose opinions are different from our own. But it helps here to see why the principle comes to be applied overindulgently.

The problem begins with a confusion between opinion and matters of pure opinion. In matters of pure opinion, there is (by definition) no argument, evidence, or credible authority through which to decide on the truth of a claim. When two people disagree on whether falling asleep is pleasant, argument and observation become bootless. Such cases lead us to say that both people are entitled to their opinions.

If all opinions were about matters of pure opinion, then people would be entitled to all their opinions. But the fact that you hold an opinion on a subject does not by itself imply that the subject is a matter of opinion—you may just as easily hold an opinion about a factual matter. An opinion is the first word on a subject, not the last word: We need to go on to classify the subject as a factual matter or not. Resorting to the plea of tolerance on opinions stops us from taking this next step.

TIPS ON APPLICATIONS

One of the first obstacles to studying critical thinking is the perception that the issues it takes up are either trivial or impossible. On one hand, we find simple examples about whether there's a dog in Pat's garage, or whether this brand of toothpaste will promote dental hygiene better than that one. You'd think that anyone old enough to take a course like this can already handle such issues.

On the other hand, we find debates that come down to questions of what policies a government should pursue, or what makes one action morally preferable to another, or what kinds of experiences the human mind is logically capable of. Most of these come down to questions of *value:* What makes something good, right, beautiful, just, wise? The rest of the questions seem to speculate about knowledge beyond any ordinary experience. They have that familiar sound of issues we could argue about forever without arriving at any truth.

Set aside the simple cases for now. As you continue to study critical thinking you will find many of them possessing more complexity than first met the eye. What about the insoluble questions? Why discuss what can't be settled? Why not admit that we have different opinions and leave things there?

At this point it is crucial not to reach for inexpensive skepticism about the equality of all positions. (Such skepticism as it arises during discussions is called the *subjectivist fallacy:* see Chapter 5 for more information.) In the first place, adopting such skepticism leads not to a different way of thinking about difficult issues, but rather to not thinking about them at all. When all opinions are equally good, we have no need to find reasons or arguments for one opinion instead of another. Without the attempt at finding such reasons, all that remain are dogmatic assertions.

Second, the intractability of certain issues is only half of the truth about them. Yes, there are questions that people have always stumbled over, and that no one has settled once and for all. But it's just as true that people have always felt compelled to ask and discuss them. Human beings have this tendency to ask what knowledge is, or whether God exists, or what makes a given action wrong, or what makes art valuable, or what makes some public policies more just than others. To ask such questions is to crave more than mere opinion: It is to ask whether our opinions are right. Anyone satisfied by the "information" that every answer is as good as every other answer never felt gripped by the question in the first place. Suppose someone says, "I've always thought of democracy as the best form of government. Now I wonder whether I was right." This person will never accept the reply that it all depends on your opinion, because the motive behind the worry was precisely the desire for *more than habitual opinion.*

If we may identify a single central purpose behind the study of critical thinking, it is the improvement of our ability to go beyond habitual opinion and find good reasons for one side of an issue or another.

EXERCISES

Sample Exercises from the Book

1-1, 1. What is a claim?

A claim is a statement that is either true or false. Note two things: The word "sentence" works as well as "statement" in defining a claim; and the word "claim" by itself does not imply that something is a factual matter.

1-2, 1. Let me tell you why Hank ought not to take that math course. First, it's too hard, and he'll probably flunk it. Second, he's going to spend the whole term in a state of frustration. Third, he'll probably get depressed and do poorly in all the rest of his courses.

The primary issue is (a), whether Hank ought to take that math course. The other possibilities may look like issues, because people could disagree about them. But that only shows that the reasons one gives on one side of a claim can themselves become issues in a further discussion.

1-6, 4. Diet soda will help you lose weight better than regular soda.

Matter of fact. In a sense this might count as a controversial claim, or at least a vague one as it stands: Washing down two pizzas with a diet soda will not help you lose weight better than having a regular soda by itself. To make the sentence a good clear claim about a factual matter, you would have to add the right qualifiers—for instance, "assuming that your diet otherwise remains the same" (see Chapter 2 on *vagueness*). Still, the vagueness does not make the claim a matter of opinion.

1-9, 19. We need to make clear that sexual preference, whether chosen or genetically determined, is a private matter. It has nothing to do with an individual's ability to make a positive contribution to society.

No argument. The first sentence communicates the claim under discussion; the second initially seems to support that claim, and so it gives the appearance of offering an argument. But a little thought should show that the second sentence merely restates the first, spelling out the meaning of "private matter" as something irrelevant to "an individual's ability to make a positive contribution to society." Think of it this way: Any reasons for accepting the second sentence are reasons for accepting the first, and vice versa. (See Chapter 6 on the type of pseudoreasoning called *begging the question.*)

1-10, 7. If you're going to buy a computer, you might as well also sign up for some lessons on how to use the thing. After all, no computer ever did any work for its owner until its owner found out how to make it work.

The issue is whether a person who buys a computer should take lessons on its use. The second sentence offers a reason for believing the first.

1-12, 1. Urbanite: The new requirements will force people off septic tanks and make them hook up to the city sewer. That's the only way we'll ever get the nitrates and other pollutants out of the groundwater.

Suburbanite: You call it a requirement, but I call it an outrage! They're going to charge us from five to fifteen thousand dollars each to make the hookups! That's more than anybody in my neighborhood can afford.

Depending on how you define the issue, Suburbanite either speaks to it or misses the point. If the issue is whether to approve the new sewage requirements, they both address it. If the issue is *more narrowly* whether the new requirements will have good environmental effects, Suburbanite's complaint about the cost misses the point. Why take the issue more narrowly? Because Urbanite's remarks about pollutants support the narrower claim; so Urbanite should be taken as addressing that issue.

Additional Exercises

A. Which of the following are claims? If they have a purpose besides that of making a claim, state that purpose.

1. What a day!

2. I could eat a horse.

3. There's nothing like mustard for a hot dog.

4. Watch out for the loose wire.

5. You ought to watch out for the loose wire.

6. Who told you I left town?

7. How long have you been out of jail?

8. I've never seen a better film than *American Beauty*.

B. Classify the following as claims about factual matters or claims about matters of pure opinion.

1. A sheet of transparent vinyl over your windows will reduce heat loss by 25 percent to 50 percent.

2. A sheet of transparent vinyl over your windows will make your home more comfortable all winter long.

3. A sheet of transparent vinyl over your windows will produce the kinds of temperatures that make most people feel more comfortable.

4. The new mandatory sentencing laws have reduced levels of the worst kinds of crimes.

5. The new mandatory sentencing laws have increased the country's prison population.

6. This 1200 is a motorcycle that will make you happy.

7. This 1200 is the most fun motorcycle to ride.

8. This 1200 is a motorcycle!

C. Identify the main issue in the following passages. Does the speaker offer an argument in support of one side of that issue?

1. This year's Super Bowl begins around 6:00 P.M. today, but the Fox pre-game programming will start at 1:00. Why? "Because we can sell it," said Ed Goren, co-executive producer of Fox Sports. "The Super Bowl is about more. It is about excess." (Reported in the *New York Times*, January 26, 1997.)

2. They should never have referred to the savings and loan deregulation as getting the government out of business decisions. All those deposits were insured by the government, which made public policy the biggest issue in the S&Ls' decisions.

3. Plenty of opportunities still exist for making money. You can't throw a rock without hitting one. All you have to do is keep an open mind.

4. Cars are not as safe as they used to be. They're more fuel-efficient, more environmentally sound, and better at surviving a 5 m.p.h. collision. But none of that adds up to safety.

5. "For many students, dropping out of school is a gradual and unintentional process. . . . A student might start staying away from school—a day here and three or four days there—because he just doesn't feel like going. Then, before he knows it, he's missed so many days and so much work that he figures he'll fail the year anyway. Why not just pack it in? Students who drop out are not usually thinking about how this will affect their job prospects and their future lives." (Albert Shanker, President, American Federation of Teachers)

6. "[We must] recognize that the entire future of American civilization and the American people is at stake. . . . If we renew American civilization, we will almost certainly lead the human race to freedom, safety and prosperity." (From the Newton Gingrich history course, "Renewing American Civilization")

D. Identify the issue under discussion. Has the second speaker addressed the same issue as the first?

1. Big: Don't worry about coming into the pool. It's only eight feet.
    Little: That doesn't make me feel any safer. You could drown in your bathtub.

2. First critic: I can't believe Jay opened his reading with that terrible poem. What a disaster!
   Second critic: Oh, it wasn't so bad. He had his Italian suit on.

3. Young: What's wrong with eating with my hands? Hands were around before forks.
   Old: Yours weren't.

4. Owner: How could you slam the door like that? It's not your car.
   Rider: I know.

5. Pro: These new term limits will give us better elected officials. We'll finally have a choice other than the candidates the party machine trots out for us.
   Con: I don't see how it can be democratic for the people who passed these term limits to restrict other voters' choices.

6. Pro: These new term limits will give us better elected officials. We'll finally have a choice other than the candidates the party machine trots out for us.
   Con: All it promises is that new party hacks will get on the ballot.

7. Potato: The networks have really come through with quality programming this fall. Every night of the week there are shows with literate writing and skillful acting.
   Potato's spouse: You sound like a sucker. They'll put on anything that they think will keep you glued to the screen.

Answers to Additional Exercises

A. 1. Not a claim. The claim "Today has been an exhausting day" is probably implied by the utterance, but as it stands it makes no assertion.

2. Claim. For any human speaker and any single meal, it is of course a false claim. It has the purpose of expressing, in colorful language, the quite possibly true claim, "I have an exceeding great appetite"; it also has the purpose of amusing.

3. Claim. Unless the speaker has previously unknown health benefits in mind, this is a subjective claim about a matter of pure opinion.

4. Not a claim. This is a sentence in the imperative mode, and such sentences can't be either true or false. (Compare: "Shut the door!" "Help!")

5. Claim. This sentence differs from the last one in its declarative form, which makes it capable of having a truth value.

6. Not a claim. Questions cannot be either true or false. The purpose is to elicit information, and probably also to issue a warning about loose lips.

7. Not a claim, for the same reason as the preceding. But notice that the present question implies certain claims: that the other person had been incarcerated, has been since released, has probably not been out of jail too long.

8. Claim. Whether or not this counts as a matter of pure opinion is itself a matter of some dispute; but even if it does, it is still a claim (though a subjective one). In addition to communicating, the sentence has the purpose of praising the movie.

B. 1. Matter of fact.

2. Matter of pure opinion: Some people may prefer the feeling of cool, refreshing drafts.

3. Matter of fact.

4. The answer here depends on how unambiguously we can define "worst kinds of crimes." Given the widespread agreement that acts of violence are worse than non-violent ones, this should probably count as a matter of fact.

5. Matter of fact.

6. Matter of fact (though open to being false).

7. Matter of pure opinion.

8. As stated, a matter of fact. But it is so obviously factual that we suspect its real purpose is to praise the motorcycle as better than others; so in its actual use, the sentence works as a matter of pure opinion.

C. 1. Issue: why pre-game programming for this year's Super Bowl will take up five hours. Ed Goren gives two reasons for his network's action.

2. Issue: whether deregulation of savings and loans institutions amounts to getting the government out of business decisions. The speaker offers an argument.

3. Issue: whether money-making opportunities still exist. There is no argument. This is an example of the common phenomenon of basing a claim on alleged reasons and examples without giving one.

4. Issue: whether cars are as safe as they used to be. No argument.

5. Issue: whether students who drop out of school are thinking about how this will affect their job prospects and future lives. Although Albert Shanker spends some time explaining that the process is gradual, that claim itself is a reason for believing that students are not thinking about the consequences of their action. The paragraph delivers an argument.

6. Issue: whether renewing American civilization has good consequences. As stated, the congressman's statements offer no argument.

D. 1. Issue: whether it's safe to go into the pool. Both sides address the issue, although they have different standards of water safety.

2. Issue: whether Jay's reading was a disaster. The second critic intentionally changes the subject, treating the reading as a fashion appearance rather than as a cultural event.

3. Issue: whether people may eat with their hands. Both sides address the issue. Old is implicitly saying: If what matters is what was around first, then the long-standing existence of forks gives Young a good reason to use them.

4. Issue: whether Rider should slam the car door. Rider intentionally misses the point, making nonownership a reason to slam rather than a reason to respect the car.

5. Issue: whether new term limits will lead to better elected officials. Con misses the point by focusing on whether the term limits are democratic. (Con is still giving a reason against the term limits, and maybe that reason should outweigh Pro's argument. But Con is not speaking to the matter of better officials.)

6. Issue: whether new term limits will lead to better elected officials. Both sides address the issue.

7. Issue: whether the networks have come through with quality programming this fall. Potato's spouse misses the point. The two are not really disagreeing at all, because the networks may have decided to broadcast quality programming as their tool for keeping viewers glued to the screen.

Answers to Review Questions

1. A claim is a sentence that is either true or false. We can respond by accepting the claim, rejecting it, or suspending judgment. When accepting or rejecting, we may do so with varying degrees of confidence. There is no contradiction in accepting a claim but doing so very tentatively—in fact, it's often the most reasonable course of action.

2. A fact is a true claim. A factual matter is an issue concerning a fact. The right answer about a factual matter will be a fact, whether or not anyone now knows that fact, even whether or not anyone is likely to in the future.

3. An argument is not a disagreement, but a series of reasons that support a claim. The supporting reasons go by the name of premises; the claim becomes the conclusion of the argument.

4. People may confuse themselves by considering a group of issues in the wrong order, with minor issues coming ahead of major ones. People may confuse each other by discussing matters that are not the real issues at hand. Very often this occurs when two issues bear a relation to one another.

5. An opinion is someone's belief on an issue, or someone's belief about a specific claim. That issue may well be a matter of fact. For the issue to be a matter of pure opinion, there must be no factual matter involved in it.

CHAPTER 2

CRITICAL THINKING AND CLEAR WRITING

The argumentative essay is the kind of writing that most demands critical-thinking techniques. An argumentative essay aims at *defining* and *defending* a position; and principles of critical thinking help us keep the essay focused on its subject, with arguments that genuinely support its position. Thus Chapter 2 will first devote itself to organization, which can help your writing overcome the illogicality and irrelevance that often plague argumentative essays. We then turn to clarity in communication, and the threats to clarity from ambiguity and vagueness.

CHAPTER SUMMARY

I.   The **argumentative essay** tries to support a position on an issue.

    A. Our purpose is to produce essays that persuade people, not by tricking them, but by presenting claims that support their conclusions.

    B. A good argumentative essay is well organized and clear: It is then both easier to understand and more persuasive.

II.   Good argumentative writing is *organized*. Clarity of structure is most often threatened by eccentric organization of material; lack of clarity is best prevented through reliable writing practices.

    A. The writer of an organized essay will focus its issue, stick to that issue, arrange the parts of the essay logically, and be complete.

        1. An organized essay begins with a clear statement of the issue to be addressed and the position taken on that issue.

        2. Every claim made in an organized essay bears on the issue.

        3. The parts of the essay follow a logical sequence. Normally the position being defended comes first and then the supporting reasons, with additional material as the need for it arises.

        4. A good essay is as complete as space permits. Every argument referred to gets developed; every disputable claim comes with some defense.

    B. Good writing practices make it easy to stick to these guidelines.

        1. After completing a draft, outline the essay. Evaluate your outline for coherence and focus.

        2. Revise an essay repeatedly.

        3. Get comments on the essay from someone else.

4. Read the essay out loud to catch problems with grammar or punctuation.

5. After finishing, set the work aside for a while and return to it for more revisions.

C. Another good general writing practice is the avoidance of certain common pitfalls of the argumentative essay. Watch out for these.

1. Windy preambles waste time with broad opening remarks about the importance of the issue to be discussed, the centuries that have been spent debating it, and so on.

2. Stream-of-consciousness rambles are found in disorganized essays that simply list thoughts as they come to the writer's mind.

3. Knee-jerk reactions emerge in essays written by people who record their automatic response to some issue without thinking it over.

4. A glancing blow deals with a topic tangentially—the writer takes on the subject of U.S. foreign policy by chatting about that nice Micronesian family that moved in next door.

5. Another kind of essay lets the reader do the work, offering bits of argumentation or abrupt shifts of direction and expecting the reader to see the logical structure behind them.

III. Good argumentative writing is also *clear*. A piece of writing can be hard to understand when it uses words poorly.

A. We can avoid certain kinds of problems by defining the key terms in a claim.

1. Definitions serve a number of purposes, but they almost always aim at the general purpose of facilitating understanding.

a. **Stipulative** definitions assign a meaning to a word: "We will call those data that help predict the economy's future 'leading indicators.'"

b. **Explanatory** definitions illustrate the implications of an already known but difficult concept: "Every use of the word 'beauty' implies some suitability to a purpose."

c. **Precising** definitions narrow down the meaning of a potentially unclear term: "By 'walking' we will specifically mean 'moving under one's own power while keeping at least one foot on the ground.'"

d. **Persuasive** definitions aim at influencing their audience: "That word 'casualties' refers to our sons and daughters killed in battle."

2. Different structures of definitions can achieve these purposes.

a. One may **define by example,** naming representative members of a group: "Ants are typical insects."

b. One may **define by synonym,** substituting a word or phrase with the same meaning: "'Ophidophobia' is the fear of snakes."

c. One may **define by analysis:** "Precipitation is water that reaches the earth's surface from the atmosphere as the result of meteorological causes."

3. Whatever kind of definition you use, be aware that many words also carry an **emotive** or **rhetorical force,** that is, the coloration of feeling that a word arouses. "Steed" and "horse" have the same literal meanings but different emotive force.

B. We can avoid other problems simply by not loading our writing down with too many words or too many twists in grammatical structure. Avoid complexity and prolixity.

IV. Clarity at the level of meaning (in words and phrases) is most often threatened by **ambiguity** and **vagueness.**

A. A claim is ambiguous if it can have more than one meaning, without clues from the context about which meaning to assign.

1. We call the claim **semantically ambiguous** if its multiple meanings result from the ambiguity of a word or phrase.

a. This is an ambiguity about what the parts of a claim mean when taken individually.

b. "Our cabdriver is green" may mean that the driver seems to be carsick, or lacks experience: The word "green" has not been pinned down.

c. The best solution to semantical ambiguity is the replacement of an ambiguous term with an unambiguous one.

2. When the sentence's ambiguity derives from its structure, we have a **syntactically ambiguous** claim.

a. Syntactical ambiguity arises more often as the sentence grows more complex, for modifying phrases and pronouns leave room for multiple interpretations.

b. The words in "This is a small men's college" are all perfectly clear on their own, but the arrangement lets them refer either to a small college for men or to a college for small men.

c. Replacing a word will not remedy most syntactical ambiguities: We need to rewrite the sentence (e.g., "This is a small college for men").

3. **Grouping ambiguity** occurs when the reference to a group of individuals may be taken as applying either to the individuals taken separately or to the group as a whole.

a. This is a type of semantical ambiguity.

b. "Flies outweigh humans" takes the individuals separately if it says that one fly outweighs one human; it refers to the collection as a group if it says (truly) that the mass of all flies exceeds that of all humans.

4. The unclarity in grouping ambiguities makes possible certain fallacies that we may therefore classify with ambiguities.

   a. The **fallacy of composition** is the mistaken belief that what holds of things individually must hold of them collectively—for example, the conclusion that a shirt made of the best material must be the best shirt.

   b. The **fallacy of division** attributes the group's characteristics to all of the group's members: "America is rich, so all Americans must be rich."

5. Classifying ambiguities correctly is far less important than spotting and avoiding them.

   a. Common sense often tells us the intended meaning of a claim. But you are still better off writing so as to keep ambiguity to a minimum.

B. A claim is vague when its meaning is excessively inexact.

1. Whereas an ambiguous claim has too many meanings (all of which may be clear), a vague claim has no clear meaning at all.

2. We can't avoid certain degrees of vagueness in ordinary speech and writing; but we must take pains to avoid undesirable degrees of vagueness.

3. Intrinsically vague words have no defining borders: "bald," "rich," and "heap" all have some quantitative meaning, but no precisely delimited one.

4. Vagueness can also enter a claim at the level of **vague comparisons.** Especially in advertisements and political speeches, people praise an object or idea with comparisons that leave out essential information (such as what the thing is being compared to). Five critical questions help us evaluate such comparisons:

   a. Is important information missing? That is, has the comparison left out some relevant data?

   b. Is the same standard of comparison being used? The "apples and oranges" problem.

   c. Are the items comparable? In such instances, you should watch for the appeal to exceptional cases, such as the safety record of one company's heaviest car as opposed to another company's lightest.

   d. Is the comparison expressed as an average? Here too, information may be missing.

   e. What does the comparison mean by "average"? The word "average" is ambiguous in that it can refer to a **mean** (arithmetic average), a **median** (halfway point), or a **mode** (most frequently occurring figure).

V. Persuasive writing differs from argumentative writing in aiming mainly at winning agreement from others, rather than (the argumentative ideal of) establishing objective grounds for a claim.

A. Assuming a perfect audience of critical thinkers, the best persuasion is good argumentation.

B. In imperfect circumstances, it helps to remember some principles of persuasion, handy both for strengthening your own arguments and for spotting in someone else's essay.

C. Still, all writing is writing for an audience, and certain principles of persuasion will help you get a good argument across.

    1. Discuss your opponent's point of view but not your opponent as a person. (The alternative is ad hominem rhetoric, both bad argumentation and offensive to readers; see Chapter 6 for more information.)

    2. Discuss what opponents of your position might say.

    3. Speak sympathetically of views opposed to your own.

    4. Concede the merits of an opponent's argument.

    5. When more issues exist than you have room to handle, focus on the important ones.

    6. Rebut objections to your view before presenting your own arguments.

    7. Open with the best argument you have.

VI. Good writing avoids reinforcing biases about race and gender.

A. There are ethical and nonethical reasons for writing this way.

    1. Our writing and speaking habits may reinforce unjust stereotypes.

    2. Writing that avoids biased language is also more effective by achieving greater precision and eliminating even the appearance of prejudice in the author.

B. The most common bias involves treating one type, usually the white male, as the standard or norm.

    1. This often translates into people's mention of someone's race or ethnicity only when that person is not a white European. Mention the group a person belongs to only when it is relevant.

    2. In cases of gender, the bias involves using male pronouns as generic pronouns. This practice contributes to the invisibility of women in language.

        a. One remedy is to replace "he" by "he or she," and so on.

        b. A more natural-sounding remedy puts sentences into the plural, thus eliminating any need for gendered pronouns.

        c. In many instances, you can rewrite a sentence so that it requires no personal pronouns at all.

KEY WORDS AND IDEAS

Ambiguity. The openness of a word or claim to more than one interpretation; the quality of possessing more than one meaning. Ambiguity is usually either semantical or syntactical.

Argumentative essay. A work of nonfiction prose that aims at stating and defending a position on some issue.

Definition by analysis. A definition that breaks a term down into its essential elements.

Definition by example. A definition that provides a representative example of a term.

Definition by synonym. A definition that explains a term by means of a word or phrase that has the same meaning.

Emotive or **rhetorical force.** Also known as "connotation"; the overtones of feeling that a word arouses, as separate from its literal meaning.

Explanatory definition. A definition intended to elucidate some feature of a complex concept.

Fallacy of composition. The mistaken assumption that what holds true of the members of a group, taken separately, will hold of the group of them taken together.

Fallacy of division. The mistaken assumption that what holds true of a group, considered as a whole, will hold of its members taken separately.

Grouping ambiguity. A type of semantical ambiguity that consists of referring to a group of individuals without clarifying whether one means the group as a whole or the individuals in it taken separately.

Mean. A type of average arrived at by adding up a group of numbers and dividing by the number of them; also known as "arithmetic mean." The mean of 3, 5, 7, and 9 is 6.

Median. A type of average arrived at by finding the midpoint in a set of numerical values. If A is 6′ tall, B is 5′10″, and C is 5′3″, the median height is 5′10″.

Mode. A type of average arrived at by finding the most frequently occurring value or number in a group. If 3 people in a class receive an A, 15 receive a B, and 9 receive a C, the mode is B.

Persuasive definition. A definition intended to influence its audience's sentiments on a subject.

Precising definition. A definition intended to make a vague concept more exact.

Semantical ambiguity. A type of ambiguity caused by the multiple meanings of words.

Stipulative definition. A definition intended to assign a meaning to a (new or existing) word by fiat.

Syntactical ambiguity. A type of ambiguity caused by the grammatical structure of a sentence; most often caused by pronouns with unclear referents and by qualifying phrases.

Vague comparison. A type of vagueness produced by a comparative claim whose basis for comparison is unclear, or which in some other way omits essential information.

Vagueness. The failure of a word or claim to possess any precise meaning.

REVIEW QUESTIONS

1. Distinguish between ambiguity and vagueness, giving an example of each.

2. Does grouping ambiguity count as a type of semantical ambiguity, or syntactical? Why? What fallacies does grouping ambiguity lead naturally to?

3. How can vagueness enter a sentence, other than through the use of intrinsically vague words? What can you do in such cases?

4. Define "house" by example, by synonym, and with an analysis.

5. Rewrite three ways, eliminating the exclusively masculine pronoun: "A doctor completes his medical education by serving as an intern."

COMMONLY ASKED QUESTIONS

Can I eliminate vagueness in my writing with stipulative definitions?

Sometimes. Stipulative definitions pose an attractive temptation to writers who want to narrow down their discussion: Say how you will use a word, and you can leave out all sorts of distracting details. But this move can free your writing from one problem only to leave it open to others.

Stipulative definitions work best when they fix the meaning of a neologism or abbreviation: "I will use 'STS' to refer to Socrates' theory of the state"; "Let 'Constable green' mean the color of lawns in Constable's landscapes." Such definitions free the author from having to repeat a long phrase or explain a concept every time it comes up. As long as one does not sprinkle abbreviations and technical terms through every paragraph of an essay, stipulative definitions that do this work make writing clearer.

Problems arise when a stipulative definition narrows down an existing word. If you intend to prove that there is no cure for baldness, and begin by defining baldness as "the absence of hair from 80 percent of the scalp or more for at least ten years," you will probably reach your desired conclusion, but only by first having narrowed down the significance of that conclusion.

You may also find yourself *begging the question* (see Chapter 6). If you define "age-appropriate reading skills" as "those reading skills achieved by most people of a certain age," you will be able to conclude that most American students have age-appropriate reading skills, but only because you have already embedded that conclusion in your stipulative definition.

Finally, a surprising number of authors begin with stipulative definitions only to forget them as they write. This happens especially with extremely abstract concepts like beauty. You may begin by stipulating that beauty, in your discussion, will imply only "the quality of an object that arouses pleasure without appealing to self-interest"; in all likelihood, you will wind up discussing beautiful things that do arouse self-interest, because the word "beauty" in fact applies to them.

If it's so hard to eliminate vagueness, how can I always do it?

No one can. Vagueness makes language possible: Without it we could never use old words to describe a new experience. Such vagueness does not threaten clear writing as long as no substantial points depend on a vague term. To call a claim excessively vague is to say that it leaves its implications inappropriately undefined. Thus, one should ask political candidates who vow to eradicate all unjust taxes how they plan to define "unjust": They may be calling for as much as the elimination of income tax, or as little as the repeal of sales tax on shoes.

Our legal system offers an example of how to treat vagueness. On one hand, many laws, such as those defining fraud and libel, appeal to what "a reasonable person" would believe. Judges and juries have to make judgments about what that hypothetical person might conclude in any specific case, but good judgments are the rule rather than the exception.

On the other hand, the legal system will strike down a law as "void for vagueness" if its application has been left so unclear as to invite capricious and unpredictable use. "Disturbing the peace," as defined in some jurisdictions, can be taken so broadly that attorneys may well defend someone arrested on that charge on the grounds that people never know when they disturb the peace.

Why do we treat clarity as the only virtue in argumentative writing?

Good writing possesses a number of virtues besides clarity. A lively style, the judicious choice of words, the well-turned phrase, all contribute to the best writing. This is not to mention such essential elements as evidence for factual claims and logical coherence, both of which will receive attention in coming chapters.

The present chapter emphasizes clarity for three reasons. First, it is a necessary condition of good argumentative writing. When we turn soon to the validity of arguments and the basis for factual claims, we will have to presuppose that someone can integrate that material into writing that has already achieved sufficient clarity.

Second, good argumentative writing aims at communicating its points, and clear writing, by definition, communicates well.

Third, even though other elements of writing—which may reduce its clarity—contribute to the overall effect of an essay, clarity is the hardest to accomplish. If the best writing lies on a spectrum somewhere between excessive clarity (tedious to read, insensitive to the subtleties of an issue) and excessive obscurity, nearly everyone's writing improves by aiming at the former extreme in order to avoid the latter.

TIPS ON APPLICATIONS

It is hard to improve on the book's guidance in clear argumentative writing. You may (with a little forcing) boil that guidance down to one overwhelming characteristic of clear writing and one fundamental practical tip.

1. More than anything else it needs, clear writing needs a *goal*. An essay must have a point, a purpose, a thesis, and must always work toward demonstrating that thesis. It would not hurt to think of an essay as a machine for producing its conclusion. Make sure all the parts are there to bring about the conclusion, and that they're all in the right place.

2. No practical tip can serve you better than the constant reminder to revise. Practice can ruin many other activities: Start throwing a ball or playing a guitar with the wrong motions, and long practice will instill bad habits along with the good ones. Writing, by comparison, almost never gets worse with practice. Anyone who keeps at it will find the sentences coming out more easily and sounding more natural; the points will go together more logically.

In addition, it may help to suggest one exercise that speeds the way to effective argumentative writing: the précis, or summary, of someone else's essay. The best objects of practice are newspaper editorials and opinion columns. (See "Additional exercises" for an example.) Editorials are short and aim at defending a point, so they provide excellent material. But the demands of reaching a wide audience and persuading readers generate certain features of editorials that you will not want in your essay. Editorials commonly don't begin with a statement of their position; they tend to dwell on some of their arguments more than on others, even repeating points within an argument; and they very often make additional comments en route to defending their main point.

When giving a précis of an editorial, you have the benefit of beginning with already existing claims and the reasons for them. Rather than worry about that part of the enterprise, you can concentrate on assembling the parts into a tightly reasoned essay. You may not agree with the editorial's conclusion or arguments, but that only means you have the opportunity to present a view with some detachment.

Begin by identifying the editorial's conclusion. Next, identify those arguments or factual claims that directly support the conclusion. Identify the argumentative passages that reply to existing or possible objections to the conclusion. Finally, identify and discard the sections that either repeat points or digress to tangential issues.

Once you are clear on the parts of the editorial's argument, you can reassemble them into your own essay. State the conclusion first. Follow that with the considerations that support the conclusion, beginning with the strongest and proceeding until they have all been stated. Then take up the replies to objections: Name the possible objections to the editorial's conclusion, and outline the responses to them.

You will probably wind up with an essay that looks very different from the original editorial, though it argues for the same point. If you have done the précis properly, it will give readers the same arguments that they would have gotten from reading the editorial: It will be as if they had read the original.

A précis sounds too simple for a college student to write. The work of actually producing one should convince you otherwise. After finishing three or four, you will notice a marked improvement in both your skills of organization and your willingness to sit down to write an argumentative essay.

EXERCISES

Sample Exercises from the Book

2-2, 1. Weintraub's findings were based on a computer test of 1,101 doctors 28–92 years old.

2. She and her colleagues found that the top ten scorers aged 75–92 did as well as the average of men under 35.

3. "The test measures memory, attention, visual perception, calculation, and reasoning," she said.

4. "The studies also provide intriguing clues to how that happens," said Sandra Weintraub, a neuropsychologist at Harvard Medical School in Boston.

5. "The ability of some men to retain mental function might be related to their ability to produce a certain type of brain cell not present at birth," she said.

6. The studies show that some men manage to escape the trend of declining mental ability with age.

7. Many elderly men are at least as mentally able as the average young adult, according to recent studies.

7-6-4-1-3-2-5. Several different clues give you this answer. A full name usually comes the first time a person is named **and** has to come before pronouns. So you know that (4) comes before everything but (6) and (7). (6) and (7) make the most general points, which means that they precede everything else; of the two, (7) is more general than (6). Of the remaining sentences, (1) and (3) describe the test, while (2) and (5) state and discuss its results so (1) and (3) come before (2) and (5). Of (1) and (3), the former refers to a "computer test," while the latter merely speaks of "the test": Now you know that (1) is before (3). As for the last two sentences, (5) is speculative, trying to account for the concrete results; so it comes last, after (2).

2-4, 10. Newspaper headline: "Police Kill 6 Coyotes After Mauling of Girl."

6 Coyotes That Maul Girl Are Killed by Police. You want to avoid the unintended implication that the police mauled the girl.

2-4, 19. If you crave the taste of a real German beer, nothing is better than Dunkelbrau.

Dunkelbrau—for those who crave the best-tasting real German beer. A little observation will show you how many ambiguities the word "nothing" can create. Consider the argument: Nothing is better than complete happiness in life. A nickel is better than nothing. Therefore, a nickel is better than complete happiness in life.

2-6, 4. The recent changes in the tax code

   a.   will substantially increase taxes paid by those making more than $200,000 per year

   b.   will increase by 4 percent the tax rate for those making more than $200,000 per year; will leave unchanged the tax rate for people making between $40,000 and $200,000; and will decrease by 2 percent the tax rate for those making less than $40,000

   c.   will make some important changes in who pays what in taxes

   d.   are tougher on the rich than the provision in the previous tax law

   e.   raise rates for the wealthy and reduce them for those in the lowest brackets

From vaguest to least vague: c, d, e, a, b. You probably had little trouble with this, so stop and think about how you reasoned. The presence of numbers in (a) and (b) make those obviously the least vague, and the greater detail about numbers in (b) sets it apart as least vague of all. (c)'s "important" not only puts an evaluative spin on the news item but also functions, as such words often do, to paper over the details. As for deciding between (d) and (e), the crucial matter is not the word "tougher" but the fact that both speak of what happens to the wealthy, while (e) also explains what happens to the lowest tax brackets.

Additional Exercises

A.   Identify the ambiguity in these examples and rewrite the claim so as to make it unambiguous.

   1.   This morning I shot an elephant in my pajamas.

   2.   Hands were around before forks were.

   3.   Our mothers bore us.

   4.   I thought your driveway was longer than it is.

   5.   Newspaper headline: Unskilled Workers Get Shot at Jobs.

   6.   Americans have shown themselves willing to drop nuclear weapons.

   7.   Dad, for my lunch tomorrow you should peel the star fruit and then cut it into pieces and put them in a plastic bag. It's easier that way.

   8.   Sign in front of a vacant lot: Fine for Littering.

B.   Look for the vagueness in these examples. Are they vague in themselves, or do they offer vague comparisons?

   1.   Please don't make any more late-night phone calls.

   2.   Please don't make any more unpleasant phone calls.

   3.   Whiskey is no worse a drink for you than beer.

   4.   Overheard after a piano recital: Well, you did it again!

5. Korn just can't do what the Rolling Stones did.

6. This warranty becomes void if the owner uses the hammer improperly.

7. It's not the heat that gets you, it's the humidity.

8. When persons voluntarily hold a property for others, they may avoid a charge of negligence by taking reasonable care of the property.

C. Rearrange the sentences in these two examples so that they make a coherent passage.

Example 1

1. Ohm Eye's new lenses all come tinted a bright rose color.

2. Have you ever lost a contact lens?

3. "Part of the problem is that you're looking without both lenses in," says Dr. Seymour Goode of Ohm Eye Laboratories.

4. One solution is a box of disposable lenses, but they still cost more than most people want to spend on contacts.

5. "We think you'll feel more optimistic about taking out your contacts now," Dr. Goode says.

6. The other problem is the dim light in most bathrooms.

7. Wherever they land, you'll see them.

8. It can take half an hour to find it, assuming that you don't give up in disgust.

9. Dr. Goode devoted a year of research to solving the problem of lost lenses; the result is something contact wearers everywhere can cheer about.

Example 2

1. Meredith Broughton doesn't lay on the horn, but she does leave the car windows down at night.

2. "I don't even cheat on my recycling," she told our reporter.

3. For over thirty years, it's been illegal to honk your horn except to avoid a collision or other substantial damage.

4. So last month Mayor Gid Tanner had the ordinance bumped up to the status of a moving violation.

5. "Maybe if they let me explain about Esmerelda, I'll get off with a warning," Meredith says—but she doesn't sound too hopeful.

6. Yesterday the city started treating her like a common criminal, with a summons delivered to her door by a uniformed policeman.

7. It seems the problem began with the city's good intentions of enforcing its ban on the unnecessary use of car horns.

8. Meredith Broughton has always thought of herself as a law-abiding citizen.

9. Last week her cat decided to sleep in the car, and it whiled away the night using the horn as a toy.

10. The fact that most people don't even know the law shows how seldom it gets enforced.

D. Identify the conclusion and supporting ideas in this editorial ("State of the Sleaze," *New York Times*, January 28, 1997). Rewrite the piece in a short précis that begins with the conclusion and organizes the supporting ideas to follow. See "Tips on Applications."

> Give the two major parties this much. They both have the faith of a misbehaving child in the everybody-does-it defense, and indeed, in today's Washington, Democrats and Republicans alike are slopping like hogs at the corporate trough. . . .
>
> The Democratic National Committee wrote playbooks for bartering face time with President Clinton. Meanwhile, the Republican National Committee was selling its rent-a-staffer plan to executives with $250,000 to plunk down. The final score in this orgy of influence-peddling was $141 million in soft money for the Republicans and $122 million for the Democrats.
>
> A White House tangled in ethics inquiries has seized on the Republican superiority as a defense of its own behavior, but that is an adolescent response to a serious national problem. These numbers do not add up to evidence of virtue for any participant in the Beltway sleaze orgy. Rather they expose the current fund-raising system for what it is—a legalized sale of a controlled substance called political influence. Under this system, wealthy individuals and corporations can buy a weighted vote in national affairs. . . .
>
> We can thank the financial disclosure laws passed during the 70's for documenting the corruption of the system. They are good laws, but flawed in their presumption that disclosure would lead to self-restraint by politicians. The financial record of 1996 proved that neither the parties, Congress nor this White House can be shamed into giving up the money they get through the sale of access and influence. That is why . . . you have not heard [Al Gore] or his President take the lead to change the current system. It has been good to them. It has been good to Mr. Gingrich and Haley Barbour, creator of the $250,000 "season ticket" for those who want the R.N.C. to open Capitol doors. It has been good to everyone except citizens who want to see Government that cannot be bought or rented.
>
> Mr. Clinton's defenders say this White House has done nothing different, but in fact it has broken down the compartmentalization and fund-raising protocols that have existed for decades. It is unfair to previous administrations to say that they would have invited in potential contributors in the banking industry to meet their Comptroller of the Currency and air their regulatory problems in the presence of the party finance chairman during the campaign fund-raising season. In this instance, and in his trade conversations with Asian contributors, Mr. Clinton has invented a new format for discussing policy. Call it Renaissance Weekend with dollars.

Does the Attorney General read the papers? What does it take to add up in her head to "credible evidence" required for appointment of a special prosecutor to study the relationships between contributors and officials at the White House and the D.N.C.? Does anybody in America believe Lanny Davis, the White House scandal team's latest flak-catcher, when he says there was nothing wrong with the banking meeting? . . .

But the lasting answers must come from higher up. Mr. Clinton has a reputation in need of repair. There have been reports that he is thinking of launching a Nafta-style crusade to get candidates and the parties out of the trough. That would be a smart move politically and a true service to an electorate weary of checkbook government.

Answers to Additional Exercises

A. 1. Syntactical ambiguity. Write: This morning, in my pajamas, I shot an elephant.

 2. Grouping ambiguity. Take "hands" and "forks" as groups.

 3. Semantical ambiguity. Write: Our mothers gave birth to us.

 4. Syntactical ambiguity. Write: Your driveway is not as long as I thought it was.

 5. Semantical ambiguity. Write: Unskilled Workers Get Job Opportunity.

 6. Grouping ambiguity. Take "Americans" as a group.

 7. Syntactical ambiguity. Write: It's easier for me to eat that way.

 8. Semantical ambiguity. Write: $100 [or other amount] Fine for Littering.

B. 1. No vagueness: "late-night" may not have a precise definition, but it's clear enough.

 2. "Unpleasant" needs more explanation.

 3. Vague comparison. If the comparison refers to the total alcohol in one whiskey drink and one bottle of beer, it is true (but such details ought to be provided). If other claims are implied about potential for abuse and relative rates of absorption, the claim requires still more information.

 4. The vagueness here lets the comment work as either compliment or insult. The word "it" needs to be fleshed out.

 5. Vague comparison. Does the comparison refer to how well the musicians play their instruments? How culturally important they can become? How innovative the two groups are? (And how would that be determined?)

 6. Given what a hammer is—an object made to hit things with—"improperly" needs a more precise definition. Does it refer only to propping up a car with the hammer? Or is it enough if you try pounding nails into extremely hard walls?

 7. Vague comparison: Far too much information is missing. Would the speaker prefer 5 percent humidity at 105 degrees to a muggy day at 65?

 8. No vagueness: Most people know how to judge reasonable care.

C. 1. 2-8-4-3-6-9-1-7-5.

   2. 8-2-6-7-3-10-4-1-9-5.

D. Sample précis for "State of the Sleaze"

(Note: Don't worry if your précis does not look exactly like this one. Any number of essays can communicate the same ideas. Focus on the main form of this example: the conclusion first, the arguments second, responses to objections third. Notice the effort to prune away comments that do not directly further the progress of the argument.)

President Clinton should lead the effort to reform campaign funding laws to prohibit the sale of political influence. The present solicitation of private money has reached such egregious levels that such new laws have become both ethically necessary and politically judicious.

Both parties have drawn huge amounts of money from corporate donors and wealthy individuals. The Democratic National Committee developed the strategy for selling time with the President, while the Republican National Committee arranged meetings with congressional staffers for executives who would pay $250,000. All told, the Republicans collected $141 million, and the Democrats $122 million. American citizens want a federal government that does not so brazenly offer to trade its power for money.

Besides being unjust, the present system is imprudent for a leader like President Clinton to acquiesce in. His reputation is now so shaken that he ought to separate himself from the open sale of political influence. If he launches a campaign to end that sale, as some have reported him to be thinking of doing, he would enhance his political standing.

It is no objection to this assessment of things to claim, as the White House has, that the greater money collected by Republicans excuses the behavior of Democrats. On the contrary, the huge numbers show that the present fund-raising system lets wealthy contributors gain control over the policymaking in both parties.

The White House has only made itself look worse by trying to avoid blame. Spokesperson Lanny Davis says there was nothing wrong with a meeting at which potential contributors in the banking industry met the U.S. Comptroller of the currency and discussed their regulatory problems with the Democratic Party's finance chairman. No one in the country believes him; and no previous administrations engaged in such behavior. Despite the claims of Mr. Clinton's defenders, this White House has violated long-standing traditions of how campaign money can and cannot be raised. The President's trade conversations with Asian contributors offer only a further example of impermissible ventures toward the goal of collecting contributions.

Nor can one claim that existing financial disclosure laws put off the need for reform. The existing laws are good as far as they go, to reveal the extent of the corruption; they err in assuming that such disclosure would shame politicians into self-restraint. Recent evidence shows that no such shame is at work. The present system benefits the leaders of both parties so much that they cannot be expected to protest it.

Answers to Review Questions

1. A vague claim has no clear meaning at all; an ambiguous claim has too many, that is, more than one. "He didn't use one French word in the whole book" is ambiguous, because it can mean either "He didn't use any French words in the whole book" or "There is one French word he didn't use in the book." "He didn't use one improper word in the whole book" is vague, because "improper" needs more clarification.

2. Grouping ambiguity is a type of semantical ambiguity, because although the ambiguous word in question ("horse," "Dane") may not seem unclear, it might refer either to a group of individuals or to the individuals belonging to that group. Grouping ambiguity leads to fallacies of composition and division.

3. Vagueness can enter a sentence by way of a vague comparison. In such cases you can demand further information, ask which standard of comparison is being used (if the items are comparable in the first place), or specify the meaning of "average" in the comparison.

4. By example: "That's a house." By synonym: "A house is a residence or domicile." With analysis: "A house is a free-standing building that people can live in."

5. A doctor completes his or her medical education by serving as an intern. Doctors complete their medical education by serving as interns. The internship marks the completion of a medical education.

CHAPTER 3

EVALUATING INFORMATIVE CLAIMS

If the full use of critical thinking involves the construction and evaluation of various forms of argument, the first step toward that skill requires looking at the building blocks of arguments, namely claims. We have already considered the clear *form* that a claim must take; it is now time to turn to the claim's *content*, and how we know whether to accept or reject it.

When a claim arrives in the context of a developed argument, we will have to examine that whole argument before passing judgment on the claim. That will be the project of Part 3 of *Critical Thinking* (Chapters 8 and following). But plenty of claims get asserted on their own, without backing from arguments, factual statistics, or anything else. To guide our judgment about such alleged information, we apply more elementary, more foundational principles.

Part 2 begins the process of determining how we may treat isolated claims. In the present chapter, we look at those claims that purport to deliver information, and measure them against a single flexible rule. Although that rule cannot work as a simple test that claims pass or fail, it does provide a framework for bringing the weight of what we already know, and the weight of our evaluation of authorities, to bear on a sentence's claim to truth.

CHAPTER SUMMARY

I.   One general rule helps us judge unargued-for claims.

    A.   Thinking critically does not mean predisposing ourselves to disbelieve everything we hear: We have to believe some things, and often enough we may justifiably believe what we hear.

    B.   Other things being equal, *it is reasonable to accept claims that fit with other things we have reason to believe, and that come from credible sources.*

        1.   A claim fits with other things we have reason to believe if it does not conflict with observation, with background knowledge, or with other credible claims.

        2.   A claim comes from a **credible source** if we *do* have reason to believe that source is informed, and we *do not* have reason to suspect **bias** in the source.

    C.   This rule is easily stated, but often tricky to apply. Even matters as apparently obvious as observation contain complications, although the subtlest issues here have to do with credible sources and their knowledge.

II. A reasonable bias exists against claims that deny direct **observation.**

    A.   Direct observation makes a solid basis for knowledge, not easily made up for by other sources.

B. Still, several factors can render observations unreliable, and it is wise to consider such factors before rejecting a competing claim.

    1. Observations depend on the conditions under which they are made.

        a. What you hear in a noisy room is less reliable than what you hear in quiet, and so on.

        b. Distractions, emotions, and fatigue can diminish the reliability of observations.

        c. Observations that call for the use of measuring instruments are only as trustworthy as those instruments.

    2. The power of observation can differ with people's expertise and experience.

    3. Expectations often influence observation.

        a. You are more likely to hear a knock at the door if you know someone plans to come.

        b. Your emotional relationship to a person creates expectations about what that person is doing, and why, and how well.

        c. You will call an action successful more often if you want it to succeed, and call it useful more often if it's something you want to do anyway.

    4. An observation made in the past suffers from the same dangers of unreliability as memory in general.

III. A similar bias exists against claims that deny **background information.**

A. Background information includes all the facts, general and specific, that we have learned through our lives, very often without being able to say where we learned them.

    1. Together with direct observation, background information forms the ground against which to pose any new claim.

    2. An assertion has more **initial plausibility** the more it fits with our observations or our background information.

    3. We say that when two claims conflict, the *burden of proof* (see Chapter 6) lies on the one with less initial plausibility.

    4. Since initial plausibility comes in degrees, we accept a plausible claim with different degrees of confidence.

B. No one possesses a perfectly broad and perfectly true body of background information; so this criterion needs to remain flexible.

    1. Although a claim that directly conflicts with what we believe should not necessarily be accepted, it may provide a reason for us to check those old beliefs.

2. The greater our store of background information, the more reliable this test becomes. There is no substitute for knowing a broad range of things.

IV. The reasonable acceptance of a claim also ought to depend on the credibility of its source, which typically means a person's knowledge.

A. This principle even holds in cases of eyewitness accounts.

1. We have seen that the quality of direct observation can depend on the observer's knowledge. Artists will be better than nonartists at remembering the color of someone's shirt.

2. Untrained observers are more likely to exaggerate their observations, partly because unusual features of a person or thing are more noticeable, and partly because reports of unusual features are more entertaining to describe.

B. Since knowledge makes one more credible, **expert** knowledge makes for the most credible sources of all.

1. Experts have had the education, training, or experience to possess special knowledge on a subject.

2. Whether or not a matter concerns direct observation, the expert's claim should be accepted over the nonexpert's.

C. In order to avail ourselves of experts, however, we must know how to assess expertise.

1. *Education* is most important; this typically means what degrees a person may possess, but also where they received them. It may also mean some other form of training.

2. *Experience* counts heavily in making someone an expert, as long as it amounts to more than just many years at a job.

3. *Accomplishments* figure somewhere on this list below the first two factors: Remember that accomplishments should pertain to the subject on which the expert is speaking.

4. *Reputation* matters when it has been earned among reliable persons, usually other experts in the field. In considering reputation, we treat this community of peers as experts about who the experts are.

5. Closely related to reputation is one's *position* in a field of expertise—for example, a prestigious academic or scientific title.

D. Even after judging someone an expert, we need to remain aware that several factors can diminish that person's credibility.

1. Expertise in one subject rarely prepares a person to make reliable assertions about another subject. Make sure the expertise is relevant to the claim.

2. All sources, even experts, lose credibility when we have reason to suspect them of bias. Bias most often arises when the expert has a financial stake in an issue.

3. Experts lose some credibility when their claims conflict with those of another expert. Ask two further questions:

   a. Does one of the expert opinions agree with what the majority of experts in that field believes?

   b. Can we assess one of the experts as more authoritative or more biased than the other?

E. Because expertise doesn't guarantee infallibility, it is often wisest either to suspend judgment, or to accept a claim while still keeping an open mind about whether it could turn out false.

V. Credible sources can also include the news media and the Internet.

A. Newspapers, newsmagazines, radio, and television make good sources of information about contemporary events, but they need to be used carefully.

   1. These media vary in the depth and breadth of coverage they provide, and the selective presentation of facts can slant a story.

   2. Most reporters get their information not through investigation but from governmental and private press releases and press conferences. So they depend on what their sources want to divulge, and on retaining good relations with those sources.

   3. Being private businesses, the news media have to make a profit.

      a. They need to take care not to offend or criticize their advertisers.

      b. The media also can't lose their audience; so they tend to simplify issues and present more entertaining or sensationalistic stories.

B. The Internet has produced an unprecedented flow of informative claims. Depending on their origin, they may possess as much credibility as the claims of news media, or substantially less.

   1. Commercial and institutional sources, such as Lexis-Nexis and other online services, belong in the same group as newspapers and newsmagazines.

   2. Individual and group Web sites, on the other hand, may have any origin at all; you should consider them as reliable as any other stranger.

   3. Auction houses on the Internet make numerous claims that their users ought to be careful about. Take precautions before spending money online.

KEY WORDS AND IDEAS

Background information. The broad and vague collection of our general and specific beliefs about the world, typically arrived at through years of education and experience, and typically without our ability to say where it came from.

Bias. An inappropriate personal motive that casts doubts on one's own observations, the firsthand observations reported by someone else, or the claims of an expert.

Although "bias" commonly means any prejudice or strongly held belief, we will use the word more narrowly. The critical judgment of an expert's claim cannot rest on the statement "Scientists are biased against the occult" or "Economists have a bias toward economic explanations." These statements may correctly describe someone's habits of thought. But habits of thought do not imply bias, which usually entails irrelevant emotional factors (e.g., friendship with someone whose views one supports) or material self-interest (employment by the corporation whose product one calls safe).

Credible source. A person who makes a claim that we thereby have good reason to accept. Most often, the cause of credibility is knowledge.

Expert. A person with knowledge beyond that of educated laypersons on some specialized subject. Experts make especially credible sources for information, as long as (1) the area of their expertise is relevant to the issue at hand, (2) their claims do not conflict with those of other experts, and (3) we have no reason to suspect their bias. One becomes qualified as an expert by means of education (not necessarily obtained in a school), experience, accomplishments, reputation, and position.

Initial plausibility. The agreement of a new informative claim with things we already have good reason to believe. A claim's initial plausibility depends more specifically on its agreement with our own observations and our store of background information.

Observation. The immediate perception of a thing or event. Other things being equal, observation produces the most solid grounds for accepting a claim, and the most solid grounds for rejecting one that denies one's own observation. But many circumstances can render even observation unreliable.

REVIEW QUESTIONS

1. What traits make someone an expert, and what traits let you identify someone as an expert?

2. What factors can influence memory, to produce a false sense of knowledge?

3. Name three jobs you have some familiarity with. How would people holding those jobs make more reliable everyday observations than other people?

4. What factors should a juror consider in evaluating a witness's account of overhearing a conversation?

COMMONLY ASKED QUESTIONS

I agree that experts have greater credibility than nonexperts when both are observers of something; but how can I trust an expert who wasn't there over a nonexpert who was, or even over my own eyes?

In many cases, of course, there's nothing like being there. Suppose a locksmith installs a new lock in your door, but two days later your key won't open it. You call to complain, and the locksmith says, "Impossible. Those locks always work." That expert assurance is not worth much when you've been battling the lock for fifteen minutes.

That example doesn't quite prove enough, though, mainly because a stuck lock is the kind of thing you don't need experts to detect. A surprising number of what we think of as direct observations actually involve theoretical assumptions or generalizations about experience. For instance, if you stand watching the eastern horizon at dawn, you will see the sun come up. What could be more obvious? So, many people who first heard of the Copernican theory that the earth goes around the sun would have thought, "What does Copernicus know? I saw the sun go up with my own eyes. Was he there?" We would have to answer them that the "observation" of sunrise amounted to an interpretation, based on the assumption that the earth stood still.

Closer to home, a lot of men believe that their beards grow faster if they shave than if they don't. Five or six days of nonshaving simply doesn't appear to produce the quantity of facial hair that comes off in five or six days' shaves. (Almost no man ever runs the experiment of shaving one side of his face every day, washing and collecting the shavings, and letting the other side grow for a year, then washing and collecting *those* shavings.) A doctor or biologist could explain that hair follicles grow at a steady pace regardless of how often they are clipped. Despite the conflict with observation, the scientific explanation simply has more credibility.

When can all the experts in a field be wrong about something, and what do we do about that possibility?

Drastic changes have a way of leaving experts high and dry, especially when they hit scientific theories. Whether it is the abandonment of Newton by Einstein and other physicists, or the change in geology to say that continents move, a ground-level scientific revolution renders the majority of experts in its field suddenly and retroactively wrong.

But when it takes something as dramatic as a scientific revolution to make experts collectively wrong, suspended judgment is the wrong response to an expert's claim. It is one thing not to buy one psychologist's account of forgetfulness when other psychologists reject it; it is quite another thing to shrug off a chemist's analysis of some material on the grounds that the next century could bring a revision of chemical theory. When a field of experts speaks with near-unanimity, you need a substantial reason not to believe them. The mere possibility of some new theory or other does not count as a substantial reason, unless you have worked out a coherent new chemical or physical theory by yourself (and good luck with that).

We may say, more broadly, that suspending judgment is not a fail-safe response to claims. When different experts make competing assertions about which foods belong in a healthy diet, you have no choice but to agree with some of them—you have to eat *something*. Nor are you always justified in suspending judgment, as the example from science shows.

This discussion raises two related issues. First, different fields have different relationships to facts of the matter, and the claims of their experts call for different responses. English professors may all agree about which novels in English are the great books, but that agreement isn't worth much just as a fact (knowing which books are deemed great has value only if it gets us to read those books) and remains open to reevaluation without the kind of drastic change that happens in a scientific revolution.

Second, watch for mere references to experts. (See Chapter 4 on *proof surrogates*.) Although news sources almost never pass along false claims, they can use unnamed experts to give the claims one context or another. "Experts say that the radiation leak poses no health risks"; "Experts warn that reported embezzlements represent only 10 percent of corporate crimes." You may assume that the media evaluate the credentials of their sources. But when two experts might disagree on an issue, you need more than a word to assure you of the truth of a claim. *Take an appeal to experts more seriously when the news source supplies you with a name.*

TIPS ON APPLICATIONS

Advertising offers a perfect opportunity for evaluating claims, because advertising aims at getting you to believe things and because the limitations of time prevent a commercial from spelling out an argument. The quickly stated claim has to sound believable on its own, or with abbreviated support. Furthermore, you will not face the same obstacles you do in other cases, because laws about truth in advertising prohibit a commercial from making clearly false specific assertions about matters of fact. Thus you possess enough background information, simply by having reached adulthood, to judge an advertising claim's initial plausibility.

The next time you watch an hour of television, practice applying the tests spelled out in this chapter. Take notes on all the commercials you see, including all the factors that can influence your evaluation of their claims. Keep the following considerations in mind, and think about where they may enter into your treatment of a commercial.

What conflicts arise with background information? There is nothing wrong with believing that some dish detergents work better than others. So some product probably is the most effective dish detergent, and one product's claim to that honor does not challenge our assumptions about how the world works. Likewise, some automobiles protect you better than others. When one model declares itself among the ten safest in the world, you know that (1) some cars belong in that group, and (2) the assertion is too specific to be permitted without factual support. (You also know that the model probably is not the world's safest or second-safest car, or the commercial would say so.)

On the other hand, some alleged differences probably don't matter as much as the advertisers profess them to. Although aspirin and an aspirin-free pain reliever probably do take effect at different rates, two brands of aspirin will have a hard time distinguishing themselves from one another. (When one aspirin manufacturer claims its aspirin to be mixed with a second ingredient to enhance the aspirin's effect, read the fine print on the screen. That second ingredient is usually caffeine, which does affect how well aspirin works, but which you can also get from a cup of coffee.)

How high are the stakes? Factors here include the cost of an object. If you let yourself get taken in by claims about the crunch in one brand of peanut butter, the most you can lose is the price of one jar. More turns on your acceptance of a claim about how smoothly a car rides. One decision can matter more than another in other respects as well. It is hard to imagine having a day ruined by a bad choice of soap; the wrong kind of hair coloring will bring more obvious effects.

How credible is the source? Here lies the largest category of questions you may ask about advertising. Watch for strategies by which a commercial presents a claim so as to imbue it with the air of authority.

What is the sex of the person who makes the claim? Does it vary with the product? If so, does this variation suggest that we commonly presume different sexes to have authority over different matters? Whom would you expect to tell you about motor oil? laundry detergent? Ask similar questions about the age of the person. Whom do you believe about amusement parks? What about financial investments? What if claims about the product come from a voice-over? What effect does it have on your belief to hear a voice without seeing its source? Why do you suppose disembodied voices can have their effect?

Finally, does the commercial contain an expert, or present someone as an expert? When actors endorse shampoo, you can expect them to possess special knowledge, because the appearance of their hair makes a substantial difference to their success. On the other hand, they are getting paid to make the endorsement, so you have to weigh their reasons for bias.

If a man appears touting a quasi-medical product—a cold remedy, antacid, or dandruff shampoo—what is he wearing? Probably a suit and tie, maybe even a white lab coat. Why do some people in commercials stand in front of bookshelves, or walls with diplomas on them? In one advertisement for a brand of imitation jewels, a man screws up his face to hold a magnifying lens against one eye and pronounces himself unable to tell this jewel from the real thing. Although a commercial cannot legally call the speaker an expert, it can still surround the person with the trappings of expertise in order to suggest that point.

In all likelihood, you will find that your observations did not change the evaluations you would have come to without a critical-thinking course. We are deluged with so much advertising that we learn how to judge it. That is no failing of the exercise; on the contrary, it shows that most people think critically without realizing what methods they use. By making yourself conscious of what you were doing unconsciously, you will improve your application of the same criteria in more difficult cases.

EXERCISES

Sample Exercises from the Book

3-5, 3. The Surgical Practices Committee of Grantville Hospital has documented an unusually high number of problems in connection with tonsillectomies performed by a Dr. Choker. The committee is reviewing her surgical practices. Those present during a tonsillectomy are

    a. Dr. Choker

    b. the surgical proctor from the Surgical Practices Committee

    c. an anesthesiologist

    d. a nurse

    e. a technician

The most credible observers are (b), (c), and (d). The two surgeons on this list (Dr. Choker and the proctor) possess the greatest knowledge; since anesthesiologists and surgical nurses possess both medical training and experience in surgery, their observations rank close behind. The technician has other matters to focus on during surgery, and probably received no training in interpreting what a surgeon does at any given moment. The proctor's freedom from bias exceeds that of (c), (d), and (e) because it is possible for those persons to feel intimidated by a surgeon.

3-6, 3. Issue: What was the original intent of the Second Amendment to the United States Constitution, and does it include permission for every citizen to possess handguns?

    a. a representative of the National Rifle Association

    b. a justice of the United States Supreme Court

    c. a constitutional historian

    d. a United States senator

    e. the president of the United States

Judging from the knowledge each is likely to have, we rank (c) as most reliable, with (b) close behind, and (d) and (e) somewhere on the spectrum. The knowledge that an NRA representative possesses is more than offset by that person's obvious bias. Bear in mind what this question does and doesn't ask. One question informed people ask about the Constitution concerns the original intent of its provisions; others include how well interpretations of an amendment cohere with the rest of the Constitution, what the amendment's words mean literally, and what those same words mean in the common-law tradition. A constitutional historian will give the best answer to the historical question of original intent, which is the question that most admits of a clear and factual answer. But just because other issues are harder to answer factually does not make them less important; it only makes expert information more useful to them.

3-12, 12. "Cats that live indoors and use a litter box can live four to five years longer."

In addition to the problem of determining exactly how long cats live outdoors, we face the need for more information that arises with every vague comparison. In this case, two things are claimed as the source of longer feline life: living indoors and using a litter box. Probably very few cats today live indoors and do not use a litter box; so the comparison does nothing to isolate the effects of the litter box.

Additional Exercises

A. Do the following claims have initial plausibility? If not, do they conflict more with observation or with background information?

   1. Your kids will grow faster with two ginseng supplements a day.

   2. Vomiting is your body's way of getting rid of something harmful.

   3. You actually walk better in shoes that fit a little too tightly.

   4. When a restaurant paints its walls red, customers eat faster.

   5. If your gas gauge says "E," you have two gallons left in the tank.

   6. Cold weather alone does not make someone catch cold.

B. Choose the subjects, associated with each expert, to which the person's expertise is relevant.

   1. Professor Bekker served as a Church of Christ minister for twenty years before retiring from that to teach religion at Northern University, a public institution.

      a. the existence of God

      b. the theology of the Church of Christ

      c. the history of American religion

      d. Roman Catholicism

   2. Elaine Rivera inherited her family's gun store, which she has operated on her own for nine years.

      a. the difficulty of enforcing gun-control laws

      b. which guns are most often bought for criminal purposes

      c. which guns are most often bought by amateurs

      d. which guns are easiest for an amateur to use

   3. Xerxes Darius went to Stanford University law school, worked as a tax lawyer for three years, and then became a criminal defense attorney.

      a. whether his present client is guilty as charged

b. whether the quality of the defense attorney makes a difference to a defendant's conviction or acquittal

c. whether existing exceptions for admitting illegally seized evidence are constitutional

d. when to accept a plea-bargaining arrangement

C. On Monday you meet Professor Armstrong, who received a Ph.D. in economics from UCLA and went on to a career at Duke University that included the publication of influential articles on market theory and a textbook on markets. Professor Armstrong tells you that inflation will rise slightly next year, to about 4 percent, but that unemployment will decrease dramatically. "Next year will see recovery and a strong stock market."

On Wednesday you meet Professor Babba of Vanderbilt University. After receiving a Ph.D. in economics from Columbia, Professor Babba published articles on work and wages and a textbook on labor economics. Professor Babba warns you that next year will be the beginning of a severe downturn, with an unhealthy rise in unemployment and deep losses in the stock market. "The only good news," says Professor Babba, "is that inflation will fall to rare levels, less than 1 percent."

Leaving out anything else you learn that week, what would you believe on Friday if you applied the rules explained in this chapter? What does your answer imply about the principles of critical thinking?

D. René Descartes (1596–1650) set the modern tradition of philosophy in motion with his attempt to discover irrefutable foundations for knowledge. In the following passage (paraphrased and edited from the first two paragraphs of the *Meditations*), Descartes outlines the problem with everything he has thus far accepted as knowledge and the strategy by which he plans to test his old beliefs.

> For years I've known that as a young man I accepted many false statements as true, that what I built on that foundation was untrustworthy, and so that I'd eventually need to tear down everything and begin again from those foundations if I wanted to reach stable and lasting knowledge. . . . Today, having arranged for peace and quiet, I will set about to overthrow all my old beliefs. . . . Since I should refuse to accept what isn't obviously true as much as what is obviously false, I can reject every belief in which I find some ground for doubt. It would take forever to examine my beliefs one at a time; but I don't have to. I will go to the principles on which they rest, rejecting every belief that lacks support.

1. What arguments does Descartes use that remind you of the material in Chapter 3?

2. Where does he go beyond Chapter 3's reasons for suspending judgment about claims?

Answers to Additional Exercises

A. 1. No plausibility. Both ordinary observations and what we know about biology entail that growth rates are not affected by supplements.

2. Some initial plausibility. But this claim conflicts with background information about causes of vomiting—for example, motion sickness—that work independently of the presence of harmful substances in the stomach.

3. No initial plausibility. Observation cuts this one down.

4. Some initial plausibility. Both observation and background information may have nothing to say on this subject; so there's no conflict.

5. Fairly strong initial plausibility. This fits with many drivers' experience and with our best guess about how a manufacturer is likely to think. (Better to build a gauge that warns you too early than one that warns you too late.)

6. Mixed initial plausibility. Colds come in cold weather, so observation leans one way; but we know that colds are caused by viruses and not by temperature alone. (Background information may include awareness of the immune system and the strain that cold weather may put on it.)

B. 1. Certainly (b), probably (c); as for (d), Professor Bekker is likely to be a better source than a layperson. The existence of God does not admit of expertise; but we could expect Bekker to know the arguments.

2. (Note that all this information is relevant to gun-control legislation.) In the case of (a), Rivera knows something about what happens in gun stores, but her bias probably disqualifies her. We hope that Rivera has no evidence about (b); she possesses expertise about (c) and (d).

3. In the case of both (a) and (b), Darius's bias disqualifies him. He has the greatest reason for bias in (a); but even in the case of (b), he may want to represent his profession as more important than it is. Darius must count as an expert about (d) and has better-than-usual information about (c).

C. Other things being equal, you have good reason on Monday to accept Professor Armstrong's claim, which comes from a credible source and probably conflicts with nothing you know. Professor Babba's claim comes from an equally credible source and conflicts with what Professor Armstrong said, which makes both experts lose some credibility.

But there is a further consideration: Your background information on Wednesday includes what you learned from Professor Armstrong on Monday. So you have less reason to believe Professor Babba: You should probably tilt slightly toward Monday's belief.

This example suggests that even the best rules of evaluation leave us with some inclination to stay with what we already believe. This is not a reason to mistrust the principles in Chapter 3, only a reminder that sometimes beliefs carry more weight because we heard them first.

D. **(Bear in mind that these questions are difficult and call for nuanced answers. The following are considerations your answers should include.)**

1. Descartes adopts both rules covered in this chapter: that he should not believe

anything that conflicts with what he already knows and that he should not automatically trust what he has merely been told.

2. Descartes goes beyond those rules by beginning with *no* assumption of background knowledge and counting *no* authority as credible. Even more dramatically, he does not conclude, as our rules of critical thinking tell us to, that a claim we have no good reason to accept is a claim on which we should suspend judgment. Rather, he plans to consider all such claims positively false.

Answers to Review Questions

1. These are two distinct questions. Experts are people with special knowledge based on education, training, or experience. You identify experts on the grounds of their education, experience, accomplishments, reputation, and position.

2. Good answers include suggestion, subsequent memories (e.g., the shirts Rabih wore since two Mondays ago can dim your sense of which shirt he wore then), and the repetition of events (if you normally buy bread when you go to the store for milk, you will believe that you did so on any given day, whether or not you did).

3. A shoemaker can tell at a glance how new someone's shoes are. A doctor who has just walked up two flights of stairs with another person can tell from the sound of that person's breathing whether he or she has any history of asthma. A third-grade teacher knows if a child is hungry.

4. Bias ranks first. Conditions of observation include noise around the conversation and the witness's state of mind. The elapsed time could determine how much a witness remembers. Expertise may also figure in: If a conversation concerned plans to commit stock fraud, a witness without special knowledge would probably not realize what points were being made.

CHAPTER 4

PERSUASION THROUGH RHETORIC

Individual claims presented without support are not always ready for our tests of initial plausibility and the credibility of the source. Those tests presuppose that the claim comes in neutral form to our accepting or rejecting minds; but even lone sentences have ways of smuggling in strategies to affect our reception of them. Chapter 4 addresses these techniques of nonargumentative persuasion, which include the use of emotionally loaded language and suggestive sentence structure. Ten categories of nonargumentative persuasion help you detect its often subtle appearances; Chapter 4 then applies some of these categories to advertisements to reveal how they can persuade without seeming to.

CHAPTER SUMMARY

I. **Nonargumentative persuasion** or **rhetoric** affects its audience's beliefs without offering reasons for a claim.

   A. Rhetoric uses additional layers of unstated meaning to influence our beliefs and attitudes.

      1. Such claims frequently choose language that has a powerful and biased emotive force. (See Chapter 2 for a definition of emotive force.) The persuasion discussed in II. A–C below most clearly fits into this category.

      2. Other techniques manipulate features of communication less directly related to emotive force. The types of suggestion discussed in II. D–E, and the obfuscatory ploys of II. F–J, are nonargumentative persuasion without the emotive energy.

   B. Speaking most generally about nonargumentative persuasion, we will call words or phrases that manipulate their emotive force **rhetorical devices and techniques.**

      1. Rhetorical devices, or **slanters,** come in a variety of forms: They laud, censure, excuse, or change the subject. In general, they can dispose us to take a certain perspective on some subject.

      2. Rhetoric typically occurs in the absence of argument, as a substitute for argument.

      3. None of this necessarily means that slanters mislead—that nonargumentative persuasion is persuasion to falsehood. Bear the following points in mind:

         a. We examine slanters to hone our ears for the shadings that language can take, not in order to produce flat and tepid language.

         b. Rhetorical techniques should not make us dismiss claims out of hand; but they should also not make us accept them uncritically.

       c.   We distinguish between language with emotive force and language that arouses an emotional response.

           i.   "He's an angel to the downtrodden" employs slanters.

           ii.   "He has donated $13 million to programs for the homeless" may inspire the same emotions, but it contains no slanters.

       d.   Rhetoric does not always mean there is no argument, for arguments may contain rhetoric; they can be perfectly good arguments regardless.

II.   Nonargumentative persuasion through the use of rhetorical techniques tends to either strengthen or weaken a claim, or to either elevate or disparage its subject.

   A.   **Euphemisms** and **dysphemisms** replace one expression with another that carries, respectively, more positive or more negative associations.

      1.   "Escort" is a euphemism for "bodyguard"; "thug" is a dysphemism.

      2.   Entirely neutral language can function as a euphemism or dysphemism, if it replaces a more common term that carries associations.

         a.   "Delivery system," neutral as it sounds, is a euphemism for "missile."

         b.   Likewise, the neutral language of "payment for nonwork" does not stop it from being a dysphemism for "welfare."

      3.   Euphemisms can have acceptable uses, when they foster civility and diplomacy.

   B.   **Persuasive comparisons, definitions,** and **explanations** are cases in which those modes of speaking slant what they say.

      1.   A persuasive comparison links our feeling about a thing to the thing we compare it to: "He had a laugh like an old car trying to start."

      2.   A persuasive definition uses loaded language while ostensibly trying to clarify a term: "Animals are our fellow conscious beings."

      3.   Persuasive explanations use loaded language while pretending merely to tell the reason for an event: "She smiled at you so she'd have an edge when you hand out raises."

   C.   Emotional associations, usually negative ones, connect to a person or thing described with a **stereotype,** a popularly held image of a group that rests on little or no evidence.

      1.   Stereotypes are often involved when someone lumps people under one name or description, especially when it begins with "the": the conservative, the Asian.

      2.   Many times a stereotype arises because it serves an interest, as when one nation goes to war with another.

D. **Innuendo** belongs among those techniques that employ not certain words but ordinary features of linguistic communication. An innuendo works by implying what it does not say.

   1. Sometimes an innuendo suggests while pretending or even claiming not to: "Far be it from me to call my opponents liars."

   2. Along the same lines, one may condemn with faint praise. Imagine a letter of recommendation that says only, "Richard was very seldom tardy."

E. A **loaded question** follows the logic of innuendo, illegitimately suggesting something through the very existence of the question.

   1. Whereas every question rests on assumptions, a loaded question rests on unwarranted or unjustified assumptions.

   2. Another feature of the loaded question is that the answer it seeks will not address the assumption. For instance, a "No" answer to "Are you still illiterate?" does not challenge the assumption that the person *had been* illiterate.

F. When the persuasive device aims at shielding a claim from criticism by qualifying it, we may call that device a **weaseler.**

   1. Words like "perhaps" and "possibly," and qualifying phrases like "as far as we know" or "within reasonable limits," most commonly signal the work of weaselers.

   2. Claims that might otherwise convey strong and specific information, but possibly be false, can be made more nearly true through the use of weaselers, though for the same reason weaker and more nebulous: "She is quite possibly one of the most gifted students I am now teaching."

   3. Weasely words can also plant an innuendo: "It's not impossible for him to have ulterior motives."

   4. But such words have a proper place in communication, where we ought to qualify our claims

      a. At best the mere existence of qualifying words should serve as a first warning that some weaseling might be afoot.

      b. To ascertain that it occurs, assess the speaker, the subject, and the context.

G. A **downplayer** is a rhetorical move to make something seem less important than it really is.

   1. Stereotypes, persuasive comparisons, persuasive explanations, and innuendo can all have this purpose.

   2. We also find downplaying at work in the use of words like "mere," "merely," and "so-called," or the placement of a word in quotation marks:

       a.   "Evolution is merely a theory."

       b.   "Professor Economou has a new 'method' for measuring inflation."

   3.   More complex downplaying happens when a speaker uses conjunctions like "however" and "although" to diminish one claim in favor of another.

       a.   As often occurs when a persuasive technique uses grammatical structures instead of words, this form of *relative* downplaying is harder to spot.

       b.   "Despite the persistent growth of algae, the lake's water must be judged perfectly safe for drinking."

H.   The **horse laugh, ridicule,** or **sarcasm** is a way to avoid arguing about a position by laughing at it.

I.   **Hyperbole** means exaggeration.

   1.   Not all strong claims count as hyperbole. "Michael Jordan is the best professional basketball player of all time," while a strong claim, is either true or close enough to truth not to involve hyperbole.

   2.   Hyperbole can turn up in a variety of other persuasive maneuvers, such as dysphemism, persuasive comparison, and ridicule.

   3.   The greatest danger that hyperbole poses is that, even when you recognize it as false, you prepare yourself to accept a weaker version of the same claim.

J.   Suppose a claim comes to you with no support except for the speaker's assurance that some support exists: This assurance takes the name of **proof surrogate.**

   1.   A proof surrogate may be as little as an adverb (e.g., "obviously") tacked on to a sentence.

   2.   The complete proof surrogate, however, refers to the evidence, argument, or authority that carries the day on some issue, without delivering details: "Philosophers agree that God does not exist"; "Studies suggest that people with arthritis don't actually feel aches when the weather changes."

III.   Advertising nearly always depends on rhetoric and must be received critically.

A.   Remember that advertising sells more than consumer goods.

   1.   It may try to sell a political candidate or policy, a way of life, a habit.

   2.   Advertising acts by creating desires, and so uses every persuasive technique available to excite those desires.

B.   The critical response to advertising rests on the question: "Does this ad give us a good reason to buy this product?"

   1.   This question fundamentally means: Will I be better off with the product than without it, or better off with the product than with the money it costs?

C. Many advertisements give no reasons why you should buy their product.

    1. They try to associate pleasant feelings with the product, show it being used or endorsed by people we identify with, or show it in situations we would like to be in.

    2. With the exception of ads that notify us of a product's existence when we already have reasons for wanting it (see E below), such advertisements never provide a justification for buying their product.

D. But just because some advertisements give reasons for their claims does not mean they give **good** arguments or reasons.

    1. The typical reason found in an advertisement is vague, ambiguous, misleading, or exaggerated.

    2. Moreover, these reasons come unsupported: We have no way of knowing whether to believe the advertised claim.

E. One kind of advertisement provides a justifiable reason to buy its product.

    1. This occurs when the ad tells you of the availability of a certain product you already want, or its availability at a price you can afford.

    2. Such ads derive their justification from whatever justification you antecedently have for wanting the product.

KEY WORDS AND IDEAS

Nonargumentative persuasion. The influence that a claim may have above and beyond the literal meanings of the words in it. Nonargumentative persuasion works in the absence of explicit reasons for accepting a claim; it often involves emotive force.

Rhetoric. Language used to persuade or influence beliefs or attitudes, rather than to prove a claim logically.

Rhetorical devices and techniques. Words or phrases that manipulate their emotive force to encourage us to take a certain perspective on some subject. Rhetoric is not always bad and does not necessarily lead us into false beliefs; these techniques are, rather, characterized by their ability to say more than the words' literal meanings convey.

Slanters. Rhetorical techniques.

See the outline above for definitions of all rhetorical techniques covered in Chapter 4.

REVIEW QUESTIONS

1. What is the difference between innuendo and a downplayer?

2. Name the single case in which advertising gives you a good reason to buy its product.

3. Give examples of a dysphemism that is also a stereotype, hyperbole that is also a persuasive comparison, and a loaded question that contains innuendo.

4. What factors might contribute to the inclusion of proof surrogates in news stories? What about stereotypes?

5. What makes a weaseler a weaseler?

COMMONLY ASKED QUESTIONS

Is there a method for telling one kind of rhetorical technique from another?

First some advice about how precisely we can draw such distinctions. As with the classifications of pseudoreasoning we come across in the next two chapters, you will find here that the distinctions are partial, often overlapping, and to some extent intrinsically vague. Rhetorical techniques are not automobile models, and critical thinkers are not car enthusiasts who look at the headlights to tell a '93 Mustang from a '94. Chapter 4's organization of rhetorical techniques into types is ultimately meant to assist critical reasoning, not obstruct it with terminology or replace it with rote acts of labeling.

That said, we may give some rough guides to choosing the best name for the spin being used in a given example. First, eliminate those possibilities whose form gives them away: A loaded question must first be a question; a persuasive comparison is a comparison; persuasive definitions and explanations are, likewise, definitions and explanations before they are anything else. If none of these categories fits the case, the technique (assuming there is one) must be euphemism, dysphemism, stereotype, innuendo, weaseler, downplayer, hyperbole, or proof surrogate.

But even if you have found the structure of, say, a definition, you do not yet have a slanter. As a next step, look for loaded words that convey more than the literal meaning the claim needs from them. (See "Tips on Applications" for more on the difference between appropriately and inappropriately loaded words.) Remember as you do this that unusually *unloaded* words may function as slanters when they are not the most natural words for a context. "Assault rifles are a kind of manually operated firearm, as are shotguns and hunting rifles" is a definition that becomes persuasive precisely by *not* pumping up your reaction to its words—the most charged word in that sentence is "assault"—but by describing the same item in less emotive terms.

If the language you are looking at falls into one of the categories already named, you have your answer: loaded question, persuasive comparison, persuasive definition, or persuasive explanation. If it does not, ask whether the loaded words produce a positive or negative effect. Where it is positive, you have either a euphemism or hyperbole; where negative, a dysphemism, a stereotype, or (again) hyperbole. Once you have narrowed down your example this far, it is not hard to pick the name that fits best.

Suppose no obviously charged language is present, nor any cues to a loaded question or the other grammatical giveaways. Check to see if the speaker appeals to vaguely described authorities—that tells you a proof surrogate is at work. Otherwise, look for the intended effect of the claim. If it aims at suggesting something about a person or thing, it is innuendo. If it more generally diminishes the importance of a claim or a description, it is a downplayer. If it tries to evade precision, it is a weaseler.

To summarize: You will look for (1) obvious structural cues; (2) loaded language; (3) intended effects. The process of elimination will lead you to the best description of the slanter.

TIPS ON APPLICATIONS

Using the information in this chapter takes one very important kind of sensitivity—namely, sensitivity to the difference between illegitimate nonargumentative persuasion and the appropriate use of lively or emotively charged language. Without a nose for this difference, you may condemn a claim when it doesn't deserve condemnation; or you may censor your own writing so scrupulously that you wind up with astringent, unreadable prose.

Some rhetorical techniques have no appropriate uses, or almost none. Innuendo might add humor when it alludes to innocuous items, such as the colorfulness of someone's clothing. But true innuendo busies itself with things salacious and has no proper uses: Either spell out the accusation or leave it unsuggested.

It's just as hard to imagine good reasons for flinging stereotypes about. Even where people should not get offended—for example, the image of the impractical professor or the shrewd lawyer—stereotypes are to thinking what a cliché is to writing: probably unavoidable in some form, but never welcome, and a sign of laziness.

Most of the other categories in this chapter have their good uses. But what are they? Two general principles, while not exhausting the subject, help sort the sheep from the goats.

In the first place, you may evaluate the emotive force in language to see if it constitutes real slanting. Emotive force alone does not make a word or phrase a slanter. Consider "mother"—what connotations that has! But we would not call "female parent" a better choice of words in a sentence like "I promised my mother not to try cigarettes." "Mother" becomes a slanter in other contexts. "Recycling: Do It for Mother Earth." "The state is responsible for your existence as much as your mother is, so obey it as you would your mother." Or even, "Support Medicare reform today and help take care of your mother tomorrow."

Similar things happen with the word "suicide." "More teenagers commit suicide today than ever before" is a claim with emotive punch, the same punch that strikes in "His immigration policies will lead to widespread suicide" and "This mouthwash is social suicide." But the first claim, unlike the next two, contains no slanters.

This is partly a matter of the literal use of words rather than their metaphorical use, but not entirely. It is more illuminating to say that the words with emotive force become slanters when some other word or phrase would be more natural in their place.

Not that identifying the more natural word can always happen so easily. The debate over abortion includes many accusations from both sides of slanters on the other side. Is "fetus" a euphemism for "unborn baby," or the most natural description? Does the phrase "right to life" imply a persuasive definition—the embryo is a human being with the right not to be killed—that unfairly characterizes the significance of the debate? In such cases the accusation of slanter-use is as controversial as the use of the slanters.

These cases, though they are important, do not make it impossible to identify the natural use of most words. Ask whether a claim would have a stronger rhetorical effect if you replaced its emotively charged word with a more neutral synonym. What's wrong with "More teenagers commit the self-induced cessation of bodily functions today than ever before"? That claim, much more than the equivalent claim with the word "suicide" in it, is trying to do something with its words. *Here,* and not in the other case, we have a slanter.

You may think of the second general principle as a broader version of the first. *Nonargumentative persuasion is appropriate when it has already been justified.* Say someone asserts: "Alcoholism is a disease like any other." You may take this for a persuasive definition. But suppose the person has already argued that some people have a genetic predisposition toward alcoholic behavior or are otherwise powerless to will it away; that their alcoholism follows a progressive and debilitating growth; that it responds to treatment, including medical treatment. Now that the definition is not being made to do the work of persuading—now that it functions as a conclusion, however controversial, to other claims—it cannot be accused of slanting.

Or take this sentence: "Tonight they'll present their so-called original idea." On its own it downplays the idea. But imagine that the sentence before it said, "Our school board spent the last two months preparing a list of books to be removed from the high school library." "So-called" is just right. The downplayer turned into an appropriate expression as soon as we saw a good reason for it.

In short, don't let the persuasive effects of language, by themselves, become the goal of your critical evaluation. Use them as a first sign that a further justification is called for. Then look for it.

EXERCISES

Sample Exercises from the Book

4-7, 4. Although it has always had a bad name in the United States, socialism is nothing more or less than democracy in the realm of economics.

Persuasive definition. Note that, as in this case, persuasive definitions can promote an idea as easily as they disparage it. Also note the downplaying function of the sentence structure: It's not unusual for a downplayer to get objections out of the way before another slanter does its work.

4-7, 6. It's fair to say that, compared to most people his age, Mr. Beechler is pretty much bald.

No slanter present. Two answers you might have given are euphemism (or dysphemism) and weaseler. But "bald" and "pretty much bald" are really the most natural words to use. As for the qualifiers—"it's fair to say," "compared to most people his age"—the inherent vagueness of baldness makes them reasonable.

4-8, 1. "If the United States is to meet the technological challenge posed by Japan, Inc., we must rethink the way we do everything from design to manufacture to education to employee relations." (*Harper's*)

"Japan, Inc." is a dysphemism. You may have called it a stereotype, because it plays on certain images of the industrial complex in Japan. It is better to say dysphemism here, mainly because the stereotype is not a standard one.

Additional Exercises

A. Name the nonargumentative persuasion at work in these examples. Where more than one fits, name them all.

1. Your teacher might have called this paper on capitalism independent thinking. I call it a spoiled kid not appreciating what he's been given.

2. I don't know what my opponents will base their speeches on; I'm basing mine on love for my country.

3. Economists say this layoff is Cleveland's final readjustment to a service economy.

4. At the end of the day, the reasons for our view tend to preponderate over the reasons for the contrary view.

5. Of course she told you it'll run smoothly. Car salespeople will tell you whatever they think you want to hear.

6. For all practical purposes, there has basically been only one worthwhile idea in the history of philosophy.

7. Are you here to beg for another favor?

8. Open this envelope and you'll get a check for three million dollars, if your name appears on our list of winners.

9. Letter to the editor: We can thank ivory-tower professors like Mr. Fosl for all the head-in-the-clouds ideas our society has to contend with.

10. Is this going to be another bright suggestion like your proposal that we take scuba lessons?

11. Who was that young woman with the Senator last night: his niece?

12. You can't sleep with the covers over your head. All the medical journals will tell you that's harmful.

13. Taxation is the oppressive practice of taking other people's hard-earned money.

14. We will fund this new program through revenue enhancements from the sale of beer and cigarettes.

15. Overheard: You know why the subway is so dirty, don't you? They're getting people on welfare to clean the cars.

B. Look for slanters and other forms of nonargumentative persuasion in this portion of an editorial (from "McCall Puts On His Partisan Hat," *New York Post*, February 10, 1997).

> State Comptroller Carl McCall has a choice to make.
>
> Does he want to be the state's principal elected watchdog—by tradition a non-partisan position? Or does he want to become a mover and shaker in the Democratic Party?
>
> One thing's for sure: McCall can't be both.
>
> On Saturday, McCall blasted Mayor Giuliani in a tendentious speech delivered in a Black History Month celebration in The Bronx. He accused the mayor of responsibility for the "disappearance" of 4,000 blacks from the city payroll. . . .
>
> Arguably analysis of the city's employment practices could be considered part of the comptroller's oversight responsibilities. But taken in the context of McCall's recent actions, this doesn't seem likely. McCall surely recognizes that New York's economic health rests on a dynamic private sector—not on people who nestle themselves into lifetime sinecures on the city payroll. And trimming the bureaucracy, reducing taxes and getting the city budget under control are the keys to private sector growth.
>
> McCall would surely further recognize that Mayor Giuliani has cut the city work force by more than 20,000 jobs, held by individuals of all races. . . . While slicing the payroll, City Hall has helped spur considerable private sector job growth—not least in Harlem, which is undergoing what some have described as an economic "renaissance." . . .
>
> The state comptroller, by definition, oversees the fiscal affairs of every municipality in the state. . . . So his political warnings amount to a kind of threat—which his targets are unable to ignore.

Answers to Additional Exercises

A. 1. Criticism of a euphemism, followed by a dysphemism.

2. Innuendo.

3. Euphemism; proof surrogate.

4. Weaseler.

5. Persuasive explanation.

6. Weaseler.

7. Loaded question.

8. Downplayer.

9. Stereotype; dysphemism.

10. Loaded question; also persuasive comparison.

11. Innuendo; *not* a loaded question.

12. Proof surrogate.

13. Persuasive definition; dysphemism.

14. Euphemism.

15. Stereotype.

B.   Answers may vary widely; but they should include most of the following:

Paragraph 2 contains a persuasive definition: The State Comptroller's office is a nonpartisan position. Its second question may also count as loaded, because it implies ambitions in the present comptroller.

Paragraph 4 contains at least one dysphemism, "blasted"; "tendentious" may be a second. The quotation marks around "disappearance" work as a downplayer.

Paragraph 5 opens with the structure of a downplayer, to mute the possibility of Carl McCall's right to make his argument. It continues with a persuasive explanation about economic health and a dynamic private sector, which then turns into dysphemism (especially the words "nestle" and "sinecures").

Paragraph 6 contains a proof surrogate: "what some have described as an economic 'renaissance.'"

Answers to Review Questions

1.   Both innuendo and downplayers can be negatively suggestive. But a downplayer suggests that a thing is worth little, or relatively unimportant, whereas innuendo suggests something more specific about a person or thing, some particular characteristic (usually a factual matter) and not just unimportance.

2.   Advertising gives you a good reason to buy its product when you already have a good reason to desire it, but don't know where to find it or whether you can afford it. The preview of a movie you've been waiting for falls into this category; also a specifically described sale on an air conditioner you want.

3.   A dysphemism that is a stereotype: robber baron; terrorist. Hyperbole that is also a persuasive comparison: "*Star Wars* is the Bible of action films." A loaded question that contains innuendo: "Have you ever acknowledged your drug habit?"

4.   Proof surrogates may enter news stories when the story is compressed to avoid losing an audience, or because of the source of the news, as when a government official has spoken off-record to reporters ("sources in the White House say"). Stereotypes in news stories can arise when the effort to retain a potentially bored audience induces a reporter to speak of "right-wing extremists" or "hard-line feminists."

5.   A weaseler weakens a claim *in order to protect it*. So, in the first place, it is a phrase or word that makes a claim say less, or say something less confidently, than it otherwise would. In the second place, the purpose of this qualification is not to make the claim more accurate or more modest, but to let the speaker get a strong idea across without actually being committed to it

CHAPTER 5

MORE RHETORICAL DEVICES

We are now beginning to look beyond individual truth claims to the support that people offer for what they say. Chapters 5 and 6 take a first step toward the study of arguments with what you may call "would-be arguments," reasons people have or adduce for their beliefs that do not in fact support them. Pseudoreasoning comprises two kinds of would-be arguments—those that appeal in a misguided fashion to emotions (Chapter 5), and those constructed like real arguments but not working like them (Chapter 6).

CHAPTER SUMMARY

I. **Pseudoreasoning** is a kind of rhetoric that aims at supporting a claim. That is, it offers considerations meant to persuade you to accept the claim.

  A. Whereas a good argument gives a justification for accepting its conclusion, pseudo-reasoning is likely to have *some* connection with the claim it's meant to support, but it does not in fact support the claim.

  B. Because pseudoreasoning is defined in terms of what it is not, it does not lend itself to technical or exhaustive categorization in the way that good argumentation does.

    1. Thus the classifications offered in these chapters may overlap in places, or fail to capture precisely what has gone wrong in an argument.

    2. The point of these chapters is to alert you to a number of ways in which reasoning may fail.

  C. Within the broad group of pseudoreasoning, the main distinction to keep in mind is the one between thinking that has been distorted by misplaced emotions and thinking that has been led astray by **fallacy** (error).

II. While most pseudoreasons introduce **irrelevant** considerations into a discussion, a **smokescreen** or **red herring** may be more specifically defined as an irrelevancy that

  A. does not fall under any of the more specific categories of pseudoreasoning, and

  B. typically is introduced deliberately in order to throw a discussion off course.

III. The **subjectivist fallacy** occurs when one seeks to dismiss someone else's claim by turning all disagreement into differences of opinion.

  A. Its most common form is, "That's true for you but not for me."

  B. This fallacy builds on the truth that people have different opinions. But it erroneously assumes that differences of opinion resemble differences of taste (e.g., between coffee and tea) that cannot be settled.

IV. The **appeal to popularity (*ad populum*)** takes several different forms, in each of which one is told to accept a claim or practice because it is accepted by other people.

    A. This rhetorical device is a distorted version of the quite reasonable practice of accepting claims from reliable authorities (Chapter 3).

        1. Only now we consider not what experts believe but what everyone thinks.

        2. In most cases, of course, the fact that everyone believes a claim does not make it true.

    B. Three variants of the appeal to popularity are worth giving special names to.

        1. The appeal to **common practice** also seeks to justify something on the grounds of its popularity; it differs from the appeal to popularity in calling an action acceptable without mentioning anyone's beliefs. The most common form is "Everyone does it" (or, when the speaker wants to sound cultured, "Everyone in Europe does it").

        2. Appeals to **peer pressure** begin with the desire for approval, and illegitimately make that desire the reason to hold a belief.

            a. It is not pseudoreasoning simply to act as your friends do in order to gain social acceptance, for then you are reasoning correctly about what will get you accepted (whether or not you ought to value acceptance that highly).

            b. Going along with others turns into pseudoreasoning when the reaction of others becomes your reason for accepting a claim as true.

        3. In the similar case of the **bandwagon,** we find ourselves supporting a political candidate or liking a consumer product just because they are popular.

            a. Again, acting so as to feel at one with your community may be unwise, but it does not constitute pseudoreasoning.

            b. The bandwagon effect amounts to pseudoreasoning (as in every version of the *ad populum*) only when the beliefs or actions of others are cited as reasons for the truth of a claim or the rightness of an action.

V. In the case of **wishful thinking,** one accepts a claim because one wants it to be true.

    A. One may equally reject a claim as false on the grounds that it is unacceptable. This form of wishful thinking often proves harder to identify, because there are more disguised ways of calling a claim unacceptable (e.g., "that intolerable idea").

    B. People rarely offer such considerations in a discussion with others. Wishful thinking typically works on our deliberations when we don't even notice it.

VI. When the emotion being appealed to is fear, we call the gambit **scare tactics.**

    A. As with many of the examples in this chapter, you need to watch for the differences between justified and unjustified appeals to fear. "If you don't check your parachute before jumping, you may die" is an excellent argument.

B. The difference lies in the relevance of the danger cited.

VII. The **appeal to pity** works like a scare tactic, except for the different emotion at stake. Exactly as in the last case, this appeal becomes pseudoreasoning when the pity is irrelevant.

VIII. When someone appeals to your vanity, the pseudoreasoning goes by the name of **apple polishing.**

    A. Note that this move can take subtle forms—for instance, "You're too smart to believe in telepathy."

    B. Appeals to vanity have fewer legitimate versions (because vanity has fewer good purposes than pity or fear), but they do exist—for example: "You should wear the gold sweater tonight, because it brings out your beautiful eyes."

IX. A would-be argument contains an **appeal to indignation or anger** if it obscures the relevant issues by arousing one's anger, particularly at some person or group.

    A. Bear in mind that expressions of anger do not by themselves make something an appeal to anger or indignation.

    B. Most commonly, such appeals arouse anger against a person before getting to the specifics of the argument, rather than expressing indignation after showing that something wrong has been done.

X. Support for a position rests on the assumption that **two wrongs make a right** when one justifies some action that hurts another person on the grounds that the other person has done (or is likely to do) the same kind of harm.

    A. This may be the trickiest kind of pseudoreasoning to distinguish from legitimate reasoning, because many people will see justice in cases of returning harm for harm.

    B. It often helps to bear in mind that "two wrongs make a right" is not identical with a general conception of revenge, but applies specifically to those circumstances in which the revenging act is illegitimate.

        1. Responding to rude service at a restaurant by telling your friends not to eat there may be vengeful, but does not fall under this category of pseudoreasoning.

        2. If you slip out without paying and justify yourself on the grounds that the waiters were rude, you are engaging in pseudoreasoning.

KEY WORDS AND IDEAS

Irrelevance. In cases of pseudoreasoning, the failure of a motivation to justify one's believing a given claim or acting in a given way. The feelings or other motives appealed to in pseudoreasoning are not necessarily illegitimate feelings. Therefore, to call the feeling invoked irrelevant is not to claim that a person shouldn't have it. The point is rather that the motivation does not bear on the truth of the claim in question. Indeed, the distinguishing mark that sets this chapter's pseudoreasoning apart from good reasoning is the incorrect connection between the motivation and the conclusion.

Pseudoreasoning. Alleged support given for a claim that does not in fact support it, whether because the reasons given are irrelevant to the claim's truth, or because something has gone wrong in the structure of the argument.

See the outline above for definitions of all types of pseudoreasoning covered in Chapter 5.

REVIEW QUESTIONS

1. Explain the difference between an appeal to common practice and an appeal to popularity.

2. Which type of pseudoreasoning can you most often apply in any given case, and why?

3. Name four emotions appealed to by pseudoreasoning, and the type of pseudoreasoning connected to each.

4. What is the difference between seeking revenge and arguing on the grounds that "two wrongs make a right"?

5. Why is anger out of place in an argument against someone's wrongdoing, when it is appropriate to be angry at the sight of wrongdoing?

COMMONLY ASKED QUESTIONS

Why is the subjectivist fallacy a fallacy?

A question like this arises out of the suspicion that the subjectivist fallacy speaks common sense. There is no arguing over matters of taste, is there?

When a matter does reduce to taste alone, the retort "That's true for you but not for me" is not pseudoreasoning. If someone has just praised the mixture of milk and coffee as better than coffee alone, you are free to answer that you have different tastes.

In matters that look like real truth claims at first blush, the subjectivist fallacy assumes the truth of relativism, the view that ethical and aesthetic claims boil down to matters of taste. "Stealing is wrong for you, not for everyone else." Now, relativism might be a true theory. It continues to be debated by philosophers, so one can call it a live issue. But even if relativism is true it is not obviously true, and one can't simply assert it. (See Chapter 13 for more.) The subjectivist fallacy goes wrong by helping itself to the truth of relativism, as if that theory had been proved true, without doing any of the work of proving it. The advantages of the subjectivist fallacy thus amount to all the advantages of theft over honest toil.

Why does the study of pseudoreasoning give us a list of categories, without more systematic organization?

This appearance is actually misleading (see the next question). But to the extent that it's true, there is a sound reason. We study pseudoreasoning to learn how arguments go wrong, how proposed defenses for a claim fail to defend that claim. And the study of failures takes us in more scattered directions than the study of successes.

Suppose someone asks you how a car runs, or how the human digestive system works. Without being an expert, you can give a general answer. But if someone asks how a car may fail to run, or how the digestive system may go awry, even an expert cannot give a single overarching answer. At most, experts will list the most common failings of the car or gastro-intestinal tract, with tips for diagnosing them.

So, too, with reasonable argument. When it works, it follows a well-defined set of rules. When it doesn't, any number of things may have gone wrong. It happens to be the case that the types of pseudoreasoning covered in Chapters 5 and 6 occur more commonly than others. You might encounter more unusual false steps; some misfired supports for a position fit in more than one category; but as a rule of thumb, the categorizations here provide the best guide to diagnosing the pseudoreasoning that you will probably confront.

What general characteristics underlie this chapter's categories of pseudoreasoning?

Recognizing the two characteristics of the pseudoreasoning covered in this chapter will help guide your diagnoses of where these arguments go wrong—where reasoning has malfunctioned. Some sort of emotion is being appealed to, but that emotion (or comparable motivation) is irrelevant to the truth of the claim under discussion. Reason may also malfunction when nothing is happening emotionally, but reasonable thinking still makes a mistake (see Chapter 6).

In every example given in Chapter 5, some emotional factor interferes with the critical assessment of truth claims. That factor may look obviously like an emotion, as with the desire present in wishful thinking, or the fear, pity, vanity, and anger that kinds of pseudoreasoning appeal to. In other cases (bandwagon, common practice, appeal to popularity), the interfering element is the common human willingness to believe what others believe and act as they do. You may think of this as the motivation that makes us social animals.

Like fear and pity and other emotions, the impulse to agree with our neighbors offers excellent advantages to human life and good behavior. We do not need to expunge these motivations from our lives: Thinking critically certainly does not have to mean turning into unemotional creatures. It does mean recognizing when such motivations belong in an argument and when they do not, where they offer reasons for believing or acting a certain way and when they cloud the issue.

Moreover, the motivations that these cases of pseudoreasoning appeal to are irrelevant to the truth or falsity of the claim being considered. So the most general strategy for identifying pseudoreasoning of this sort begins by identifying the motivation appealed to and asking whether it pertains to the question at hand.

A final comment about irrelevance. Because it haunts all of these bad reasons, there is a vague sense in which you may call any of them a smokescreen. When tackling the exercises in this chapter, you might find yourself frequently reaching for "smokescreen/red herring." Watch out. Although some examples do count as smokescreens, be careful not to use the label for just any case in which you're not sure what has gone wrong. The true smokescreen contains an intent to mislead, a deliberate act of changing the subject, often with the purpose of avoiding an accusation.

TIPS ON APPLICATIONS

People often feel torn when trying to apply what they have learned about pseudoreasoning in ordinary contexts. This is not a matter of being able to spot the pseudoreasoning in editorials, a newspaper's or magazine's letters to the editors, and so on: You will soon discover that you have no trouble finding and identifying such argumentative missteps.

The trick arises in conversational contexts. On the one hand, your knowledge of pseudoreasoning makes it tempting to call another person's statement "apple polishing" or "subjective fallacy." On the other hand, simply throwing out these labels is rude at best, not to mention confusing and weird. It doesn't help anyone's critical thinking to give a name to what someone just said.

Watching for pseudoreasoning therefore works best if you notice the category that a would-be argument falls into, and use that information to tell yourself that an emotion has been irrelevantly appealed to. If you then want to say something in the conversation, it is more useful to say, "That pity [or anger, vanity, concern for the opinions of others, and so on] is not relevant to the truth or falsity of what you're talking about."

EXERCISES

Sample Exercises from the Book

5-1, 4. I've come before you to ask that you rehire Professor Johnson. I realize that Mr. Johnson does not have a Ph.D., and I am aware that he has yet to publish his first article. But Mr. Johnson is over forty now, and he has a wife and two high-school-aged children to support. It will be very difficult for him to find another teaching job at his age, I'm sure you will agree.

Appeal to pity. However, notice that the speaker is not trying to convince his or her audience of the truth of a claim, only to play on their pity when they are to decide about rehiring. Although pity should not be the uppermost concern in a rehiring decision, it probably does have some role to play.

5-2, 1. Is the fact that a brand of toothpaste is advertised as a best-seller relevant to the issue of whether to buy that brand?

No. Popular toothpastes gain nothing by being popular. By comparison, a popular college is worth looking at. If a school is popular enough, it will get more applicants and raise its admissions standards; then going to that college will probably mean being surrounded by better fellow students, which benefits your own education.

Keep one thing in mind with all the questions of 5-2: There is nothing inherently wrong with paying attention to what other people believe and do. You may fall into conformism if you base all your decisions on what other people do, out of a desperate urge to fit in; but, while no one would recommend such a life, no pseudoreasoning is involved. Obedience to popular tastes counts as pseudoreasoning only if you assert or believe something to be true solely on the basis of the beliefs of others.

5-4, 4. Aw, c'mon, Jake, let's go hang out at Dave's. Don't worry about your parents; they'll get over it. You know, the one thing I really like about you is that you don't let your parents tell you what to do.

Apple polishing. The opening sentence sets up a peer-pressure context. The second sentence offers a reason for going to Dave's—your parents will get over it—that is *not* pseudoreasoning. (The argument that an action will have no bad consequences is, from this point of view, reasonable thinking.) Only the last point falls into the pseudoreasoning trap, by flattering its listener.

5-4, 10. Reporter Cokie Roberts: Mr. Cheney, aside from the legal issues that stem from the various United Nations resolutions, isn't there an overriding moral dimension to the suffering of so many Kurdish people in Iraq?

(Former) Secretary of Defense Dick Cheney: Well, we recognize that's a tragic situation, Cokie, but there are tragic situations occurring all over the world. (Adapted from an interview on National Public Radio's *Morning Edition*)

Smokescreen/red herring. Other answers fit here to some degree: two wrongs make a right, if Secretary Cheney means to imply that some of the existing "tragic situations" result from Iraq's own behavior; also common practice, in that he plays down the import of U.S. actions by making them seem customary. But Mr. Cheney does not explicitly try to defend a U.S. action, so neither of those two works exactly.

Ultimately, smokescreen applies best because (1) neither of the others fits in an unambiguous way, and (2) the speaker has brought in considerations that could get the conversation far off track, out of a deliberate intention not to answer the question.

5-5, 10. One local to another: I'll tell you, it's disgusting. These college students come up here and live for four years—and ruin the town—and then vote on issues that will affect us long after they've gone somewhere else. This has got to stop! I say, let only those who have a genuine stake in the future of this town vote here! Transient kids shouldn't determine what's going to happen to local residents. Most of these kids come from Philadelphia . . . let them vote there.

Appeal to indignation. The trick here is to separate the legitimate argument from the pseudoreasoning. The speaker does have an argument, based on the principle that people should not vote on issues that don't affect them. You can dispute this principle—what would follow about the right of childless couples to vote on school spending? But you would need to show the problems with that principle separately. The speaker's words also contain, however, inflammatory and biased language against students; that makes the argument pseudoreasoning.

5-6, 4. Don't risk letting a fatal accident rob your family of the home they love—on the average more than 250 Americans die each day because of accidents. What would happen to your family's home if you were one of them? Your home is so much more than just a place to live. It's a community you've chosen carefully . . . a neighborhood . . . a school district . . . the way of life you and your family have come to know. And you'd want your family to continue sharing its familiar comforts, even if suddenly you were no longer there. . . . Now, as a Great Western mortgage customer, you can protect the home you love. . . . Just complete the Enrollment Form enclosed for you.

Almost scare tactics. The advertisement plays on our fear, but mortgage insurance does protect against the danger of losing your house. Since this is an advertisement for one kind of mortgage insurance, though, we have to ask whether this danger will strike anyone who does not buy Great Western mortgage insurance.

Additional Exercises

Classify the pseudoreasoning at work in these examples.

1. Biker: I refuse to buy a Japanese motorcycle. I don't believe in doing business with Communist countries.
   Reporter: But Japan isn't Communist.
   Biker: Well to me they are.

2. Officer: Excuse me, sir. Do you know how fast you were going?
   Driver: I never get over the sight of you mounted policemen. How do you leap down off the horse's back so fast? And you must have them well trained, not to run away when you dismount.

3. Dear Editors: When Al Zacharkiw wrote in to criticize city workers, he didn't mention his occupation. Maybe he's a millionaire without a care in the world, that he has the time to criticize people working for him—if he's even a taxpayer.

4. Ladies and gentlemen of the jury: My client stands before you accused of three bank robberies. But the prosecution has not told you about three little children in this story, who will have a hard time getting food on their table if their daddy goes to prison.

5. My opponent would like to see TV networks label their programming, on the grounds that violent shows make children who watch them violent. But everyone knows a couple of shows can't change your personality.

6. I had to get a garage built last summer. Who wants to be the last person on the block to park his car in the open air?

7. There must be life on other planets. Imagine how lonely we'll find the universe if we discover that we're the only ones here.

8. Judge Cunningham keeps striking down our state gun-control laws. She had better say good-bye to any hopes for a Supreme Court appointment, as long as we have a Democrat in the White House.

9. I'm a disabled Vietnam veteran. Why can I only get a six-month license to sell pretzels from my pushcart? You have to be a foreigner with a green card to make a living in this country.

10. The United States is under no obligation to pay its debts to the United Nations. Here we are, the biggest contributor to the UN budget, and we only get one vote out of 185.

11. How can Moslems be opposed to alcoholic beverages? People have been drinking them since before the beginning of history.

12. Why do you take a bus to work when most people drive?

13. Give that woman a dollar. I see her on this corner every day crying. And she seems to be ill.

14. Ladies and gentlemen, that concludes my proposal. You know that I trust and honor your judgment. Even if you do not approve my request, I am happy just to have had the chance to present this proposal to such qualified experts. Thank you.

15. Letter to the editor: Your magazine expresses sympathy for Annie Larson, a putative "fashion victim" because "animal rights terrorists" splashed paint on her mink coat. But when I think of those dozens of animals maimed and anally electrocuted to satisfy someone's vanity, I know who the real victims are, and who's the terrorist.

Answers to Additional Exercises

1. Subjectivist fallacy.

2. Apple polishing. This also counts as smokescreen, but that's not the best answer here.

3. Appeal to indignation.

4. Appeal to pity.

5. Appeal to popularity.

6. No pseudoreasoning. The person wants to keep up with the neighbors, but is not asserting that a garage is a good thing in itself.

7. Wishful thinking.

8. Scare tactic.

9. Appeal to anger and appeal to pity.

10. Two wrongs make a right.

11. Common practice.

12. Common practice.

13. No pseudoreasoning: Pity is relevant to giving money away.

14. Apple polishing.

15. Two wrongs make a right.

Answers to Review Questions

1. Although the two are closely related, the appeal to popularity begins with the premise that people in general consider something to be true. The invocation of common practice begins with the observation that people act a certain way, whether or not those people would call their behavior right. (Maybe all jobseekers do pad their résumé, but it's not the case that they all consider that practice morally right.)

2. The smokescreen fits more cases than any other kind of pseudoreasoning. This is because smokescreen simply means the introduction of extraneous or irrelevant information, and nearly every type of pseudoreasoning contains some such irrelevancy.

3. Four emotions appealed to by pseudoreasoning are fear (scare tactics), vanity (apple polishing), pity (appeal to pity), and anger (appeal to anger or indignation).

4. One may argue that two wrongs make a right when one feels motivated by the thirst for revenge. But such arguing gets classified as pseudoreasoning only in the more specific circumstances of an argument intended to justify an illegitimate act. The revenging act has to be wrong for it to fall under the category of "two wrongs."

5. The appeal to anger or indignation counts as pseudoreasoning because it reverses the appropriate relationship between wrongdoing and anger. It is one thing to get angry because you see something wrong being done; but the appeal to anger tries to make you call something wrong because you feel angry.

CHAPTER 6

MORE PSEUDOREASONING AND OTHER RHETORICAL PLOYS

Many types of pseudoreasoning do not begin with an emotional response to an issue. The types listed in Chapter 6 often follow the structure of a good argument, but with some element of that argument distorted. In general, the speaker makes a genuine argument, but one that lacks a proper connection with the truth-claim at stake.

As in Chapter 5, the categories of rhetorical ploy presented here cover the most common kinds of **fallacy**—so common, in fact, that the major terms of Chapter 6 have entered everyday English.

CHAPTER SUMMARY

I. The pseudoreasoning covered in this chapter often resembles good reasoning more than the examples from Chapter 5 did.

    A. For this reason, these fallacies are often used as if they were legitimate arguments (and not necessarily with the intent to manipulate their audience).

    B. In many cases the fallacies listed here garble the structure of a good argument.

II. **Ad hominem** pseudoreasoning calls on us to reject a claim on the grounds of who has said it. All of the following forms of the ad hominem fallacy share a confusion between the merits of a claim and the merits of the person or group who put it forward.

    A. The simplest and most obvious form of the ad hominem is the **personal attack.** As its name indicates, it maligns a person in order to dismiss the person's beliefs.

    B. The **circumstantial ad hominem,** often very close to a personal attack, reduces what someone says to the beliefs of a group that person belongs to.

        1. This often becomes abusive—for example, "Of course he thinks the economy's fine: He's a Republican, and they don't care about poor people."

        2. Still, abusive treatment is not essential to a circumstantial ad hominem. "My doctor says that homeopathic cures don't work, but that's what they get drilled into them in medical school." You may like your doctor, but though the statement contains no tincture of abuse, it becomes an ad hominem by refusing to consider the truth of the doctor's opinion.

    C. A more specialized case goes by the name of **pseudorefutation.** In this case, one dismisses a claim on the grounds of the other person's inconsistency.

1. Inconsistency does bring down a position, if a person is advocating both a truth-claim and its negation. When I argue in the same breath that vigorous daily exercise is good for my health and that it wears down my organs, you can dismiss my claims on the basis of their inconsistency.

2. But in one variety of pseudorefutation, the contradiction between two beliefs reaches back to something a person said in the past: "How can you say caffeine makes people sleepless, when back in high school you told me it had no effect at all?"

3. A more common variety (the *tu quoque*) finds an inconsistency between people's statements and their behavior. "You say this sausage is loaded with cholesterol, but I notice you eat it every morning." The person may be a hypocrite, but sausage contains cholesterol nevertheless.

D. In another twist on the ad hominem, one is **poisoning the well** by impugning a person's character before that person has even said anything. Poisoning the well gives anything else that person says an unreliable sound; thus you may think of it as ad hominem in advance.

E. The broadest category of all is the **genetic fallacy,** which may attack what either a person or a group says. The genetic fallacy rejects a claim solely on the grounds of its source, its origins, or its associations.

1. In conversation, the genetic fallacy may sound as broad as "You just think that's wrong because you were brought up that way."

2. Strictly speaking, the ad hominem is a specific form of the genetic fallacy.

III. Perhaps the most difficult pseudoreasoning to detect is one that puts an inappropriate **burden of proof** on a claim. It occurs when one places the burden of proof on the wrong side of an issue, or places the burden of proof more heavily on one side than it should be.

A. Very often a discussion of some issue can turn into a discussion of which side faces the greater burden of proof. It helps to have reasonable grounds for assigning the burden of proof properly.

B. All other things being equal, the greater burden of proof rests with someone whose claim has less *initial plausibility* (see Chapter 3). Suppose one person claims that every even number less than 100 is the sum of two prime numbers, while another denies it. This claim will strike most people as implausible, so the first person faces the greater burden of proof.

C. All other things being equal, the greater burden of proof rests with someone making an affirmative claim, rather than with the one denying that claim.

1. Watch especially for someone who defends an affirmative claim by throwing the burden onto the other side, calling a claim true simply because it has not been shown to be false.

      2.   This special variety of burden-of-proof pseudoreasoning is called an **appeal to ignorance.**

  D. Finally, consider special circumstances that shift the normal burden of proof. When there is a lot at stake (life, liberty, property), we should place a higher than usual burden of proof on claims that might cause harm.

IV. The fallacy of attacking a **straw man** consists in arguing against a distorted or simplified version of what someone has said, and treating that argument as if it brought down what the person really did say.

  A. A straw man fallacy typically involves a smokescreen, because recasting another person's opinion in distorted form amounts to changing the subject.

  B. At the same time, such thinking can occur without any intent to mislead. One may misunderstand someone else's view and criticize it on inappropriate grounds. The criticism has still gone wrong, but we would not call it straw man reasoning.

V. A **false dilemma** assumes that only two alternatives exist in a given situation, so that anyone who does not agree with the first must agree with the second.

  A. The false dilemma distorts a sound logical principle, namely that when there are only two alternatives and the first does not hold, the second must. If my cat is not male, she must be female.

  B. Thus a false dilemma goes wrong by first describing a situation as though only two alternatives exist, when in fact others do.

      1.   Bear in mind that one may present the false dilemma in a grammatical form other than "either-or." Any sentence with an "or" can easily be translated into a sentence with "if-then": "A or B" becomes "If not A, then B."

      2.   Thus a false dilemma like "Either we balance the budget or we all starve" becomes "If we don't balance the budget, we'll all starve." The sentence structure changes, but not the false dilemma.

  C. The **perfectionist fallacy** uses false dilemmas in a particular way, first assuming that the only two options for action are its perfect success and nothing, and then rejecting anything that will not work perfectly.

  D. Another variation on false dilemmas, the **line-drawing fallacy,** arises when discussing vague concepts: If you cannot draw a line to demarcate the edge of the concept, it is dismissed as hopelessly unclear (see also Chapter 2).

      1.   One might bemoan the Constitution's protection against excessive bail, pseudo-arguing that we don't know where to draw the line between excessive and non-excessive amounts. (If $10,000 is not excessive, what about $10,001? and so on.)

      2.   Some authors classify the line-drawing fallacy under the heading of slippery slope, because it encourages the idea that one step in a given direction commits us to going all the way to the end. But pseudoreasoning about where to draw the line also makes a clear case of false dilemma.

VI. One invokes a **slippery slope** when predicting that if one thing happens, or is permitted to happen, another (clearly undesirable) thing will eventually result.

   A. The structure of the slippery slope argument is robustly logical. If A does imply B, and B is indeed absurd, or false, or undesirable, then you have produced an argument against A.

   B. The slippery slope makes good sense when A does imply or lead to B. For instance, a society's small restrictions on the press can lead to greater restrictions; so newspapers fight curbs on highly offensive language in order to prevent being censored themselves in the future.

   C. Such reasoning turns into pseudoreasoning when it rests on *unfounded claims* about whether A leads to B. It does not suffice to point to a conceptual similarity between A and B: One must give a reason for believing that A logically produces or permits B.

VII. The would-be defense of a claim that relies on the very claim it purports to prove is **begging the question.** This also gets called "circular reasoning," "starting too close to your conclusion," or (in certain cases) "tautology."

   A. Begging the question defeats the very idea of an argument, because premises ought to be statements the other person already accepts.

   B. Rarely does a question-begging bit of pseudoreasoning simply repeat the same words, so you should watch for such disguises as appeals to synonyms. For example: "It's impossible to believe that space goes on infinitely, because that's inconceivable."

KEY WORDS AND IDEAS

Fallacy. Pseudoreasoning, usually in the narrower sense of bad argumentation not based on irrelevant appeals to emotions. Fallacies often are *mistaken* or *distorted* versions of good forms of reasoning.

See the outline above for definitions of all types of pseudoreasoning covered in Chapter 6.

REVIEW QUESTIONS

1. Name the five species of ad hominem pseudoreasoning covered in this chapter. Which is the broadest? Which gets applied under the most specific circumstances?

2. Name and explain two tests for determining where the burden of proof ought to lie.

3. When does an ordinary false dilemma become a perfectionist fallacy?

4. Explain the difference between an appeal to ignorance and a straw man argument.

5. How would you spot the difference between a pseudorefutation and a legitimate refutation that resembles it?

COMMONLY ASKED QUESTIONS

What general principles underlie this chapter's categories of pseudoreasoning?

If you divide this chapter into two sections, the types of the ad hominem and everything else, you can see the ways in which pseudoreasoning begins with some sort of legitimate reasoning.

Ad hominem pseudoreasoning bears a certain resemblance to the concern over a source's credibility, as discussed in Chapter 3. Very often, considering the source of information provides us with a good reason not to give it much weight. In the fable of the boy who cried "Wolf!" the townspeople who finally stopped rushing to help him were justified in discounting his shouts, because he had repeatedly demonstrated his unreliability.

The ad hominem goes inappropriately beyond this habit of weighing a speaker's credibility in its habit of *denying* the claim instead of *not accepting* it. When I refuse to accept a claim, I am in principle keeping my mind open; when I deny it, I commit myself to the contrary claim. Even the fable of the hoax-happy boy shows this fact, because in the end a real wolf did chase him. If the townspeople had inferred from his shouts that no wolf was present they would have been reasoning fallaciously, despite their sound reasons for not inferring that a wolf was present. Anyone may stumble upon the truth, even if for the wrong reasons. (For the more complicated case of moral assertions, see the last question in this section.)

The remaining examples of pseudoreasoning lie even closer to good methods of argumentation; for this reason, many of them are fallacies that people fall into inadvertently, with no desire to mislead or change the subject. (Ad hominem criticisms have a way of arising out of ill will, with a bias toward defamation of character.) In just about every dispute, for example, one side faces a greater burden of proof than the other. One ought to require one's opponents to substantiate what they say, if any burden of proof lies with them; the fallacious application of this principle crosses a line that is often hard to see.

Likewise, straw man pseudoreasoning may arise unintentionally when you try to apply the excellent practice of stating and rebutting someone else's view. Complex, difficult, or obscurely presented positions find themselves mistreated in this process.

The slippery slope and false dilemma get much of their power from their own similarity to sound reasoning. A slippery slope scenario condemns an action or position because of its consequences; thus it begins with an unimpeachable pattern of argument. "Don't run into the street because a car might hit you" argues against a kind of action because of what can or probably will follow. Even reasoning closer to the slippery slope may make good sense (see "Tips on Applications" below). The slippery slope turns fallacious not because of its inherent structure, but because it rests on false or unsubstantiated predictions about likely consequences.

Finally, a false dilemma works as well as it does by resembling a true dilemma. In cases of a pair of alternatives that exhaust all possibilities, failing to agree with one binds you to agreeing with the other. Again, the structure of the argument commits no fallacy—for this reason, you should take care not to call just any appeal to a pair of alternatives a false dilemma. When you can show that a further alternative exists, however, you have a false dilemma.

Is there a simple way of telling one type of ad hominem attack from another?

Excessive fussing over classification is not the purpose of studying pseudoreasoning. Very seldom does anything hinge on whether you have spotted the precise name for a fallacy. Still, the different subcategories of the ad hominem do possess distinguishing marks.

In practical terms, it helps to eliminate obviously inapplicable possibilities. For instance, when a person is being talked about without reference to a larger group that person belongs to, you may rule out the circumstantial ad hominem. The two other, more specialized versions of this pseudoreasoning are the pseudorefutation and poisoning the well. The former requires some allegation of inconsistency, whereas the latter characteristically looks ahead to what you are likely to hear from a person.

When none of the above holds, the ad hominem in question probably counts as a personal attack. If pressed, you can fit most ad hominems under the broad construal of the genetic fallacy as any appeal to the origins of a claim. However, the genetic fallacy more precisely invokes a culture's first development of an idea—for example, "You can't trust the concept of equality, since it was invented by white male slaveholders."

Finally, more than one category might apply to a case, for either of two reasons. First, the categories themselves are not always logically independent of one another; nor do they need to be to help us understand pseudoreasoning. Second, spurious attacks on a position have a way of firing like shotguns, leveling a number of different criticisms in the hopes that one will hit the target. If you can, look for the category that fits best; when there is no such category, the fault may lie in the nature of things.

Does the label "ad hominem" really imply that we can't discount anyone's character flaws when deciding on moral issues?

Ad hominem attacks call for the greatest delicacy in cases of moral assertion. Certainly we feel entitled to ignore self-righteous posturing from a degenerate. But it is important to keep in mind what does follow from someone else's failings and what does not.

When a man you know to be habitually adulterous loudly condemns someone else's infidelity, you may well call him a hypocrite. You also have good reason to think that his hypocrisy makes him worse than if he committed his adultery in shame and embarrassment. It may be time for him to stop talking. But these are all judgments about him, not about the truth of what he is saying.

Take a more difficult case: A chronic embezzler criticizes you for eating in an expensive restaurant, when the world is full of hungry children. You are likely to reply that such moral judgments require credibility, that weighing personal gratification against the needs of others is a task for one with a more finely honed ethical sensibility than the embezzler possesses. After all, morality is not theory alone.

Even so, the embezzler's lack of credibility does not demonstrate that the claim in question is false. It gives you a reason to discount or dismiss the criticism, but not to believe the opposite. That is, you may stop worrying about eating in expensive restaurants, but you haven't shown that it is right.

If the ethical ad hominem ever works, it works when an unreliable person advises you that something you worried about is actually all right. Suppose someone who habitually lies to get out of work tells you, "A little white lie this time won't hurt." You think, maybe correctly, that it was probably a few little lies that got this person into the habit of dishonesty, and that if you follow this one piece of well-meant advice you might find yourself in the same bad habit. Now you have a reason to believe that what the person said is false. Such reasoning is sometimes sound. It is no excuse for indulging in wanton personal attacks, but it does illustrate the subtlety of ad hominem reasoning in moral contexts.

TIPS ON APPLICATIONS

It is worth spending an extra moment on the slippery slope, one of the most common of this chapter's types of pseudoreasoning and also one of the most common accusations made against someone else's position in an argument. Sometimes the participants in a discussion will label anything their opponents say a slippery slope, if it makes any reference to the effects of an action or belief.

Every such reference to effects, good or bad, rests on predictive claims, so you need to stay alert to predictions of what follows from what else, and what basis in fact those predictions may have.

Consider the following reasoning from a sleepy parent: "If I get up at 3:30 A.M. today to feed the baby, she'll be more likely to cry again at 3:30 tomorrow, or even 3:00, and then it will take her longer to fall back asleep." Although the parent may be exaggerating these dangers, the core predictive claim—that the baby will interpret being fed at 3:30 today as an incentive to cry in the middle of the night tomorrow—has a good deal of plausibility. So does the parent's belief that it is easier to stop a bad habit from establishing itself than to eradicate an existing one.

The psychology of infant behavior is much simpler than the collective psychology of an entire society, and neither element of the parent's argument applies directly to more complex questions. Claims about social tendencies, and about the difficulty of stopping them, call for more substantial evidence and analysis.

Doctor-assisted suicide provides a controversial example. Some opponents to its legalization argue on the basis of worse consequences to come. "Once we allow doctors to help people commit suicide when they clearly want to, they will provide that same assistance to patients who are incompetent to make a decision for themselves, or even try to convince undecided patients to kill themselves."

This argument makes two claims: (1) that physicians will change their behavior and their expectations from patients once a certain practice has become legal, and (2) that society will find itself unable to stop that egregious behavior. Since these are claims about fact, and debatable, they require some support.

In this particular case, those who make the argument often appeal to the example of the Netherlands, where doctor-assisted suicide is already legal. Some argue that its legality has resulted in unwanted deaths. Does this mean there is no slippery slope at work?

It depends. You should examine two matters before deciding whether to accept or reject the argument at this point: whether the claims about what happens in the Netherlands are true, and whether social circumstances present there are also present in the United States (since the consequences of a policy in one country do not always translate to another country).

What matters more to us is that this discussion has already shifted to citing and evaluating evidence. That's a sign that we have left the domain of the slippery slope. Slippery-slope arguments tend to rest on anecdotal evidence, or often no evidence at all. In many cases, a wild prediction about what will happen next lets you know that someone has conjured up a slippery slope but not really thought about it.

EXERCISES

Sample Exercises from the Book

6-1, 4. Harvard now takes the position that its investment in urban redevelopment projects will be limited to projects that are environmentally friendly. Before you conclude that that is such a swell idea, stop and think. For a long time Harvard was one of the biggest slumlords in the country.

Pseudorefutation. It is easy to spot the ad hominem thinking in this example; what some-times causes more trouble is specifying which subspecies of the ad hominem it belongs to. Circumstantial ad hominem is easily eliminated, because Harvard's past does not commit it to environmental friendliness in the present. Neither personal attack nor poisoning the well is all wrong. But this example brings up a charge of inconsistency, which points us toward pseudorefutation as the best answer.

6-4, 7. Whenever legislators have the power to raise taxes, they will always find problems that seem to require for their solution doing exactly that. This is an axiom, the proof of which is that the power to tax always generates the perception on the part of those who have that power that there exist various ills the remedy for which can only lie in increased governmental spending and hence higher taxes.

Begging the question. The long sentence of abstract nouns can make the pseudoreasoning hard to spot. It helps to begin by looking for synonyms: "ills" merely restates "problems," as "remedy" echoes "solution." Once you translate the words into their equivalents, the argument's restatement of its own conclusion becomes more evident.

6-7, 4. Overheard: Should school kids say the Pledge of Allegiance before class? Certainly. Why shouldn't they?

Inappropriate burden of proof. Although this particular exercise tips off the pseudo-reasoning with the final "Why shouldn't they?"—a common move when one misplaces the burden of proof—you should note that comments very similar to this one are legitimate. If the speaker had referred to multiplication tables instead of the Pledge of Allegiance, the remark would have sounded more appropriate. In such cases you need to apply the test of initial plausibility: It's so obvious that multiplication belongs in schools that the task of marshalling an argument rests on those who would oppose the practice.

6-9, 7. Aid to Russia? Gimme a break! Why should we care more about the Russians than about our own people?

Straw man. This makes a classic case, because it equates an unspecified quantity of foreign aid with excessive care for the Russian people. The speaker could improve the attack by filling in steps, arguing, for example, that foreign aid is money that could be spent domestically, and that all domestic problems should be solved before addressing a single foreign problem. Such an argument would have to rest on highly controversial claims, but it would get further than the specimen provided.

Additional Exercises

Classify the pseudoreasoning at work in these examples.

1. Either join in political life or resign yourself to a lonely and meaningless existence.

2. You have to discount Mr. McGill's views on abortion. As a member of the Pre-Natal Liberation Organization, he can't help being prejudiced.

3. You should bathe three times a day in a tub of whole milk to keep your skin looking young. No one has ever proved that it doesn't work.

4. Defense lawyer Robert Baker, at the O. J. Simpson civil trial: This isn't a fight for justice, it's a fight for money.

5. Letter to the editor: Now the Dallas police have dismissed the rape charges against Michael Irvin and Erik Williams. Excuse me if I'm suspicious of the Dallas Police Department. I'm old enough to remember Lee Harvey Oswald being shot to death with the Dallas police escorting him.

6. Before you go getting all excited about the ancient Greek ideal of leisure and learning, remember that it was built on the backs of slaves. How do you think they liked the sight of all those philosophers? Not much.

7. Once your kids are watching cartoons, they're also watching those toy commercials. If they see the commercials they'll want the toys; before you know it, they're obsessed with the toys and you've lost all control over them. So don't let children watch cartoons.

8. Tomorrow night you will watch my opponent on these same channels. He'll try to defend all the exhausted ideas that have landed this state in the gutter. You wait, he'll pretend he's saying something new. But that's the way it goes in politics, and I'll let him make his little speech. Freedom of choice is what America is all about.

9. Either you floss daily or your teeth look pathetic.

10. I beg to differ, Officer, but sometimes you people go overboard talking about the dangers of fast driving. If you can prove that there's actually a child near the street right now, and that the child would have stepped out in front of my car, then I'll grant you that going fifty-five was dangerous.

11. The life on other planets must be highly intelligent. After all, we've never documented a single case of aliens landing on Earth—which proves that they realize how dangerous it would be to make contact.

12. Ms. Turnier gave me extra homework for running in class. She has a rule against it. But I told her, "I wasn't running, I was walking. One foot was in front of the other." Maybe I went fast, but where is it in her book of rules that suddenly that's running?

13. Don't stay in the Army. You were ROTC instead of going to one of the academies, and that means they might promote you for a while, but you'll never get above lieutenant colonel. Why bother?

14. Ms. Ng said to tell you I'm not reading enough. But I don't think you should worry. She's a teacher, so she has reading on her mind.

15. How do you like those developers trying to raise the sales tax to pay for the new stadium? They say it's going to be profitable for the city. If it's so profitable, why don't they build it out of their own money and really get rich?

16. Do I want the police department to take charge of writing parking tickets? You mean, do I want to get shot if I pull up next to a fire hydrant? What do you think?

17. Madam President, I don't see how we can go ahead with this curricular revision. The committee is worried about students not getting a good liberal arts education; but when you look closely at the details of the proposal, you see that a shrewd student can still worm through with the right course selections and wind up uneducated.

18. What do you mean, I broke my curfew? All I did was walk to the curb. You wouldn't cite me if I stood on the porch, would you? And if I'd just stepped off the porch, that wouldn't be any different. So what's so magical about the curb?

19. Ladies and gentlemen of the jury: My client's civil rights are at stake. It's true that he pointed at the victim and told the other men with him, "That's the one who cost you your jobs. Get him!" But that was only his expression of his opinion. You have to either let a man speak his mind, or admit that we're living in a police state.

Answers to Additional Exercises

1. False dilemma.

2. Circumstantial ad hominem.

3. Inappropriate burden of proof, specifically appeal to ignorance.

4. False dilemma. Note the implicit "if-then" statement: If it's a fight for money, then it's not a fight for justice. This statement in turn becomes a standard "either-or": Either it's a fight for money or it's a fight for justice. The alternative, of course, is that one may fight for money as a way of fighting for justice.

5. Ad hominem: poisoning the well. There is an implied reference to inconsistency that might make the example count as pseudorefutation; but the writer only claims to be " suspicious," not to refute.

6. Genetic fallacy. The speaker is right to say that leisure, as known to the ancient Greeks, loses its splendor in the light of its origins. But it doesn't follow that leisure and learning based on a different social system has to be rejected as well.

7. Slippery slope. This example begins with a clearly true prediction: If children watch cartoons on television, they watch toy commercials. The predictions get less plausible as they go on.

8. Ad hominem: poisoning the well. Apple polishing to round it off.

9. False dilemma.

10. Inappropriate burden of proof.

11. Begging the question.

12. Line-drawing fallacy.

13. False dilemma: perfectionist fallacy.

14. Circumstantial ad hominem.

15. False dilemma. Note the "either-or" disguised as an "if-then."

16. Straw man.

17. False dilemma: perfectionist fallacy.

18. Line-drawing fallacy.

19. False dilemma.

Answers to review questions

1. The five species of ad hominem pseudoreasoning are personal attack, circumstantial ad hominem, pseudorefutation, poisoning the well, and genetic fallacy. Genetic fallacy is the broadest, as it applies to every situation in which one argues against a view on the grounds of its origins. Circumstantial ad hominem is probably the most specific, because it requires that someone belong to a group that customarily believes something; but poisoning the well, which requires a personal attack in advance, could also be the most specific.

2. Initial plausibility makes the first and most easily applied test. (See Chapter 3.) Which claim fits best with background knowledge and observation? Next, consider which of the two claims makes an affirmative assertion, positively declaring something to be the case, while the other claim simply denies the first.

3. An ordinary false dilemma becomes a perfectionist fallacy when one of the two options presented is an unrealistically perfect outcome of some plan or policy. So one criterion is that a plan or policy has been presented; the other is some perfect consequence that the speaker imagines.

4. In both the appeal to ignorance and the straw man argument, one strengthens one's own position by opposing it to an easily conquered alternative. In the case of the straw man, the alternative is the simplified or distorted version of someone else's claim. In appeals to ignorance, the alternative is the absence of any claims to the contrary.

5. A pseudorefutation begins with a claim of inconsistency. A person says something today that is contradicted either by that person's actions or by something incompatible with it that the person said at some point in the past. The similarly structured legitimate refutation bases itself on an inconsistency between two claims the person is making now.

CHAPTER 7

EXPLANATIONS

Our reasoning about a claim can take several forms. We will mainly occupy ourselves with arguments, beginning with Chapter 8. But before taking that step, we will spend some time on explanations, which are often mistaken for arguments but have their own distinct work to do. This chapter concentrates on identifying explanations, classifying them, and telling the good from the bad. The classification system divides most explanations into the physical, behavioral, and functional types, depending on what sort of information they offer about what sorts of phenomena. The criteria for telling good explanations from bad ones will get us looking both for the qualities we want in an explanation—testability, relevance, reliability, explanatory power—as well as the characteristics we want to avoid, such as circularity, vagueness, and dependence on unnecessary assumptions.

CHAPTER SUMMARY

I. **Explanations** are claims designed to show why something is the case, or why or how something happened.

    A. Explanations are not arguments.

        1. Arguments try to show that something is the case, or will be, or should be, not why or how it is.

        2. Explanations get offered only after we agree what the fact of the matter is.

    B. Nevertheless, explanations find themselves confused with arguments.

        1. People aren't always sure which one they intend to give.

        2. The same words can work as either an explanation or an argument.

        3. Even the words "explain" and "explanation" can be used to describe an argument—for example: "The effect of fruit on digestion explains why you should eat more of it."

        4. Explanations may legitimately be used in arguments, and also as arguments.

    C. People may also confuse explanations of behavior with justifications or defenses of it.

        1. In many instances an explanation does get offered as a justification: "I swerved off the road because someone threw a brick at my windshield."

        2. But one may also try to explain behavior, even the very worst sort, without meaning to defend it.

            a. It is important to bear this in mind, so that we do not treat legitimate explanations as excuses.

II. Three types of explanation stand out as most important and most common (although we could easily subdivide these further into an indefinitely large number of types).

   A. A **physical explanation** uses information relevant to the natural sciences to state the cause of an event.

      1. That information may include general background conditions—the weight of a thing, the weather, the properties of gases—when they need to be stated.

      2. More specifically, however, the information will try to pinpoint the *direct* or *immediate* cause.

      3. An event may result from more than one chain of causes, as when a car accident results from both a slick road (which then needs to be explained) and a tired driver (whose fatigue also then needs to be explained).

      4. Three common mistakes occur when giving physical explanations.

         a. We sometimes have to explain the immediate cause with a further causal story: Here it is important to judge when no further explanation is called for.

         b. We sometimes expect the natural sciences to provide a reason or motive behind an event; they do not include references to such things.

         c. We sometimes deliver a physical explanation at an inappropriate level of technicality, whether too advanced or too simple.

      5. Finally, remember that physical explanations may speak to general occurrences as well as to individual events. "Why does fire require oxygen?" calls for a physical explanation in the same way that "How did this fire start?" does.

   B. **Behavioral explanations** find causes for human behavior.

      1. Such explanations use the vocabulary of psychology (including "commonsense psychology"), sociology, political science, history, and economics—the social sciences.

      2. The structure of behavioral explanations resembles the structure of physical ones in both providing relevant background and identifying a direct or immediate cause. The two differ mainly in the kind of information they use.

      3. As with physical explanations, behavioral ones can address general phenomena as well as specific ones.

      4. Behavioral explanations rely on knowledge that is less exact, and admits of more exceptions, than the knowledge in physical explanations.

         a. Normally we won't expect to find a single correct explanation of a particular human action.

         b. This greater openness does not make behavioral explanations worse than physical ones.

5. The two kinds of explanations are alike in their capacity to be pitched at the wrong technical level for the context.

6. Behavioral explanations that appeal to reasons or motives speak of the future instead of the past: "I laid out my clothes because I need to get dressed fast tomorrow."

7. One mistake creeps into behavioral explanations and no others: the confusion of reasons for doing something and some one person's reason for doing it. The former is actually an argument.

C. **Functional explanations** explain what an object or event does, what role it plays in a given context.

   1. Because an object may have more than one function, or a function different from its originally intended one, it helps to provide the context in which the object performs a given function.

   2. Functional explanations typically refer to human motives and reasons; so you will find behavioral explanations closely related to functional ones.

      a. For instance, the answer to "Why did Pat buy a stamp guide?" will depend on the answer to "What is a stamp guide for?"

D. More than one type of explanation may turn up in our account of a phenomenon.

   1. This is not to be regretted: Our goal in classifying these explanations is not to keep them apart but to analyze their various purposes.

   2. When the physical explanation of an event includes a human action, that in turn may call for behavioral explanation.

   3. When the functional explanation of a thing entails complex processes, it may need a physical explanation.

III. As every type of explanation may be either good or bad, strong or weak, certain criteria help us evaluate them.

A. The **testability** of an explanation means its provability in other contexts.

   1. An explanation must have more support than the single phenomenon it purports to account for.

   2. Thus there must exist other circumstances in which the explanation will either work or fail.

      a. Specifically, we say that a testable explanation is refutable, because some situation can show it false.

      b. Nontestable explanations may be called *ad hoc* or "rubber" hypotheses, stretching to cover every case and thus remaining conveniently beyond refutation—but also, for that reason, useless.

    c.   The natural sciences provide the clearest examples of such tests: Every experiment seeks either to confirm or disconfirm some hypothesis.

B. An explanation that merely restates the thing to be explained is **circular.**

C. A **relevant** explanation adequately explains the phenomenon in question.

    1.   Relevant explanations are those whose information accounts for the *specific* phenomenon in question.

    2.   Thus, explanations are relevant to the extent that they help us make predictions.

D. Explanations must be free from excessive vagueness (see Chapter 2 on *vagueness* in general).

E. Testable explanations can be examined for their **reliability,** that is, the degree to which we confirm their predictions.

    1.   Notice that you cannot spot reliability or its opposite just from looking at an explanation: Unlike most of the other criteria, this one is applied after we have more facts.

    2.   You can think of a reliable explanation as a "true" one, except that truth calls for more extensive confirmation.

F. The more phenomena an explanation accounts for, the greater its **explanatory power;** and the better an explanation it is.

    1.   Isaac Newton's theory of gravity showed its explanatory power by accounting for both the motion of falling bodies on earth and the motions of planets around the sun.

    2.   Scientific theories especially depend on explanatory power.

G. Explanations ought to have as few **unnecessary assumptions** as possible.

    1.   Unnecessary assumptions drag unusual or implausible entities or events into the account of something that is itself less unusual.

        a.   If your keys turn up in your roommate's pocket, the explanation that your roommate put them there is freer from unnecessary assumptions than the explanation that the keys traveled by themselves.

    2.   You may ask yourself: Does the explanation itself stand in need of explanation?

H. One of the most reliable tests for an explanation—when it applies—is **consistency with well-established theory.**

    1.   Note the similarity between this criterion and Chapter 3's test of initial plausibility for informative claims.

    2.   This test applies best to physical explanations, as long as the phenomenon explained falls under a natural science.

3. Remember the difference between agreeing with an established theory and not disagreeing with it.

I. Finally, an explanation is better when no **alternative explanations** agree for a phenomenon.

1. This may be the hardest test to apply, because alternatives tend not to exist until someone thinks of them.

2. The alternative does not need to be superior to the first explanation: As long as some roughly equivalent explanation exists, we have less confidence in our original account.

3. For example: One explanation for your refusal to greet me on the street may be that you are angry with me; but once I think of an alternative explanation (you aren't wearing your glasses and don't recognize me), I find myself less inclined to believe that you're angry.

IV. **Explanatory comparisons**—also called *analogies*—explain an unfamiliar thing by pointing to resemblances between it and a more familiar thing.

A. The goal of such comparisons is not truth but clarification.

1. As long as the listener understands something better after hearing the comparison, it has (to some degree) succeeded.

2. Hence we do not strive for absolute correctness in the comparison, but for as many points of resemblance as possible.

3. When the objects being compared have vague, numerous, or complicated features, comparisons work better by communicating a general idea than by going through all the features of both things.

B. The degree of clarification is best judged by someone who knows both parts of the comparison.

1. Only that person can tell whether the comparison delivers relevant resemblances.

2. The listener who does not know the unfamiliar item may have a clear idea as a result of the comparison, but can't judge the accuracy of that idea.

C. Other sorts of comparisons do not lend themselves to these tests of explanation.

1. Metaphorical comparisons may or may not illuminate; they do not explain in the ordinary sense of the word.

2. Persuasive comparisons (see Chapter 4) do not aim at explaining, but at expressing a claim colorfully or persuasively.

KEY WORDS AND IDEAS

Alternative explanation. A second explanation of a phenomenon, whose existence casts doubt on the value of the original explanation.

Behavioral explanation. An explanation of individual or group human behavior, by means of information drawn from the social sciences, whether that information is technical or common-sensical. The knowledge being used here is less exact than that in physical explanations, so a behavioral explanation tends to remain open to broader interpretations and to admit to more exceptions.

Circularity. An undesired trait of an explanation; the explanation's repetition of the thing to be explained. Circularity adds no information to explanations.

Consistency with well-established theory. A highly desired feature of an explanation; the explanation's agreement (or lack of disagreement) with what is known or justifiably believed to be the case; related to initial plausibility.

Explanation. A claim that seeks to tell why or how a given other claim should be true; distinct from an argument for a claim and from a justification for an action.

Explanatory comparison. Also called an analogy; a type of comparison that clarifies an unfamiliar thing by juxtaposing it to something more familiar that it resembles.

Explanatory power. The capacity of an explanation to account for more phenomena than another explanation does.

Functional explanation. An explanation of what an object or event does, or what part it plays in some context.

Physical explanation. An explanation of an event by means of information drawn from the natural sciences, whether that information is technical or commonly known.

Relevance. A desired feature of explanations; the explanation's appropriate relationship to the thing being explained. An explanation is fully relevant if it permits us to predict the phenomenon's occurrence.

Reliability. The success of an explanation when facing further tests (see testability). Reliability cannot be seen in the explanation itself, but must be ascertained through further checking.

Testability. The openness of an explanation to verification or refutation in further cases; a necessary feature of explanations. An untestable explanation has as evidence only the individual event it seeks to explain.

Unnecessary assumption. An implausible entity or event invoked by an explanation; an undesired feature of explanations.

Vagueness. An undesired feature of explanations. (See Chapter 2.)

REVIEW QUESTIONS

1. When does an explanation have explanatory power? What does explanatory power tell us about untestable explanations?

2. Does a circular explanation pass the tests of relevance, reliability, and testability?

3. Which of the three types of explanations will be most testable? Why?

4. Can we give behavioral explanations of our own behavior as well as of other people's?

5. When can a physical explanation also be a functional one? Give an example.

COMMONLY ASKED QUESTIONS

What general rules might simplify the work of applying these criteria to any particular explanation?

Just for practical purposes, it helps to distinguish between the *absolute* strength or weakness of an explanation and its *relative* strength or weakness when compared with rivals. After determining these two, you can ask about an explanation's reliability.

When you look at an explanation, first see how it stands on its own. You may examine both its language and its relationship to what you already know (though in practice this is a loose distinction). "Language" means that some explanations betray their weakness just in the way they are said. Vagueness, circularity, and testability belong in this category: All you need to do to detect them is to look at what the explanation says. "Some mammals live in the sea because it is their habitat" is circular; "Some mammals live in the sea because they enjoy it more" is both vague and untestable.

Next consult what you know to determine an explanation's relevance and consistency with established theory. You must treat the latter as an inflexible test: If an explanation denies the laws of chemistry, physics, or biology, it has no hope of explaining anything. (Exceptions occur within those disciplines, when scientists worry over how to account for results that their theory says they shouldn't get. But these exceptions should not concern us.) Relevance is also determined by appeal to other knowledge. "I was late because the sky was too cloudy for me to tell what time it was" is irrelevant because, as we all know, very few people today use the sun to tell time.

Explanations become trickier to evaluate once they pass these tests of their absolute strength; at this point we have to weigh them against other explanations, both actual and possible. The criteria of explanatory power, freedom from unnecessary assumptions, and absence of alternative explanations measure an explanation's relative strength. An explanation with little explanatory power might still work well enough, if it is the only explanation in town. "Why is our mail wet?" "Because the mailbox has a hole in its lid." This explanation accounts for one home's soggy mail and nothing else; but unless you have reason to suspect your carrier of loading mail into a bucket of water, it will carry the day. Explanatory power lets you rank one explanation ahead of another; it does not let you accept or reject a free-standing explanation.

The same holds of the criterion of unnecessary assumptions, but more flexibly. When the assumptions are too outlandish, you can reject even an explanation that faces no competition. Usually, though, you will ask which of two explanations requires fewer unnecessary assumptions. Suppose your boss suddenly forgets your name, and two reasons come to mind: (1) your boss is having memory trouble, or (2) your employers have engaged in a nefarious plot to make you question your own identity. Although you would normally think of (1) as bringing in unnecessary assumptions—since stark memory loss is an unusual phenomenon—it makes incomparably more sense than (2). Here the unnecessary assumptions in (2) are measured against the competition.

Finally, you weigh the relative strength of an explanation against possible alternatives. This test requires the greatest creativity and thoughtfulness on your part (see the next question). You have to come up with an alternative and then treat it as a rival to the existing explanation. That is, you compare the explanatory power of each, and their use of unnecessary assumptions. The only difference from your usual comparison of two explanations is that, when you have thought up an alternative explanation, it often matters enough that the alternative is no worse than the original explanation.

After applying these tests to an explanation, you can take up the one that belongs in its own category: reliability. There is no way around trying an explanation out to see if it is reliable. It may succeed at passing every other criterion and simply not hold up. Of course, that is what any reasonable person should expect of explanations: They have to be true. The purpose of all our other criteria is to let you eliminate bad explanations before going to all the work of testing them.

When is it clear that an alternative explanation threatens a proposed explanation?

Any additional explanation that works as well as the one proposed will threaten the original explanation's authoritative status. It helps if the alternative supersedes the original in some specific way—if it has more explanatory power, for instance. But even given rough equivalence between the two, their mere coexistence—like the disagreement between two experts (see Chapter 3)—weakens the first explanation's exclusive claim to truth.

For example, if a diet containing plenty of fruit is linked to longer life, one person might offer the explanation that fruit contains a number of vitamins. Then someone else proposes that the fiber in fruit accounts for its healthful effects. Both explanations might be right; but the mere presence of this alternative makes the first one less decisive, and will probably weaken any further claims about how many vitamins people need in their diet.

No method will always help you concoct alternative explanations. Very often, as in the example about fruit, someone has to think of them. Still, many alternative explanations fall into one of two groups. If A has been shown to lead to B, and the first explanation singles out one feature of A as the cause, you may consider other features of A that would explain B as well. Or you may ask whether A and B are both the results of some other event, C, the common cause that accounts for both. (For much more on causal claims, see Chapter 12.)

When appealing to an alternative explanation, keep two things in mind. First, the alternative must be concrete. The all-too-common reply, "There might be other explanations," accomplishes nothing. (That reply resembles something that people say about a literary interpretation: "There might be other interpretations." Fine; so give one.)

Second, you will find many instances in which the alternative explanation merely refers to chance, a random occurrence. Suppose that out of a class of forty students, the two who ate poached eggs on the morning of a test got the highest scores on the test; someone suggests that something in poached eggs causes success on tests. Before even considering substantive alternative explanations, you will reflect that chance alone could have produced this unusual phenomenon.

Is there a contradiction between wanting explanatory power in your explanation and not wanting unnecessary assumptions?

In practice, an explanation may fail one test while doing very well on another. This question describes one such case. In order to gain in explanatory power, an explanation typically has to assume more than a single phenomenon seems to call for.

Science provides excellent examples. To explain planetary orbits around the sun, Newton postulated the existence of a gravitational force that applies both on earth (when things fall down) and among all the bodies in the universe. This force struck some of his contemporaries as an unnecessary assumption, a mysterious "action at a distance" that kept the planets moving along their paths. But if he had not invoked this force, Newton could not have explained the solar system. What seemed like an unnecessary assumption made for the explanatory power.

In the ordinary world, additional assumptions tend not to increase explanatory power. Nor is it hard to tell the difference between useful and useless assumptions. When they let us subsume one phenomenon under a broader description, they have made greater explanatory power possible; when they only explain the thing right at hand, they have no explanatory efficacy to offset their weakness.

Imagine that you find a tiny hole torn in one of your blankets. Did a mouse do it? Ordinarily, that explanation calls for too much in the way of unnecessary assumptions. But then you remember the crumbs you found scattered over the kitchen floor one morning; and last week you thought you heard a scurrying sound in the wall. The mouse-explanation now sounds better than it had, because what at first had seemed an unnecessary assumption turned out to deliver more explanatory power.

TIPS ON APPLICATIONS

You should not have much trouble finding discussions of explanations going on around you, whether in academic subjects, contemporary moral debates, or everyday life.

Daily life especially bombards us with behavioral explanations. Why did she seem so reluctant to see that movie? (Because women don't like police movies? Because, as an artist, she's sick of the distorted Hollywood portrayal of the art world?) Why didn't he tell me he'd brought a plumber over? (Because he didn't want to seem incapable of fixing the faucet himself? Because Mr. Plummer was in the room, and he always thinks people are making fun of his name?)

Nearly every academic subject comes in for debates about explanations. Can a historical explanation be tested when the background conditions only happened once? Should historical explanations focus on those causal chains that feature political leaders, wars, and laws, or give more weight to weather, diet, disease, and the length of the workday? Anthropology, sociology, economics, and literature all face analogous questions.

Biology makes a particularly good example, because it is the scene for both theoretical and political disputes about explanation. At the theoretical level, quite a few philosophers worry about the principle that physical explanations contain no room for talk of reasons. Why does a plant grow toward light? The accepted answer speaks of auxin, a growth hormone that makes the shadowed side of the stem grow faster. Biology does not countenance the explanation that the plant bends "in order to get more of the light that nourishes it." That is called a teleological explanation, and modern scientists reject it. But should they? Philosophical commentators argue that the teleological explanation adds a level of meaning to phenomena that otherwise make no sense.

Biology enters political discourse in the debate between evolution and creationism. This debate comes down explicitly to the question of which side offers the better explanation of life. Creationists argue that the evolutionary picture contains circular explanations, since "survival of the fittest" only means that those who survive, survive. They call the basic claims of evolution untestable, given that the processes in question take more time than an observation could last, and cannot be duplicated in laboratories. They charge evolutionary theory with incompleteness, as the known fossil record has not yielded all the species of plants and animals that the theory claims to have existed. Finally, creationists use an alternative explanation—the divine creation of plants and animals—to argue that evolution is based on unnecessary assumptions.

Against these criticisms, evolution defends its explanations and attacks the creationist ones. Biologists will say that even if the appearance of new species is not a testable claim, the survival of better-adapted species is; and evolution gains support from numerous other claims—about genes, mutations, and so on—that have successfully undergone laboratory testing. They defend talk of "survival of the fittest" by explaining how fitness for survival can be identified in a plant or animal by standards other than the mere fact of its survival.

Turning the critique of explanation back against creationism, evolution's defenders find too many other assumptions. Consider one: For creationism to be right in claiming a uniform date of appearance of species (a more recent date than evolution claims), our method of dating fossils must be wrong. But then substantial parts of physics and chemistry rest on error and must be rejected. Whereas evolution does not contradict the other sciences, creationism does: Hence its explanation is weaker.

You will notice how squarely this debate fits into Chapter 7's criteria for testing explanations. The fact that both sides of the debate use the same criteria shows that even very deep disagreements about the world coexist with agreement about how to reason. It also shows—a useful warning for everyone—that evaluating explanations requires careful judgment. Not every criticism is as good as it first appears. Not every explanation collapses because it fails one test.

EXERCISES

Sample Exercises from the Book

7-1, 4. The reason Collins was ill is that she ate and drank more than she should have.

Explanation. Context matters. The example can be an argument if the person is trying to convince you that Collins was ill, or if the person wants to convince you not to eat and drink too much ("Look at what happened to Collins"). But if you know that Collins was ill and want to know why—the natural way to take the example—it is an explanation.

7-7, 7. In Southern California the grass turns brown in the summer because there is no rain.

Physical explanation. Sometimes this throws people off, because the reason given is something that did *not* happen or does *not* exist. But there's no difference between the two: The absence of oxygen will cause death just as surely as the presence of too much carbon monoxide.

7-11, 7. Alcoholics find it so difficult to give up drinking because they have become physiologically and psychologically addicted to it.

Poor explanation; circular. Some further explanation along these lines may be reasonable, but it would have to flesh out the concept of addiction. For instance, you might explain physiological addiction in terms of a brain chemistry that creates obnoxious symptoms when the alcoholic goes without alcohol.

Additional Exercises

A. Are the following examples arguments, explanations, or justifications? If they are explanations, what group do they belong to?

1. The coach is being especially hard on you, all right, but that's only because you're such a gifted athlete.

2. Thanks to that fatty meat I had for lunch, I've been dragging myself around all afternoon.

3. The stomach churns harder with meat in it so that the meat will get broken down.

4. He sprinkles tarragon on his tuna salad because tarragon gives it an undefined extra zest.

5. Bicycles stay vertical as easily as they do because their wheels work as gyroscopes.

6. The rose's thorns keep predators from eating it.

7. You know you can trust Bear-Lee-Breax dishes, because their superheated construction is designed not to shatter.

8. I'm a better singer than Caruso, because I can hold my breath longer.

9. They hosed down the walls of their house to prevent it from catching fire.

B. Evaluate the following explanations.

1. Elephants cover the corpses of dead fellow-elephants with branches, because they understand what death is.

2. Things burn because the phlogiston in them is being driven off. It's true that metals get heavier when they burn; but that's because the phlogiston sometimes has negative weight.

3. When you leave your cereal standing for a few days, the flakes on the milk's surface dry first. That's because they're closer to the sun.

4. All living things have souls, because the soul is the principle of life.

5. He acts unfriendly because he has an inferiority complex.

6. Our television reception is terrible! I'll bet it's the Browns with their power tools.

7. Rome declined because its people had lost their zest for empire.

8. Rome declined because every civilization, like every plant and animal, has a built-in life span.

9. The Christians may have been persecuted for the great fire in Rome because they thought it was the end of the world and rushed into the streets to celebrate.

10. The plants in western Africa match with those in eastern South America because the two continents were once parts of a larger land mass.

11. Protestantism began because communication was so hard in those days, and people in northern Europe didn't know what the pope was commanding them to do.

12. She solved that math problem because she had a sudden burst of insight.

13. Every few weeks I throw away our extra wire clothes hangers; before you know it they're back again. They must reproduce.

14. Opium causes sleep because it possesses a dormitive virtue.

15. You're hungry again because you ate in front of the TV.

16. I've had boils all summer. There could be a problem with my heart.

Answers to Additional Exercises

A. 1. Justification with a behavioral explanation.

2. Physical explanation, perhaps used as justification.

3. Physical explanation.

4. Functional explanation, perhaps used as justification.

5. Physical explanation.

6. Functional explanation.

7. Argument with a functional explanation.

8. Argument.

9. Behavioral explanation.

B. 1. Fair explanation, if it's testable (if you put sleeping elephants in front of them and see how they respond).

2. Untestable.

3. No relevance, given the insignificant difference in nearness to the sun between cereal flakes on top and those below. Look for alternatives.

4. Circular.

5. Good explanation. "Inferiority" can apply to other situations, and so it is testable.

6. Good explanation, if reliable.

7. Vague.

8. Unnecessary assumptions. Alternative explanations are possible.

9. Untestable, though imaginative.

10. Good explanation; it especially benefits from explanatory power.

11. Vague and almost certainly irrelevant.

12. Untestable.

13. Inconsistent with well-established theory; and there are many alternative explanations.

14. Circular: "dormitive virtue" just means the power to cause sleep.

15. Inconsistent with established theory.

16. Irrelevant.

Answers to Review Questions

1. An explanation has explanatory power when it accounts for a greater number of phenomena. Explanatory power comes in degrees—one explanation typically covers a broader range of things than another. Untestable explanations are as bad as they are because their explanatory power extends only to the single thing they explain. They don't lead to the next thought, "If that X is true, I should start noticing Y." If counting to four before I picked up the bat is what got me on base, it should work again the next time I'm at bat; if counting to four "explains" my base hit only on that one occasion, I have an untestable hypothesis with no explanatory power.

2. A circular explanation is, in the strict sense of the words, both relevant and reliable. It is about the thing explained, since it repeats the fact of the thing's existence; it is reliable insofar as no observation could refute it. But these features only show the circular expla-

nation's triviality. A circular explanation is not testable, because it can never be disproved through further observation. I'm healthy because I'm not sick—how do I test that?

3. Physical explanations admit of the greatest degree of testability, because the laws of nature that they depend on are the most exact and broadest of all explanatory information. Moreover, scientists are the people most commonly engaged in testing explanations.

4. Because behavioral explanations apply to all human behavior, we can make them of ourselves as well as of others. However, we should not assume that explanations of our own behavior are necessarily truer than another person's explanations of us.

5. A physical explanation can be a functional one if its account of why or how something happened also explains how something works. "The car stopped quickly because its antilock brakes pump instead of freezing up, and hence prevent skidding" is a physical explanation of the car's stopping and a functional explanation of the antilock brakes.

CHAPTER 8

UNDERSTANDING AND EVALUATING ARGUMENTS

There are claims, and then there are claims with supporting arguments. Chapters 8–12 fill out the work of critical thinking by doing for arguments what we have already done for claims: spotting them, identifying their parts, and finally evaluating them.

The evaluation of arguments plays a relatively small role in Chapter 8, just as the evaluation of claims played only a small role in Chapter 1's account of what a claim is. But it is even more true of arguments than it was of claims that you will not get far in judging their merits until you have first gotten clear on what they are and how they should work. This chapter sets the project in motion by showing how to clarify and analyze an argument. Arguments will be divided into two broad groups, deductive and inductive, dissected into their essential parts— mainly, premises and conclusions—and characterized as strong or weak, valid or invalid, depending on how well the premises lead to the conclusions.

CHAPTER SUMMARY

I.   An **argument** comprises a **conclusion** and **premises**.

    A.   The conclusion is the claim that the argument intends to support, and the premises are all the claims offered in support of the conclusion.

        1.   An argument may have any (finite) number of premises, but it must have at least one.

        2.   When a group of arguments are presented together, the conclusion of one argument may go on to serve as a premise in another. Here one claim functions as both premise and conclusion, depending on which argument it's in.

    B.   An argument may leave a premise, or even its conclusion, unstated.

        1.   "[Conclusion] You don't want to shop at Lucky's Car Stereo. [Premise] A man has to court disaster to win the name 'Lucky.'" Unstated premise: You don't want to shop at a car stereo business owned by a man who courts disaster.

        2.   "[Premise] If old age were bad in itself, every old person would be unhappy. But [premise] I'm old and I'm happy." Unstated conclusion: Old age is not bad in itself.

    C.   An argument may contain either **dependent** or **independent premises** supporting a single conclusion.

        1.   Dependent premises need one another all to be true, to make the argument work.

    a.   The argument then works because the premises all connect with each other in the right way.

    b.   "[Premise] Joe is a chiropractor, and [premise] chiropractors are experts about human bodily movement, so [conclusion] Joe must be an expert about human bodily movement."

  2. Independent premises work individually even when one of them is false.

    a.   You may think of an argument with two independent premises as two arguments for the same conclusion.

    b.   "[Conclusion] I didn't dent your car door. First of all, [premise] I never borrowed your car. In the second place, [premise] the door was fine when I returned the car to you. And anyway, [premise] the door was dented when I borrowed the car."

    c.   No sane person would ever make that kind of argument, but note that, logically speaking, even if one or two of the premises are false, we have some support for the conclusion as long as at least one is true.

II. We evaluate arguments with the terms **good** or **bad, valid** or **invalid, sound** or **unsound, strong** or **weak.**

  A. Most generally, we call an argument good if it gives grounds for accepting its conclusion.

    1. "Good" and "bad" are relative words when applied to arguments: It is often more apt to call one argument better than another than to call one absolutely good.

    2. The following discussion will elaborate the grounds for calling an argument good or bad.

  B. When premises provide indubitable support for the conclusion, the argument is valid and perhaps sound as well.

    1. An argument is valid if, whenever all its premises are true, the conclusion is true as well.

    a.   More casually, you may say that the conclusion of a valid argument must follow from its premises.

    b.   The premises do not all have to be true for an argument to be valid. So validity does not guarantee a true conclusion. But if all the premises of a valid argument are true, then the conclusion is true.

    c.   An argument intended to be valid, but isn't, is invalid.

    2. An argument is sound if it is valid and all its premises are true.

    a.   That means that the conclusion follows from the premises, and that all the premises are true.

     b.   Given the definition of validity, it follows that a sound argument always has a true conclusion.

     c.   An argument is unsound if any of its premises are false or if it is not valid.

  3.   Whereas a valid argument is not necessarily a good one (because of the possibility of false premises), a sound argument normally is good.

C. When arguments are not intended to count as valid, they may be evaluated as strong or weak.

  1.   An argument is strong if, whenever all its premises are true, the conclusion is unlikely to be false.

  2.   Good examples of strong arguments are those that rest on prior experience or observation.

D. We may now describe a good argument more precisely as one that is either sound or strong.

  1.   Validity and invalidity are absolute terms—they either hold of an argument or don't. But strength and weakness are relative, depending on the relative likelihood of the argument's conclusion being true.

  2.   For this reason, the two sets of terms work better when kept separate: Do not call valid arguments strong or weak, or call strong or weak arguments valid.

E. We can handily distinguish **deductive** and **inductive arguments** using this vocabulary.

  1.   Deductive arguments are valid, or intended to be valid; inductive arguments are neither.

  2.   Hence, deductive arguments are those we evaluate as valid or invalid, sound or unsound, whereas inductive arguments are evaluated as strong or weak.

III. By understanding what would make an argument good, we can identify and thus evaluate its **unstated premises.**

A. Many arguments encountered in daily life contain unstated premises.

B. An unstated premise is an assumption that, when added to the stated premises, makes the argument either valid or strong.

  1.   The argument "My car won't start, so the starter wires must have shorted" becomes valid if we add "Whenever a car does not start, its starter wires have shorted." But that added assumption seems unlikely to be true.

  2.   The same elliptical argument becomes strong with the added assumption "Lately my car has not been starting, and each time the starter wires had shorted."

  3.   The second added assumption has much more plausibility, so we should go with that one and produce a strong argument rather than a valid one.

C. The merit of the argument depends on the plausibility of these added assumptions.

1. When an argument needs false or unlikely assumptions to become good, it is not a good argument.

2. It is also not a good argument if reasonable added assumptions leave it invalid or weak.

D. Hence you should respond to an incomplete argument by looking for a reasonable claim to add to its existing premises.

1. Find a general claim that would make the argument valid.

2. If that effort leaves you with an implausible premise, modify the claim to make the argument strong.

3. Reject an incomplete argument when no reasonable claim will make it either valid or strong.

E. Although the identification of missing steps in an argument makes for fine reading, fine writing calls for providing all those steps to begin with.

IV. The final step before evaluating an argument is understanding it.

A. Evaluation applies to both the argument's claims taken separately and their function in the context of the argument. We ask two questions:

1. Are the premises reasonable—that is, probably true?

2. Do the premises form a good support—that is, a valid or strong argument—for the given conclusion?

B. Some techniques of clarification repair the most common problems of understanding.

1. Arguments become difficult to understand when they go by quickly, exhibit a complicated structure, surround themselves with nonargumentative material, or have no clear structure or no good premises.

2. In each case, the argument needs to have its premises and conclusion identified, and the interrelationships among them spelled out.

C. A simple method lets you render arguments in diagrams that clarify their structure.

1. Circle all **premise and conclusion indicators**—all words that show that one claim depends on another: "for," "since," "hence," "therefore," "it follows that," and so on.

2. Bracket each premise and conclusion and number them consecutively.

3. Arrange the numbers for these claims, with the following symbols to show their interconnections:

a. An arrow from one number to another means that the first is supposed to support the second.

b. A line under two numbers, with a plus sign between them, shows that the two are dependent premises. An arrow then goes from the line to the claim they support.

c. Separate arrows from different numbers or groups of numbers indicate independent premises.

d. When a claim supports more than one conclusion, an arrow goes from it to each claim it supports.

e. An arrow from one number to another with lines through it means that the argument has included this first claim as a counterargument to its conclusion.

D. Nonargumentative material, or **window dressing,** often makes this structure harder to see.

1. The passage may not be an argument at all, but a description or explanation. Ask: Does the speaker offer reasons for the stated claim?

2. The passage might not state its conclusion.

3. When no premises seem to be present, the passage may be a piece of nonargumentative persuasion (see Chapter 4) or contain pseudoreasoning (Chapters 5 and 6).

V. The entirety of critical thinking comes into play when evaluating an argument. You need to ask whether the premises are likely to be true, and whether they support the conclusion.

A. To determine whether unsupported premises in an argument are reasonable, use the methods covered in Chapters 1–7. To review:

1. Claims should possess initial plausibility and come from a credible source.

2. Except when there are very good other reasons for accepting them, claims should not conflict with observation or background information.

3. Claims from one credible source should not conflict with claims from another: Accept neither before resolving the question of which source to believe.

4. Ambiguous, vague, or otherwise unclear claims should be clarified before being accepted.

B. Bear in mind that although two arguments may both have reasonable premises, those in one argument can be more probably true than the premises of the other. Then the first argument is better.

C. To determine the validity or strength of an argument, use the methods to be covered in Chapters 9–13.

1. In the case of inductive arguments, their relative strength depends on more than the likely truth of their premises. See Chapters 11 and 12.

KEY WORDS AND IDEAS

Argument. A set of claims consisting of a conclusion, which is to be supported, and one or more premises, which are to support the conclusion.

Deductive argument. A valid argument, or one intended to be valid.

Conclusion. The claim that is argued for.

Dependent premises. Two or more premises in an argument, all of which must be true in order to support the conclusion. We say that each dependent premise needs all the others to work in order for it to work. They work together.

Good argument. An argument that offers justification for accepting its conclusion; the most general term of approbation for arguments. Good arguments are either valid or strong.

Independent premises. Two or more premises in an argument, each of which provides the support it does for the conclusion regardless of whether the others are true. We say that independent premises do not need each other to work.

Inductive argument. A strong argument, or one intended to be strong; neither valid nor intended to be.

Invalid argument. An argument, usually intended to be valid, that is not. In an invalid argument, all the premises can be true without the conclusion's being true.

Premise. A claim that provides a reason for believing the conclusion.

Premise and conclusion indicator. A word or phrase that shows the place of a claim in an argument; examples include "because," "consequently," "for this reason," "on the grounds that," and so on.

Sound argument. A valid argument all of whose premises are true. The conclusion of a sound argument is true.

Strong argument. An argument, normally inductive, of the sort that, when all of its premises are true, the conclusion is unlikely to be false.

Unsound argument. A deductive argument that is not sound, whether because one or more of its premises is false or because it is not valid.

Unstated premise. A premise needed in an argument to make it valid or strong, but not stated.

Valid argument. A deductive argument of the sort that, whenever all its premises are true, the conclusion is true as well. We often say, informally, that the premises "make" the conclusion true, or that if the premises are true the conclusion "must be" true.

Window dressing. Nonargumentative material included within, or in lieu of, an argument; extraneous matter to be winnowed from the argument before evaluating it.

REVIEW QUESTIONS

1. What two tests show whether or not an argument is sound?

2. What do you aim for when supplying an incomplete argument's unstated premises? What do you do when you can't achieve that aim?

3. Give an example of a strong and valid argument.

4. Give an example of a valid but unsound argument.

5. What two tests show whether or not an argument is good?

COMMONLY ASKED QUESTIONS

Why so much stress on validity when it does not guarantee truth, whether among the premises or in the conclusion?

This question is natural and well motivated. The emphasis on validity can feel like a false promise, when validity delivers no truth. But our answer is just as natural: Logic almost never tells us whether a given sentence is true or false. (The exceptions are such sentences as "It is either raining or not raining," always true in any weather, because it is a tautology, and "It is raining and it is not raining," a contradiction and so always false, again regardless of the weather. But these claims convey no information.)

And why does logic not pronounce on the truth or falsity of a claim? Because it was not designed to. Logic exists in order to let us know whether a group of premises works to produce or support the argument's conclusion. Certainly validity is not everything, because a valid argument with at least one false premise may have no value at all. But without validity a deductive argument cannot be worth anything.

Perhaps the greatest appeal of validity follows from its not coming in degrees. An argument is either valid or not; and we can use strict, clear, foolproof rules to tell which to call it. Nor can you improve on the internal structure of a valid argument: As far as the relationship between conclusion and premises goes, validity is the most that an argument can aspire to, and the most it can achieve.

Many people try to express the reliability of valid arguments with special language. "If the premises are all true, the conclusion can't conceivably be false"—or "absolutely must be true," or "has to follow." Such language seeks to capture the sense one gets from a valid argument, that there is no room for doubt about the step between premises and conclusion. "All humans have lungs. All animals with lungs have hearts. Therefore, all humans have hearts." Take the premises and you have taken the conclusion, too.

The language of conclusions absolutely proceeding from premises may help you understand validity. If it does not, forget it. It suffices to say of valid arguments that their conclusion is true whenever all their premises are true. True is true; talk of guaranteed or infallible or certain truth hammers home the point that valid arguments don't fail, but it otherwise adds no information. Just know that when you have accepted all the premises of a valid argument, you will have no grounds for rejecting its conclusion.

When identifying unstated premises, how many assumptions can be put into another person's mouth?

Every day we make assumptions about other people's assumptions. You assume that the waiter who approaches your table with pen and pad assumes you will order food. The friend who gossips about a third party assumes you won't tell that third party, and you know it. Life without such assumptions belongs to those unsocialized types who need every little thing spelled out.

To a great extent, identifying unstated premises works like these ordinary interpretations of other people. Anyone who makes an argument wants it to be a good argument, and must be assuming whatever plausible claims make the argument good. We justify our act of supplying those assumptions with the *principle of charity,* according to which we interpret another person's claims so as to make them as true as possible, as coherent as possible, and—when the claims come packaged together in an argument—as valid or strong as possible.

The principle of charity goes too far only when the desire to make another person's argument valid (or strong) leads us to impute assumptions that the person could not want to hold, or could not reasonably be expected to believe. Someone says: "I'm thirsty, so I must have had salt in my lunch. Because whenever I'm not this thirsty, I've left the salt out of my food." We may lay out this argument as follows:

> If I'm not thirsty, my food has been left unsalted.
> I'm thirsty.
> Therefore, my food was salted.

This is an invalid argument, resting on a common error called the *fallacy of denying the antecedent* (see Chapter 10). You can make it valid by adding this premise: "When not being thirsty follows from not adding salt to food, then being thirsty follows from adding salt." Not a perfectly plausible claim, since we get thirsty for other reasons; but nor is it a howling error.

Do we attribute this assumption to the speaker? In all likelihood, the person is not assuming any such complex claim about nutrition, only making a little logical faux pas. The principle of charity takes us too far if we let it commit other people to all the premises that would fix their arguments.

In practice, being only human, we are more likely to make other people's arguments too bad than too good. But it will not hurt to remember that the search for unstated premises needs to be tempered not only with a recognition of which assumptions are plausible in themselves, but also with a recognition of which ones are plausible as the speaker's or writer's thoughts.

TIPS ON APPLICATIONS

Applying the concepts of Chapter 8 raises one issue that has not come up seriously before now. In order to think precisely about how (and whether) an argumentative passage works, we need to use a few technical terms, that is, words with fixed but exact meanings. The previous chapters contain their share of special vocabulary; but, especially in the case of nonargumentative persuasion and pseudoreasoning, the meanings of those terms are flexible, even elusive. The rigorous study of argument does not permit such flexibility.

Moreover, the words with such specific meanings already have common uses outside the official study of critical thinking. So we need to take care not to blur the technical vocabulary with the ordinary occurrences of the same words. The colloquial meanings of the words are not false. But they belong in contexts outside logic.

Start with "argument" itself. In ordinary parlance the word refers to disagreement, especially a heated one. In logic it means a set of sentences by a single speaker or writer, whether or not that person disagrees with anyone else. It is true that even philosophers—who make the examination of arguments their main business—reach for combative metaphors when praising a piece of reasoning. We hear of "unbeatable" arguments, even of a "knock down, drag out" argument that no one can vanquish. But though such turns of phrase show that arguments get used in debates and disputes, in verbal battles of every stripe, you should not infer that an argument *requires* any contentious context.

Then the word "valid." We speak of opinions as valid; feelings too. "Your anger was perfectly valid, since you thought he'd insulted you." No confusion here and no misuse of language. But when we enter the house of logic we check this meaning of "valid" at the door and use the word only to refer to arguments with the proper internal structure.

To a lesser degree the same cautions are in order for the adjectives "sound" and "good." When engaged in clarifying and identifying arguments, do not speak of ideas, questions, or suggestions as sound. Ideas can no more be sound, from a logical point of view, than numbers can be hungry.

Even when restricting "sound" to arguments, watch out. All sound arguments have true conclusions, but not all arguments with true conclusions are sound. So don't call an argument sound merely as a way of affirming its conclusion, nor merely as a compliment. It is a term of praise for arguments, but only in the way that "registered nurse" and "poet laureate" are terms of praise: They mean something specific and must be earned; so too soundness.

Treating certain terms in a strict technical sense will help you avoid misunderstandings now. When we turn to logic proper—and especially the truth-functional logic of Chapter 10—such exactness will prevent outright error. Logic tends to demand unchanging and narrow definitions for its terms. We give up some flexibility, some color, some freshness of phrase; we gain the clarity and precision that are logic's contribution to thinking.

EXERCISES

Sample Exercises from the Book

8-2, 10. Let's see . . . If we've got juice at the distributor, the coil isn't defective, and if the coil isn't defective, then the problem is in the ignition switch. So the problem is in the ignition switch.

Premises: If we've got juice at the distributor, the coil isn't defective. If the coil isn't defective, then the problem is in the ignition switch. Unstated premise: We've got juice at the distributor. Conclusion: The problem is in the ignition switch. The unstated premise is easier to spot once you realize that the premises are dependent on one another.

8-3, 4. When blue jays are breeding, they become very aggressive. Consequently, scrub jays, which are very similar to blue jays, may also be expected to be aggressive when they're breeding.

Conclusion: Scrub jays may be expected to be aggressive when they're breeding. Be careful with the clause "which are very similar to blue jays." This functions as a premise in the argument, not as part of the conclusion; without it among the premises, the argument isn't valid.

8-4, 9. If you drive too fast, you're more likely to get a ticket. You're also more likely to get into an accident. So you shouldn't drive too fast.

Independent. Some repetition of words in the two premises ("you're more likely to get") may obscure the logical independence of these premises. What matters is **not** whether getting into an accident leaves you more likely to get a ticket but whether the two have to occur together to give you a reason not to drive too fast.

8-11, 7. Washington, D.C., mayor Marion Barry was convicted of cocaine use; he could not have been a very effective mayor while he was using drugs.

Assumed premise: No one convicted of cocaine use could have been a very effective mayor. The trick to watch out for is the phrase "convicted of." The premise "No one who used cocaine could have been a very effective mayor" does not yield a valid argument. (And which is more plausible, that using cocaine makes a mayor less effective, or that being convicted of its use does?)

8-15, 4. They really ought to build a new airport. It would attract more business to the area, not to mention the fact that the old airport is overcrowded and dangerous.

One judgment call here: whether to break the last premise stated into two: The old airport is overcrowded, and the old airport is dangerous. Given that an airport may become dangerous for reasons aside from its overcrowding, these are really separate points. The speaker is giving three independent reasons for accepting the conclusion.

Additional Exercises

A. Identify premises and conclusions in the following arguments or argument forms.

1. Because [a] and [b], then [c].

2. Naturally [a]. After all, [b].

3. When you remember that [a] and [b], you realize that [c].

4. [a]. Since [b], then [c].

5. [a] if [b], and [b] whenever [c]. [c], so [a].

6. How could this stereo stand not be finished? I used all the parts.

7. It stands to reason that local politicians should only get two terms in office. Anyone with nothing better to do shouldn't have power.

8. The car won't start. It must not have gas in the tank.

9. The car won't start. After all, it doesn't have gas in the tank.

B. Supply premises to make these arguments valid, if possible, or sound, if they can't be valid. Or conclude that they can't be made either valid or sound.

1. It's no use going on about whether this law is just. It was passed democratically.

2. How can you be so critical of *Pride and Prejudice?* You never read it.

3. I wouldn't call her reliable. She was late with her last rent check.

4. It's not safe to let Dave drive you home. He just had a furious argument with his boss.

5. Look, it's snowing. The air will be warmer today.

6. We didn't miss the bus. It isn't 8:04 yet.

7. That isn't art. A child could do it.

C. Diagram these arguments.

1. Everyone from Artemus Ward Pre-School knows how to tie their shoes. Bradley tried and tried and couldn't do it. She must not go to Artemus Ward.

2. Put together that our uninsured children have pressing needs, and that the elderly face high medical costs, and you see that the new health care bill is the right one to pass, despite the fact that it will lead to higher taxes.

3. There's no talent here. The novel's plotlessness and its unsavory characters make it the result of just stringing together a lot of big words. And when all you have is a lot of big words strung together, there's no talent at work.

4. If he'd been perfectly innocent he wouldn't have been arrested; but he was arrested. And you've seen that suspicious smirk on his face. He's not innocent.

5. There's no way she'll be able to afford private schools for her kids. She speculated in real estate—that's been a real money loser lately. And she bought a lot of art and plowed the rest into her retirement account, which means she has no liquid capital.

6. They have no convincing alibi for the night of the fourteenth. They can't explain what happened to their shotgun. And they owed the victim money, which means they had a motive. It makes a winning case, and that's why I'm pressing charges.

Answers to Additional Exercises

A. 1. Premises: [a] and [b]. Conclusion: [c].

2. Premise: [b]. Conclusion: [a].

3. Premises: [a] and [b]. Conclusion: [c].

4. Premises: [a] and [b]. Conclusion: [c].

5. This is a bit tricky. You can say that [b] and [c] are premises, or you can say more precisely that the premises are [a] if [b], [b] whenever [c], and [c]. Conclusion: [a].

6. Premise: I used all the parts. Conclusion: This stereo stand is finished.

7. Premise: Anyone with nothing better to do shouldn't have power. Conclusion: Local politicians should only get two terms in office.

8. Premise: The car won't start. Conclusion: It doesn't have gas in the tank.

9. Premise: The car doesn't have gas in the tank. Conclusion: It won't start.

B. 1. Assumed premise: Most laws that were passed democratically are just. This makes the argument strong. The premise needed for a valid argument, "All democratically passed laws are just," is not as plausible.

2. Assumed premise: You are not justified in being critical of any book you have not read. This is plausible and makes the argument valid.

3. No assumed premise makes the argument either strong or valid. The weakest possible assumption, "If she was late with her rent check last month, she probably isn't reliable," is far too implausible.

4. Assumed premise: When Dave has just had a furious argument, it's usually not safe to let him drive. Strong argument. It isn't plausible to assume (as you'd have to for a valid argument) that Dave is an unsafe driver every time he's had a furious argument.

5. Assumed premise: When it is snowing, the air becomes warmer. Strong argument.

6. Assumed premise: If it isn't 8:04, the bus probably has not come yet. This makes the argument strong.

7. No assumed premise makes the argument either strong or valid. The weakest possibility, "Very few children could make art," is too vague to be plausible.

C. 1. (1) Everyone from Artemus Ward knows how to tie their shoes.
   (2) Bradley tried and tried and couldn't do it.
   (3) She must not go to Artemus Ward.

2. (1) Our uninsured children have pressing needs.
   (2) The elderly face high medical costs.
   (3) The new health care bill is the right one to pass.
   (4) It will lead to higher taxes.

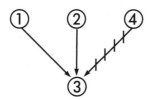

3.   (1)   There's no talent here.
     (2)   The novel has no plot.
     (3)   The novel has unsavory characters.
     (4)   The novel is the result of stringing together a lot of big words.
     (5)   When all you have is big words strung together, there's no talent.

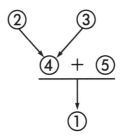

4.   (1)   If he'd been perfectly innocent he wouldn't have been arrested.
     (2)   He was arrested.
     (3)   He has a suspicious smirk on his face.
     (4)   He's not innocent.

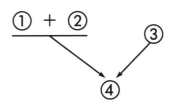

5.   (1)   She won't be able to afford private schools for her kids.
     (2)   She speculated in real estate.
     (3)   Real estate has been a money loser lately.
     (4)   She bought a lot of art.
     (5)   She plowed the rest into her retirement account.
     (6)   She has no liquid capital.

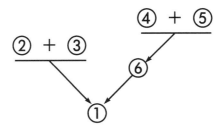

6. (1)   They have no convincing alibi for the night of the fourteenth.
    (2)   They can't explain what happened to their shotgun.
    (3)   They owed the victim money.
    (4)   They had a motive.
    (5)   It makes a winning case.
    (6)   I'm pressing charges.

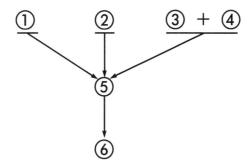

Answers to Review Questions

1. An argument must pass both of the following tests to be sound: It must be valid, and all its premises must be true. To be valid, an argument must be such that whenever all its premises are true, so is its conclusion.

2. The first aim is validity: You look for a sufficiently general or reasonable claim that, when added to the stated premises, produces a valid argument. If no plausible claim can make the argument valid, modify the claim to make the argument strong: That is the second aim. If no plausible claim makes the argument strong, reject the argument.

3. Trick question. We call no argument both strong and valid; not because valid arguments are weak, but because these are two different categories of evaluation.

4. Any example will work here, as long as the argument is valid and contains at least one false premise. (For the purposes of the example, it helps to have the premise be patently false.) "All wolves are canines. All canines have the power of flight. Therefore, all wolves have the power of flight."

5. An argument's goodness emerges in one of two ways. First, it is good if it is valid (and preferably sound). We test for validity according to the methods to be covered in Chapters 9 and 10. Second, an argument may also be good by being strong. We test for argumentative strength according to the methods to be covered in Chapters 11 and 12.

CHAPTER 9

DEDUCTIVE ARGUMENTS I: CATEGORICAL LOGIC

You may think of all the preceding chapters as preliminaries to the detailed and precise task of evaluating arguments. Chapters 1–3 examine the parts of arguments (words, claims); Chapters 4–6 look at attempted persuasion in the absence of arguments (nonargumentative persuasion, pseudoreasoning); Chapters 7–8 speak in a general way about the support we provide for claims (explanations, arguments). Now it is time to put arguments to the test. Chapters 9–13 will take up deductive arguments, inductive arguments, and then the difficult kinds of arguments concerning moral, legal, and aesthetic matters.

We begin with deductive arguments, which we have characterized as being either valid or invalid. Chapters 9–10 present two methods for testing for validity. In the present chapter, we use the logic of categorical statements, which dates back to Aristotle, and is a powerful tool for handling one large group of arguments. Those arguments are distinguished by the form of claims that make up their premises and conclusions—roughly, claims beginning with the words "all" and "some." Chapter 9 shows first how to work with such categorical statements by themselves: translating them into equivalent forms, separating them from superficially identical claims, and so on. Then we look at the standard arrangement of such statements into arguments, called categorical syllogisms. Two methods test syllogisms for validity; either one will let the reader evaluate every standard categorical syllogism.

CHAPTER SUMMARY

I. **Categorical logic** studies the relations among classes or categories of things.

   A. This theory of logical inference began with Aristotle, and developed for over two thousand years since.

   B. Like *truth-functional logic* (see Chapter 10), it helps in every situation that calls for clarification and analysis.

      1. Our evaluation of arguments most obviously will depend on logic.

      2. Many other situations—legal contracts, logical reasoning tests, and so on—call for the same skills.

II. **Categorical claims,** which make assertions about groups or categories of things, make up the subject matter of categorical logic.

   A. We will use categorical claims in their standard forms. A **standard-form categorical claim** has one of these structures:

      1. A: All _____ are _____.

104

2. E: No _____ are _____.

3. I: Some _____ are _____.

4. O: Some _____ are not _____.

B. Categorical claims have nouns and noun phrases in the above blanks.

    1. We call those nouns and noun phrases **terms.**

        a. The first term in a standard-form claim is its **subject term,** S.

        b. The second is its **predicate term,** P.

    2. Only nouns and noun phrases can work as terms.

C. Each of these forms of claims can be given a visual illustration in a **Venn diagram.**

    1. In each Venn diagram, the two overlapping circles represent the groups or categories named by the subject and predicate term.

    2. A shaded area represents an empty class.

        a. Note that this is the opposite of a shaded area in Venn diagrams you may have used to illustrate sets in math class.

    3. An area with an X represents a class that is not empty: The class contains at least one member. (In this chapter, "some" will mean "at least one.")

D. When drawing Venn diagrams for categorical claims, it helps to think of those claims in terms of empty and nonempty classes.

    1. "All S are P" (A) means the same thing as "The class of S outside of P is empty."

    2. "No S are P" (E) means the same thing as "The class of S inside P is empty."

    3. "Some S are P" (I) means the same thing as "The class of S inside P has at least one member."

    4. "Some S are not P" (O) means the same thing as "The class of S outside of P has at least one member."

E. For obvious reasons, we separate these four claims into **affirmative** (**A** and **I**) and **negative** (**E** and **O**) claims.

    1. Affirmative claims include one class within another; they contain no negation words.

    2. Negative claims exclude one class within another; they contain a negation word, "no" or "not."

III. Categorical logic begins with the task of translating claims into standard-form categorical claims.

A. This process can make a surprising number of ordinary sentences work as categorical claims.

B. Many ordinary claims need only small changes before taking on standard form.

    1. Claims about whole classes require only the addition or substitution of words like "all" and "no."

        a. "Each student is a responsible adult" thus turns into "All students are responsible adults."

        b. "Students are not idle people" turns, with equal ease, into "No students are idle people."

    2. Claims in the past tense go quickly into the present tense that characterizes standard-form categorical claims.

        a. "Some conspirators were Protestants" thus becomes (only a little stiffly) "Some of the people who were conspirators are people who were Protestants."

        b. In such cases, the past tense enters the term (the noun phrase).

    3. Ordinary claims containing "only" become A-claims; the trick is to identify subject and predicate terms correctly.

        a. "Only" by itself comes before the predicate term. "Only adults are legal drivers" is restated, "All legal drivers are adults."

        b. "The only" comes before the subject term. "The only good cars are Japanese cars" thus turns into "All good cars are Japanese cars."

C. Other translations into standard form take more thinking, especially about the terms of the claim.

    1. Many claims speak generally about times and places, and we need to make the reference to time and place explicit.

        a. "I'm loved wherever I go": "All places I go are places I'm loved."

        b. "You sometimes fall asleep at the movies": "Some times that you're at the movies are times that you fall asleep."

    2. Claims about single individuals need rephrasing before they can count as categorical claims.

        a. Such claims become A-claims or E-claims.

        b. We replace the single thing's name (N) with the phrase, "All things [people, places, and so on] identical with N."

        c. "Cleveland has the best orchestra in the country" becomes "All cities identical with Cleveland are cities that have the best orchestra in the country."

    3. Claims that use mass nouns—that is, nouns referring to some stuff in general—are best translated with a phrase about examples of that stuff.

    a. "Water is colorless": "All examples of water are examples of something col-
    orless" (A-claim).

    b. "Some meat tastes like chicken": "Some examples of meat are examples of
    things that taste like chicken."

IV. The **square of opposition** shows the logical relationships among all **corresponding** categorical claims.

   A. We say that two categorical claims correspond to one another when they have the
       same subject term and the same predicate term.

       1. The two claims may belong to any form; for example, an A-claim may corre-
           spond to an E-, I-, or O-claim.

       2. Note that the claims must have the same two terms in the same places. As they
           stand, "All experts are professionals" and "Some professionals are not experts"
           do not correspond.

   B. We can put all four corresponding claims about any subject and predicate into the
       same square of opposition:

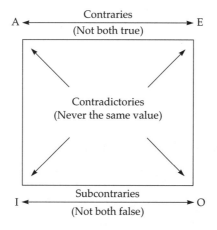

   C. Corresponding A- and E-claims are **contrary claims:** They are never both true.

       1. If "All rooms are vacant" is true, then "No rooms are vacant" is false.

       2. Both claims might be false. Neither "All cars are Toyotas" nor "No cars are
           Toyotas" is true.

       3. So if an A- or E-claim is true, you know that its contrary is false. If it's false, you
           can't draw any conclusions.

   D. Corresponding I- and O-claims are **subcontrary claims:** They are never both false.

1. If "Some rooms are vacant" is false, then "Some rooms are not vacant" must be true.

2. Both might be true: "Some cars are Toyotas" and "Some cars are not Toyotas."

3. So if an I- or O-claim is false, you know its subcontrary is true. If it's true, you can't draw any conclusions about its subcontrary.

E. Exceptions to both these rules occur when the subject class is empty. We will assume, however, that it is not.

F. Corresponding A- and O-claims are **contradictory claims,** as are corresponding E- and I-claims: They have opposite truth values.

1. If "All boxers are left-handed people" is false, "Some boxers are not left-handed people" must be true.

2. If "Some left-handed people are boxers" is true, "No left-handed people are boxers" must be false.

G. When you have a true A- or E-claim (a claim at the top of the square), or a false I- or O-claim (at the bottom), you can infer the truth values of all corresponding claims.

1. Say that "All windows are glass objects" is true. Then:

   a. "No windows are glass objects" (contrary) is false;

   b. "Some windows are not glass objects" (contradictory) is false;

   c. "Some windows are glass objects" (contradictory of the contrary) is true.

2. Say that "Some cars are boats" is false. Then:

   a. "Some cars are not boats" (subcontrary) is true;

   b. "No cars are boats" (contradictory) is true;

   c. "All cars are boats" (contradictory of the subcontrary) is false.

H. However, when you have a false A- or E-claim, or a true I- or O-claim, you can only infer the truth value of its contradictory.

1. From the false claim "All politicians are men," all that follows is the truth of its contradictory, "Some politicians are not men."

2. From the true claim "Some politicians are men," all that follows is the falsity of "No politicians are men."

V. Together with the square of opposition, three operations help us draw simple inferences from categorical claims.

A. To produce the **converse** of a categorical claim (a process called conversion), simply switch the subject and predicate terms.

1. E- and I-claims are equivalent to their converses, but A-and O-claims are not.

2. When you say, "No cats are dogs," you equally say, "No dogs are cats."

3. When you say, "Some doctors are men," you equally say, "Some men are doctors."

B. To produce the **obverse** of a standard-form claim (a process called obversion), change it from affirmative to negative, or vice versa, and replace the predicate term with its **complementary term.**

1. A term's complementary term names every member of the universe of discourse that is not in the original class.

   a. Usually, the complementary term can be formed with the prefix "non" in front of the original term: "democracy" and "nondemocracy."

   b. Sometimes you need to take care to restrict the universe of discourse. The term complementary to "drivers" is "people who are not drivers."

   c. Note: "Non" is safer than common opposites. The complement to "people who are happy" is not "people who are sad" but "people who are not happy."

2. Changing a claim from affirmative to negative, or vice versa, is the same as going across the square of opposition.

3. All claims are equivalent to their obverses.

4. "All blessings are mixed things" becomes, through obversion, "No blessings are unmixed things."

5. Similarly, saying, "Some athletes are pros" amounts to saying, "Some athletes are not nonpros."

C. To produce the **contrapositive** of a claim (a process known as contraposition), switch the subject and predicate terms and replace both by their complementary terms.

1. A- and O-claims are equivalent to their contrapositives, but E-and I-claims are not.

   a. That is, claims that are *not* equivalent to their converses are equivalent to their contrapositives.

2. "All poodles are dogs": "All nondogs are nonpoodles."

3. "Some employees are not guards"? Then "Some nonguards are not non-employees."

VI. We begin the study of **categorical syllogisms** with vocabulary.

A. In a categorical syllogism all claims are categorical claims and three terms appear, each one twice.

1. A **syllogism** is a deductive argument with two premises.

2. Each term in a categorical syllogism occurs in two of the claims (whether premises or conclusion), once in each.

3. "All poodles are dogs. All dogs are mammals. Therefore, all poodles are mammals." Note the distribution of terms.

B. In the interest of clear and uniform labeling, we refer to these three terms by standard names:

1. The **major term** is the conclusion's predicate term; we abbreviate it P.

2. The **minor term** is the conclusion's subject term; we abbreviate it S.

3. The **middle term** occurs in both premises, but not in the conclusion; we abbreviate it M.

C. Although it is easy to confuse "major" and "minor" here, what matters most is to see the function of the middle term in a syllogism. The middle term links the major term to the minor.

D. We now possess two ways of telling categorical syllogisms from impostors.

1. Make certain that all three claims have been presented in standard form.

2. Make certain that exactly three terms appear in the syllogism, each one twice. Watch out for complementary terms sneaking in.

VII. Venn diagrams provide one method for testing categorical syllogisms for validity.

A. Keep certain basic ideas in mind when using this method.

1. Recall the meaning of validity. If the premises are all true, the conclusion is true, too.

2. The method extends the Venn diagrams for single claims to illustrate how premises and conclusion work together.

3. The point of this method is simple: Once you diagram the premises, the diagram should reveal the conclusion. (This is, after all, what validity amounts to, that stating the premises of an argument means stating its conclusion.)

a. In certain cases of arguments with I- and O-claims for conclusions, the conclusion will not simply appear in the finished diagram. See below for this exception.

4. With only a few additional guidelines, the work of diagramming a syllogism will look exactly like the work of diagramming two separate claims; that is, shading and Xs will work much as they do for separate claims.

B. Every diagram begins with three overlapping circles:

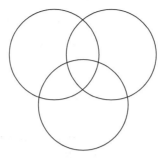

C. Add four rules to the diagramming rules you have already learned for individual categorical claims.

1. To keep all diagrams uniform, put the minor term on the left, the major term on the right, and the middle term a little below them, in the middle.

2. When one premise is an A- or E-claim and the other is an I- or O-claim, diagram the A- or E-claim first.

    a. In other words, shade before putting in Xs. Do not put an X in a shaded area.

    b. This usually helps solve the problem of where to put an X, when more than one area is available.

3. If it is still not clear where to put the X—if it could go in either of two spaces—put the X on the line between them.

4. After you have finished diagramming the premises, see if any circle has only one unshaded area; if so, put an X in that area.

    a. Remember our assumption that no class is empty.

    b. This final step permits you to go from two premises that are A- or E-claims to a conclusion that is an I- or O-claim; that step would otherwise be impossible.

D. Once the premises have been diagrammed, see if the diagram for the conclusion appears in the circles.

1. If the argument is valid, the finished Venn diagram will "state" the conclusion.

2. When the conclusion is an I- or O-claim, you need the relevant X to appear completely within its space. An X only partly in the right area does not give you your conclusion.

VIII. Many ordinary-language syllogisms can be brought within this formal structure and evaluated with Venn diagrams (or the rules method).

    A. In some cases, you need to supply unstated premises.

        1. Many categorical syllogisms we encounter in ordinary reading and conversation are missing premises, usually because a premise is considered too obvious to assert.

        2. Find a reasonable claim you can add to the syllogism's argument to make it valid. (See Chapter 8.)

        3. The subject and predicate terms of the missing premise will be the two terms that each occur once in the stated premise and conclusion.

            a. That is, if you are given a premise of the form "No A are B" and a conclusion of the form "Some C are not A," you know that the missing premise will contain the terms B and C.

            b. It takes a little more work to see how to arrange those terms to form a missing premise (in this instance, more than one form works) to produce a valid argument. Syllogisms in ordinary language usually suggest their missing premises.

    B. In all cases, begin your evaluation of the completed syllogism by abbreviating its terms.

        1. Write down a clear abbreviation key, for example, "B = baseball players."

        2. Rewrite the argument using your abbreviations. Both methods of evaluation go faster when the form is more perspicuous.

IX. A simple set of three rules provides the second test of a categorical syllogism's validity.

    A. In most respects the rules method is better than Venn diagrams.

        1. It is easier to understand the principles behind Venn diagrams, where the three rules do not wear their rationale on their sleeve.

        2. However, applying Venn diagrams can be cumbersome and slow, and often provides opportunities for small (but telling) clerical errors.

    B. To use the rules, you first need to feel comfortable with the distinction between affirmative and negative claims.

        1. A- and I-claims are affirmative; E- and O-claims are negative.

        2. Negative claims either begin with "no" or contain "not."

    C. Second, you need to become familiar with **distributed terms.**

        1. A term is a distributed term if the claim it appears in says something about all members of the class in question.

a. "All dogs are mammals" distributes the term "dog," because it obviously speaks of all dogs.

b. The same claim does not distribute "mammal," because it tells you nothing about all mammals.

2. Memorize the distributed terms of each form of claim (distributive terms are in **boldface**):

a. A: All **S** are P.

b. E: No **S** are **P.**

c. I: Some S are P.

d. O: Some S are not **P.**

D. With this terminology in place, we can state the rules. A syllogism is valid if and only if all the following are true:

1. The number of negative claims in the premises is the same as the number of negative claims in the conclusion.

2. At least one premise distributes the middle term.

3. All terms distributed in the conclusion are distributed in the premises.

E. When applying these rules, first go through the syllogism circling all distributed terms. Then you will find rules 2 and 3 easy, even pleasant, to apply.

KEY WORDS AND IDEAS

A-claim. A categorical claim of the form "All S are P." (Mnemonic: "All" begins with "A.")

Affirmative claim. A claim that includes one class within the other; an A- or I-claim.

Categorical claim. An assertion about groups of things; in its standard form it is an A-, E-, I-, or O-claim.

Categorical logic. The study of relations among categories or groups of things. Categorical logic treats categorical claims.

Categorical syllogism. A syllogism in which both premises and the conclusion are categorical claims, and in which three terms appear. Each term appears exactly twice, once in each of exactly two claims.

Complementary term. A term naming everything not in the class named by another term. If "T" is the term, "non-T" is the complementary term.

Contradictory claims. Two corresponding claims that fall into one of these pairs: Either one is an A-claim and the other an O-claim, or one is an E-claim and the other an I-claim. Contradictory claims have opposite truth values, so that if one is true the other is false.

Contrapositive. A claim formed by switching the subject and predicate terms of a categorical claim, and replacing both by their complementary terms. A- and O-claims are equivalent to their contrapositives.

Contrary claims. Two corresponding claims, of which one is an A-claim and the other an E-claim. Contrary claims are never both true.

Converse. A claim formed by switching subject and predicate terms of a categorical claim. E- and I-claims are equivalent to their converses.

Corresponding claims. Two or more standard-form categorical claims possessing the same subject term and the same predicate term.

Distributed term. In a categorical claim, a term of which the claim asserts something true of all members of the class named.

E-claim. A categorical claim of the form "No S are P." (Mnemonic: "E" means that a set is being called "empty.")

I-claim. A categorical claim of the form "Some S are P." "Some" here may mean as few as one, or as many as all. Thus in categorical logic, "Some ants are biters" does not contradict the claim "All ants are biters"; and it is fully compatible with the claim "Most ants are biters." (Mnemonic: The "I" refers to a claim that speaks of at least one "individual.")

Major term. In a categorical syllogism, the predicate term of the conclusion; symbolized by P.

Middle term. In a categorical syllogism, the term appearing in both premises but not in the conclusion; symbolized by M.

Minor term. In a categorical syllogism, the subject term of the conclusion; symbolized by S.

Negative claim. A claim that excludes one class from the other; an E- or O-claim. Negative claims in standard form either begin with a "no" or contain a "not."

Obverse. A claim formed by changing a categorical claim from affirmative to negative (or vice versa), and replacing the predicate term with its complementary term. All claims are equivalent to their obverses.

O-claim. A categorical claim of the form "Some S are not P." Note the meaning of "some" discussed under "I-claim." (Mnemonic: The claim "Some S are not P" contains more Os than any other.)

Predicate term. The second term in a standard-form claim. Note that the predicate term often cannot be identified until the categorical claim has been written in standard form.

Square of opposition. A diagram that shows the logical relations among all corresponding categorical claims. There are three such relations: contrary, subcontrary, and contradictory.

Standard-form categorical claim. A categorical claim written so as to belong clearly to one of the four groups: A-, E-, I-, and O-claims. The subject and predicate terms must be either nouns or noun phrases.

Subcontrary claims. Two corresponding claims, of which one is an I-claim and the other an O-claim. Subcontrary claims are never both false.

Subject term. The first term in a standard-form claim. Note that the subject term often cannot be identified until the categorical claim has been written in standard form.

Syllogism. A deductive argument with two premises.

Term. A noun or noun phrase functioning as either the subject term or the predicate term of a categorical claim.

Venn diagram. A diagram for illustrating categorical claims, or for testing the validity of categorical syllogisms.

REVIEW QUESTIONS

1. Using "strudel" as your subject term and "pastry" as your predicate term, state all four kinds of standard-form categorical claims.

2. How do you translate claims containing "only" into standard form?

3. When can the square of opposition tell you the truth values of all claims corresponding to a given claim? What does it tell you otherwise?

4. Explain the similarity and the difference between conversion and contraposition, with an example of each.

5. When making a Venn diagram of a syllogism, what do you do with a premise that begins with "some" (i.e., an I- or O-claim)?

6. Explain the definition of a distributed term. One form of claim has no distributed terms. Why not?

COMMONLY ASKED QUESTIONS

Are there any shortcuts to remembering these terms and methods?

One drawback of categorical logic is that it can get top-heavy with special vocabulary and rules that rely on that vocabulary. If you feel overwhelmed by the initial blitz of detail, take heart: Students of Aristotelian logic have responded that way for over two thousand years—because for at least that long, logicians have been inventing memory aids to keep the elements of logic straight.

You will probably find the logical procedures of Chapter 10 still stranger at first sight, and reminiscent of mathematics; but before long you will see that they involve less of this sort of memorization. So Chapter 9 is the one to work on.

What follow are a few tricks for getting a handle on what seem like arbitrary symbols and rules. If they strike you as far-fetched, silly, or harder to remember than the chapter's actual material, please ignore them.

A-, E-, I-, O-claims. The definitions of these terms in "Key Words," above, include suggestions for remembering them.

Converse, obverse, contrapositive. The work here is remembering which operations you may apply to which sorts of claims. No one worries about obversion, because every categorical claim is equivalent to its obverse; lea rn how to do it and apply it everywhere. You may think of obversion as a way of taking a double negative: Negate the *form* of the claim (negative to affirmative or affirmative to negative), and then negate its *content* (with the complementary term, the denial, of the predicate).

Which claims may be converted, and which need contraposition? Both operations involve switching the subject and predicate terms. But that's all you do to an E- or an I-claim, whereas A- and O-claims require that you also replace each term with its complementary term. What is it about A- and O-claims that makes the added step necessary?

E- and I-claims are symmetrical statements, whereas the other two are asymmetrical. "Some bakers are Italians" tells you what "Some Italians are bakers" does (aside from subjective emphasis), so you can trot out those terms in either order. "All bakers are Italians," on the other hand, is saying something about all bakers, and has nothing to say about Italians in general.

The Venn diagram is one way to identify symmetrical statements. In diagrams for E- and I-claims, the only marks within the two circles, whether shading or X, are made in the lens-shaped area between them. You can relabel the two circles and still have the same claim. But A- and O-claims yield diagrams in which all the action happens outside that lens-shaped space.

Here's another way of thinking about it. Some categorical claims can be naturally translated into sentences containing "S and P," but others can't. An E-claim, "No S are P," says, "Nothing is both S and P." The corresponding I-claim, "Some S are P," tells you, "At least one thing is both S and P." By contrast, the O-claim turns into "At least one thing is S and is not P"; the A-claim has no graceful translation into a claim about S and anything else.

This "and" should tip you off. If something is both S and P, it's both P and S. If nothing is both S and P, nothing can be both P and S either. So claims you can restate as being about S and P make equally good sense about P and S; hence they're symmetrical; hence you convert them and don't take the contrapositive.

Distributed terms. Some memorization helps with distributed terms, but a few little tips will help you keep them straight. In the first place, you have noticed that no two types of categorical claims distribute their terms in the same way. If you remember how terms are distributed in two types of claims, you have narrowed down the possibilities for the other two. If you remember three, the fourth type of claim will be the remaining alternative.

The general way to remember distributed terms is this: The subject term of a universal claim (one that doesn't begin with "some") is always distributed, as is the predicate term of a negative claim.

One linguistic sign is the word right before the term. If the word is either "all" or a negation ("no" or "not"), the term is distributed. If the word is "some," the term is not distributed.

Some terms have no signs before them, of course: The predicate term of an E-claim is distributed without any linguistic hint. But if you remember "all or none," you will have a signpost marking three out of the four distributed terms that arise.

What is a good way of choosing between Venn diagrams and rules as tests for validity?

Don't base your decision on which method is easier to understand, or which method's rules you can absorb faster. Venn diagrams win on both counts; but, while you may reasonably decide to use them in all cases, the rules have advantages that don't appear right away.

First of all, the rules are easier to learn than they first appear. Stated in a row, they have an alienating effect: so abstract and so complicated. But once you are familiar with distributed terms you will find yourself looking over syllogisms and quickly spotting their validity or invalidity.

Remember: When you have written a syllogism in standard form, go over it to circle all distributed terms. This will make the application of the second and third rules even faster.

Venn diagrams have the great advantage of resting on an obvious principle: Because the premises of a valid argument make the conclusion true, diagramming the premises should make the conclusion appear. However, this method is often harder to get the hang of than it looks. Before deciding to stay with it, make sure that you feel comfortable with the procedures for diagramming an entire syllogism.

One thing that leads to little errors in the use of Venn diagrams is the crucial difference between their appearance in logic and the appearance you may be familiar with from a math course. When making the diagram of a set in math, you shade in to show that an area is full. When diagramming an A- or E-claim, however, you shade to show that the area is empty.

TIPS ON APPLICATIONS

Students sometimes take critical thinking to help them prepare for standardized tests such as the GRE and LSAT. They are right to: Although no one course can transform low scores into high ones, critical thinking explicitly lays out many of the ideas and methods we use without realizing it, and so makes it easier to apply them to logical and analytical puzzles.

(This is not to say that students should take courses merely as cram sessions. But, given that critical thinking is bound to have effects on your reasoning that go far beyond exam scores, there's nothing wrong with going to it for an immediate practical purpose.)

The "Logical Reasoning" section of the LSAT bears an especially close relationship to the topics covered in critical thinking. Logical Reasoning questions include questions about a passage's main idea or conclusion, about assumptions made in the passage or inferences that can be drawn from it, and about fallacies or other flaws exhibited in the passage. We have covered these matters in earlier discussions of clear assertions (Chapter 2), argument (Chapter 8), and pseudoreasoning (Chapters 5–6). But Logical Reasoning can also ask about the structures of arguments; and here Chapter 9 can help.

Consider the following: Truck drivers are seasoned professionals. So some truck drivers will be aware of your presence when you're in their blind spot. Which is the necessary assumption for the conclusion to follow logically?

(A) All seasoned professionals will be aware of your presence when you're in their blind spot.

(B) Truck drivers are the only seasoned professionals.

(C) All seasoned professionals who remain unaware of your presence when you're in their blind spot are truck drivers.

(D) Some seasoned professionals will be aware of your presence when you're in their blind spot.

(E) Some truck drivers will remain unaware of your presence when you're in their blind spot.

It is the work of a moment to write the given premise and conclusion as:

> All T are S.
> Some T are A.

Every term in a categorical syllogism must occur exactly twice. So before even thinking about validity, you know that the missing premise must contain S ("seasoned professionals") and A ("people who are aware of your presence when you're in their blind spot"), and nothing else. Already this narrows down the possible answers to A and D.

Now try out both possibilities. The first answer gives you:

> All T are S.
> All S are A.
> Some T are A.

Valid. The second answer gives you:

> All T are S.
> Some S are A.
> Some T are A.

Invalid. (If you're using the rules, you notice that the middle term has not been distributed in either premise.) So the answer is A.

The last part of the "Additional exercises" below contains a few more such questions. When you have mastered categorical logic, you can fly through such problems much faster than if you have to stop and think about what each sentence contributes to the argument.

EXERCISES

Sample Exercises from the Book

9-1, 10. Wherever there are snakes, there are frogs.

All places having snakes are places having frogs. Let this example remind you to keep an eye open for the suffix "-ever": It should make you think of "every," that is, "all."

9-2, 10. I've had days like this before.

Some prior days are days like this day; or, Some days I've had are days like today. Claims that something **exists,** or has existed, translate into I- or O-claims, claims that begin with "some." This shouldn't surprise you: If "some" in logic means "at least one," that word makes the best way to indicate existence.

9-4, 4. Find the converse of "Some Kurds are not Christians."

Some Christians are not Kurds; not equivalent to the original claim. When taking this converse, or doing anything else to an O-claim, remember that the word "not" is part of the frame of the claim, not part of its content. The "not" stays where it is as you move terms around.

9-5, 4. Find the contrapositive of "No students who did not score well on the exam are students who were admitted to the program."

No students who were not admitted to the program are students who scored well on the exam; not equivalent. A note on the complementary terms here: Because our universe of discourse is obviously "students," all the complementary term has to do is name those students not named by the original term, not all people who didn't score well.

9-8, 4 a. No members of the club are people who took the exam.
b. Some people who did not take the exam are members of the club.

(B) becomes "Some members of the club are not people who took the exam." It may help to add a few words about strategy. You look at the original claims and notice that you have to rewrite the phrase "people who did not take the exam" so as to get the "not" out of it. That should make you think: complementary term. Only one procedure, contraposition, produces a complementary term in a claim's subject. And you can't use that here, with an I-claim. So move the phrase into the predicate by taking the converse: "Some members of the club are people who did not take the exam." Now take the obverse, which always gives a complementary term in the predicate, and you get "Some members of the club are not people who took the exam."

9-10, 9. a. Not everybody who is enrolled in the class will get a grade. (True)
b. Some people who will not get a grade are enrolled in the class.

True. Your first strategy is to make these corresponding claims. This means that (a) needs to be put into standard form, and the subject term of (b) needs to be changed into its complementary term. Notice that (a) contradicts the claim "All people enrolled in the class will get a grade." So it's the contradictory of that: "Some people enrolled in the class are not people who will get a grade."

Now onward to (b). Get that problem term into the predicate by conversion: "Some people enrolled in the class are people who will not get a grade." Clean it up with obversion. "Some people enrolled in the class are not people who will get a grade." Because the two claims translate into the same thing, (b) is true.

9-11, 7. All halyards are lines that attach to sails. Painters do not attach to sails, so they must not be halyards.

Valid. Two comments are worth making about this one. First, it illustrates the need to put syllogisms into standard form. Separate the second premise from the conclusion. Make the second premise, "No painters are lines that attach to sails"; make the conclusion, "No painters are halyards."

   Second, think of what the conclusion's diagram will look like: As an E-claim, it will have a shaded lens-shaped area between the circles for P (painters) and H (halyards). Because the completed diagram has that shaded area, the argument is valid.

9-20, 4. This is not the best of all possible worlds, because the best of all possible worlds would not contain mosquitoes, and this world contains plenty of mosquitoes!

Valid. First, specify the terms and assign abbreviations to them, for instance as follows:

> T = worlds identical to this one (i.e., this world).
> B = worlds that are the best of all possible worlds.
> M = worlds that contain mosquitoes.

Then identify the conclusion, which is the first clause of this compound sentence: No T are B. Make sure the two subsequent clauses are put into standard form with the same terms: No B are M; All T are M. As a syllogism, the argument then says:

> No B are M.
> <u>All T are M.</u>
> No T are B.

If you are using the rules method, circle the distributed terms. In this syllogism, every term is distributed except the M in the second premise. You will see that one premise is a negative claim, as the conclusion also is (rule 1); that the middle term is M and is distributed in the first premise (rule 2); that T is distributed in the conclusion and also in the second premise, and that B is distributed in the conclusion and also in the first premise (rule 3).

Additional Exercises

A. Put the following claims into standard form, then operate on them as indicated.

   1. A desk is a piece of furniture. Contrapositive.

   2. A desk is a piece of furniture. Contrary.

   3. Desks make good workbenches. Contrary of the obverse.

   4. Winged horses do exist. Obverse of the converse. (Hint: Start the sentence with "some.")

   5. Winged horses do exist. Obverse of the subcontrary of the converse.

   6. The wicked flee when no man pursueth. Contrapositive.

   7. The righteous are bold as a lion. Contrapositive of the contradictory.

8. None of my friends wanted to help me move. Contrapositive of the contrary.

9. There are people who can be honest without being offensive. Contradictory.

10. There are people who can be honest without being offensive. Converse of the subcontrary.

11. There are people who can be honest without being offensive. Converse of the contrary of the contradictory.

B. Where necessary, put these claims into standard form. Then, based on what you are told about the truth value of the first one, say whether the second claim is true or false, or has undetermined truth value.

1. a. It never rains but it pours. (False)
   b. Some times that it rains, it doesn't pour.

2. a. Sandwiches with mayonnaise go bad. (True)
   b. Some sandwiches that go bad are sandwiches with mayonnaise.

3. a. There are bald eagles in America. (False)
   b. Some bald eagles are birds outside America.

4. a. If you're not a psychiatrist, you're not a doctor. (False)
   b. A psychiatrist is a doctor.

5. a. What you don't know can't hurt you. (True)
   b. Some things that can hurt you are things you know.

6. a. Nothing but cabbage soup will help me lose weight. (False)
   b. Some food besides cabbage soup will help me lose weight.

C. Put these syllogisms into standard form. Then test them for validity.

1. All men are mortal; Socrates is a man; Socrates is mortal.

2. There's never been a car that could fly. Flying things are all made of aluminum. So nothing made of aluminum is a car.

3. Some harmonica players are also ventriloquists. Harmonica players love to perform on the radio. So some ventriloquists love to perform on the radio.

4. I've seen the only existing Tucker. So some of these guys must be driving something else, because I haven't seen what they're driving.

5. Milk is white. Some ghosts are white. So, some ghosts are milk.

6. Cats are not friendly animals. Friendly animals respond to the sound of their names. So no animal that responds to the sound of its name is a cat.

7. Gloves are not essential to life. After all, Plato's *Republic* mentions all of life's essentials, and it has nothing to say about gloves.

8. You'll find that all statisticians are professionals. After all, no nonprofessional is employed by this company; and everyone employed by this company is a statistician.

9. All educated people respect books. Some bookstore personnel are not truly educated. So some bookstore personnel don't respect books.

D. The following questions resemble some questions from the "Logical Reasoning" section of the LSAT. Use the materials and methods of Chapter 9 to arrive at your answer.

1. No shoes but loafers are sold in this store. The shoes sold here can be expensive. Which of the following conclusions can logically be inferred from these sentences?:

   (A) Only expensive shoes are sold in this store.

   (B) All expensive shoes are loafers.

   (C) All loafers are sold in this store.

   (D) Some loafers are expensive.

   (E) No expensive loafers are sold in this store.

2. Only only children are trapeze artists. Some circus performers are only children. Therefore, some circus performers are trapeze artists.

   Which of the following exhibits the same logical flaw as the argument above?:

   (A) All toddlers are big eaters. Some girls are toddlers. Therefore, some girls are big eaters.

   (B) Only human beings cool off by perspiring. Some team mascots are human beings. Therefore, some team mascots cool off by perspiring.

   (C) Only you are an expert on soft-coal mining. Some experts on soft-coal mining are consultants. Therefore, only you are a consultant.

   (D) Only Hard-Lee-Hott air conditioners are energy-efficient. My air conditioners are Hard-Lee-Hott air conditioners. Therefore, my air conditioners are energy-efficient.

   (E) Any friend of Pat's is a friend of mine. Any friend of mine is a friend of philosophy. Therefore, any friend of Pat's is a friend of philosophy.

3. Every successful mechanic uses cast-iron wrenches. Some mechanics use wrenches made of something besides cast iron. So some mechanics are not successful.

   Which of the following most closely resembles the reasoning given in this argument?:

   (A) All valid syllogisms are incapable of surprising you. Some syllogisms are not at all able to surprise you. So some syllogisms are not valid.

   (B) Everything worth doing is worth doing right. Everything boring is not worth doing right. So boring things are not worth doing.

   (C) Every good bicycle has hand brakes. Some messengers' bikes are not good bicycles. So some messengers' bikes don't have hand brakes.

   (D) Every happy adult was once a grouchy teenager. Grouchy teenagers fly into fits of anger. So some happy adults fly into fits of anger.

(E) A tape recorder is a sophisticated piece of equipment. Some home appliances are unsophisticated pieces of equipment. Therefore, some home appliances are not tape recorders.

Answers to Additional Exercises

A. 1. Standard form: All desks are pieces of furniture. Contrapositive: All nonpieces of furniture are nondesks.

2. Standard form: as in (1). Contrary: No desks are pieces of furniture.

3. Standard form: All desks are things that make good workbenches. Contrary of the obverse: All desks are things that don't make good workbenches.

4. Standard form: Some horses are winged creatures. Obverse of the converse: Some winged creatures are not nonhorses.

5. Standard form: as in (4). Obverse of the subcontrary of the converse: Some winged creatures are nonhorses.

6. Standard form: All wicked people are people who flee when no man pursueth. Contrapositive: All people who don't flee when no man pursueth are nonwicked people.

7. Standard form: All righteous people are people who are bold as a lion. Contrapositive of the contradictory: Some people who aren't bold as a lion are not nonrighteous people.

8. Standard form: No friends of mine are people who wanted to help me move. Contrapositive of the contrary: All people who didn't want to help me move are nonfriends of mine.

9. Standard form: Some honest people are not offensive people. Contradictory: All honest people are offensive people.

10. Standard form: as in (9). Converse of the subcontrary. Some offensive people are honest people.

11. Standard form: as in (9). Converse of the contrary of the contradictory: No offensive people are honest people.

B. 1. a. All times that it rains are times that it pours. (False)

   b. Some times that it rains are times that it doesn't pour. Obverse of the contradictory of (a); hence true.

2. a. All sandwiches with mayonnaise are sandwiches that go bad. (True)

   b. Already in standard form.

   Begin with (a). Contrary: No sandwiches with mayonnaise are sandwiches that go bad (false). Contradictory: Some sandwiches with mayonnaise are sandwiches that go bad (true). Converse: Some sandwiches that go bad are sandwiches with mayonnaise (true).

3. a. Some bald eagles are birds in America. (False)

   b. Already in standard form.

   Begin with (a). Obverse: Some bald eagles are not birds outside America (false). Subcontrary: Some bald eagles are birds outside America (true).

4. a. No nonpsychiatrists are doctors. (False)

   b. All psychiatrists are doctors.

   Undetermined.

5. a. No things you don't know are things that can hurt you. (True).

   b. Already in standard form.

   Begin with (a). Contradictory: Some things you don't know are things that can hurt you (false). Converse: Some things that can hurt you are things you don't know (false). Obverse: Some things that can hurt you are not things you know (false). Subcontrary: Some things that can hurt you are things you know (true).

6. a. All things that will help me lose weight are examples of cabbage soup. (False).

   b. Some nonexamples of cabbage soup are things that will help me lose weight.

   Take (a). Contradictory: Some things that will help me lose weight are not examples of cabbage soup (true). Obverse: Some things that will help me lose weight are nonexamples of cabbage soup (true). Converse: Some nonexamples of cabbage soup are things that will help me lose weight.

C. 1. All men are mortal beings.
      <u>All people identical with Socrates are men.</u>
      All people identical with Socrates are mortal beings.

      Valid.

   2. Invalid. C = cars; F = flying things; A = things made of aluminum.

      No C are F.
      <u>All F are A.</u>
      No A are C.

   3. Valid. H = harmonica players; V = ventriloquists; R = people who love to perform on the radio.

      Some H are V.
      <u>All H are R.</u>
      Some V are R.

   4. Valid. S = things I have seen; T = Tuckers; C = cars these guys are driving.

      All T are S.
      <u>No C are S.</u>
      Some C are not T.

5. Invalid. M = examples of milk; W = things that are white; G = ghosts.

    All M are W.
    Some G are W.
    Some G are M.

6. Invalid. C = cats; F = friendly animals; R = animals that respond to the sound of their names.

    No C are F.
    All F are R.
    No R are C.

7. Valid. E = things that are essential to life; M = things mentioned in Plato's *Republic*; G = gloves.

    All E are M.
    No G are M.
    No G are E.

8. Invalid. S = statisticians; P = professionals; E = employees of this company.

    All E are P.
    All E are S.
    All S are P.

9. Invalid. E = educated people; R = people who respect books; B = bookstore personnel.

    All E are R.
    Some B are not E.
    Some B are not R.

D. 1. (D). Let S = shoes sold in this store, L = loafers, and E = expensive shoes. In standard form, the two premises then say

    All S are L.
    Some S are E.

    You can tell immediately that the conclusion must contain the terms L and E; so (A), (C), and (E) are out. Then try the argument with the other possibilities. (B) fails, on the rules test, because it distributes the term E, and E is not distributed in a premise. With (D) as the conclusion, however, we get a valid syllogism.

2. (B) The trick, of course, is to spot the logical flaw. When people are not trying to deceive each other, their logical errors usually occur in arguments that look very much like valid arguments, but with a small and crucial difference. The present argument may be abbreviated,

    All A are B.
    Some C are B.
    Some C are A.

This is invalid, for the middle term is not distributed. But note that a very similar-looking argument is valid:

All B are A.
Some C are B.
Some C are A.

(You will get this form for the first premise if you neglect the rule for translating "only.") Now look through the five arguments for an A-claim in the first premise. Since they all have that, look for an I-claim in the second premise. Now you are down to (A), (B), and (C). Next, look at those I-claims to find one whose predicate term is the same as the predicate term of the first premise. The answer is (B).

3. (E). Note that this is a valid argument:

All S are C.
Some M are not C.
Some M are not S.

This time, start with the conclusions of the five sample arguments. Which ones are O-claims? There are three: (A), (C), and (E). Of these, which have an O-claim for a second premise? You may be tempted to say they all do, but look more closely at (A)—it's an I-claim in disguise. This leaves us with (C) and (E). You can satisfy yourself that (C) takes the invalid form,

All G are H.
Some M are not G.
Some M are not H.

But (E) comes out:

All T are S.
Some H are not S.
Some H are not T.

Not only valid, but substantially the same argument as the one about mechanics.

Answers to Review Questions

1. A-claim: All strudels are pastries. E-claim: No strudels are pastries. I-claim: Some strudels are pastries. O-claim: Some strudels are not pastries.

2. All such claims become A-claims. When the word "only" appears alone, the term after it is the predicate term of the A-claim. When the claim contains the phrase "the only," the term that follows is the subject term of the A-claim.

3. The square of opposition can get you from the truth value of one claim to the values of all corresponding claims when the first claim is either a true A- or E-claim or a false I- or O-claim. When the claim you begin with is either a false A- or E-claim or a true I- or O-claim, the square of opposition tells you only the truth value of the claim's contradictory.

4. Both conversion and contraposition involve switching the subject and predicate terms of a claim. But when taking the contrapositive, you also replace each term with its complementary term. All E- and I-claims are equivalent to their converses (and nothing else is); all A- and O-claims (and nothing else) are equivalent to their contrapositives.

5. In the first place, you leave that premise to be diagrammed after the A- or E-claim. Then the shading you have done either specifies a single area in which to put an X, or it does not. If not, the diagram will contain two areas that could equally take the X; you put the X on the border between them.

6. A term is distributed within a claim if the claim makes an assertion about all things called by that name. If the claim is true, it continues to be true when the term is replaced by a term naming a subset of the class originally referred to; thus, if a true claim contains "plants" as a distributed term, that word can be replaced by "trees" without making the claim false. The claim distributes what it says of that term over all members of the class.

    I-claims have no distributed terms. "Some presidents are left-handed people" simply makes no assertions about either the class of presidents or the class of left-handed people. The corresponding O-claim, "Some presidents are not left-handed people," tells you something about all lefties, namely that you can look through the whole group of them without ever stumbling over a president.

CHAPTER 10

DEDUCTIVE ARGUMENTS II: TRUTH-FUNCTIONAL LOGIC

Despite the power and rigor of categorical logic, it lacks flexibility. Its methods really only apply to syllogisms in which each of the two premises can be translated into a standard-form categorical claim. For this reason, even an introductory treatment of logic calls for some discussion of modern symbolic logic. Truth-functional or propositional logic is the simplest part of symbolic logic, though you will find it both rigorous enough to let you carry out systematic proofs and broad enough to handle a wide range of ordinary arguments.

This chapter shows how to work with complex arrangements of individual sentences. You will use letters to represent sentences, and a few special symbols to represent the standard relations among sentences: roughly speaking, the relations that correspond to the English words "not," "and," "or," and "if-then." Truth tables and rules of proof show how the truth values of the individual claims determine the truth values of their compounds, and whether or not a given conclusion follows from a given set of premises.

CHAPTER SUMMARY

I. **Truth-functional logic** is a precise and useful method for testing the validity of arguments.

   A. Also called propositional or sentential logic, truth-functional logic is the logic of sentences.

   B. It has applications as wide-ranging as set theory and the fundamental principles of computer science, as well as being useful for the examination of ordinary arguments.

   C. Finally, the precision of truth-functional logic makes it a good introduction to non-mathematical symbolic systems.

II. The vocabulary of truth-functional logic consists of **claim variables** and **truth-functional symbols.**

   A. Claim variables are capital letters that stand for claims.

      1. In categorical logic, we sometimes used capital letters to represent terms (nouns and noun phrases). Keep those distinct from the same capital letters that now represent whole sentences.

      2. Each claim variable stands for a complete sentence.

   B. Every claim variable has a truth value.

1. We use T and F to represent the two possible truth values.

2. When the truth value of a claim is not known, we use a **truth table** to indicate all possibilities.

3. Thus, for a single variable P, we write:

   P
   T
   F

C. Whatever truth value a claim has, its **negation** (contradictory claim) has the opposite value.

   1. Using ~P to mean the negation of P, we produce the following truth table:

P	~P
T	F
F	T

   2. This truth table is a definition of negation.

   3. ~P is read "not-P." This is our first truth-functional symbol.

D. The remaining truth-functional symbols cover relations between two claims.

   1. Each symbol corresponds, more or less, to an ordinary English word; but you will find the symbols clearer and more rigid than their ordinary-language counterparts.

   2. Accordingly, each symbol receives a precise definition with a truth table, and never deviates from that definition.

E. A **conjunction** (indicated by "&") is a compound claim asserting *both* of the simpler claims contained in it.

   1. More precisely, a conjunction is true if and only if both of the simpler claims are true. We write:

P	Q	P & Q
T	T	T
T	F	F
F	T	F
F	F	F

   2. Notice that this truth table needs four lines, not two, to capture all the possible truth values of P and Q.

   3. We often say there's only one way for a conjunction to come out true, but many ways for it to come out false.

   4. As the ampersand (&) should indicate, "and" is the most common way to describe a conjunction in English. But:

    a. Other English words translate just as well into &: "but," "although," "while," "even though."

    b. "And" sometimes has connotations that & lacks. "I had dinner and went to bed" suggests that one thing happened before the other; the logical conjunction carries no such suggestion.

F. A **disjunction** (indicated by "v") is a compound claim asserting *either or both* of the simpler claims contained in it.

  1. In rigorous language, we say that a disjunction is false if and only if both of the simpler claims are; and we write:

P	Q	P v Q
T	T	T
T	F	T
F	T	T
F	F	F

  2. Aside from the different arrangement of truth values in the final column, this table is set up like the last one.

  3. It's as hard to make a disjunction false as it is to make a conjunction true.

  4. "Or" captures the core meaning of the wedge, "v," but:

    a. "Or" sometimes means that both of the simpler claims can't be true—for example, "You may take the lottery prize in a lump sum or receive payments over twenty years." The logical disjunction never forces us to choose between the disjuncts.

    b. Other English words, like "unless" (see p. 134), also get translated into disjunctions.

G. A **conditional claim** (indicated by "→") is a compound claim asserting the second simpler claim on the condition that the first simpler claim is true.

  1. To define a conditional more exactly, we first need to define its parts.

    a. The claim before the arrow is the **antecedent,** the one after it the **consequent.**

    b. A conditional claim is false if and only if its antecedent is true and its consequent is false. Or:

P	Q	P → Q
T	T	T
T	F	F
F	T	T
F	F	T

  2. We read "P → Q" as "If P, then Q." In many cases the logical conditional will strike you as different from the ordinary English "if-then" construction.

a. The essence of our definition is that the conditional only *must* be false under one set of circumstances, when the antecedent sets up a promised condition and the consequent does not deliver on it. In other cases we are not pressed to call the compound claim false. See "Commonly Asked Questions" below for further discussion.

III. Three rules permit you to construct a truth table for any well-formed combination of claim variables and symbols. Use parentheses when you need them; put enough rows in the table to capture all combinations of truth values; make columns of the parts of the expression.

A. Parentheses specify where a truth-functional operation is doing its work.

1. $5 + 3 \times 2$ makes no sense in arithmetic. It must be written either $(5 + 3) \times 2$, in which case it equals 16, or $5 + (3 \times 2)$, in which case it equals 11.

2. Similarly, the symbols that link claim variables make no sense when strung together without separation, as in P & Q v R → S. Write (P & Q) v (R → S) or whatever you mean.

B. The truth table must capture all possible combinations of truth values for the individual sentences contained in the complex expression.

1. Remember that the truth table is designed to show all the conditions under which a given expression is true or false. Because each of its component claim variables is independent of each other one, the table must reflect every combination.

2. Make a column at the left of the table for each of the claim variables. These are the reference columns.

3. If you have *n* claim variables in an expression, you will need 2^n rows: 2 variables require 4 rows, 3 require 8 rows, 4 require 16 rows, and so on.

4. The rightmost column alternates Ts and Fs; the column just to its left goes T-T-F-F; the column to the left of that, T-T-T-T-F-F-F-F, and so on. The left-hand column is half all Ts and then half all Fs.

5. Here are the reference columns for a truth table built to handle three variables, P, Q, and R:

P	Q	R
T	T	T
T	T	F
T	F	T
T	F	F
F	T	T
F	T	F
F	F	T
F	F	F

C. The truth table must contain columns for the parts of the final complex expression, if any of those parts is not a single claim variable.

    1. For example, if you are building a truth table for the expression (P v Q) → R, you should first make a separate column for P v Q and determine its truth values.

    2. You will then refer to those columns in calculating the truth values for the final expression.

IV. Truth tables so constructed produce a truth-functional analysis of more complex claims, and show whether two claims are equivalent.

A. As an example, take the sentence "Either Peleg and Queequeg will both go harpooning, or Queequeg won't."

    1. We first render it, with obvious symbols, (P & Q) v ~Q.

    2. The truth table contains two claim variables and thus needs four rows; and it must have columns for P & Q and ~Q:

P	Q	P & Q	~Q	(P & O) v ~Q
T	T	T	F	T
T	F	F	T	T
F	T	F	F	F
F	F	F	T	T

    3. Now we can say that the complex expression is false only in row 3, that is, only when P is false and Q is true.

B. When two expressions containing the same claim variables have identical columns in truth tables, we call them **truth-functionally equivalent** (see definition (1)).

    1. You may think of equivalent expressions as claims that mean the same thing.

    2. Consider the truth table for "If Queequeg goes harpooning, so will Peleg," symbolized Q → P:

P	Q	Q → P
T	T	T
T	F	T
F	T	F
F	F	T

    3. Note that this final column is identical to that for "Either Peleg and Queequeg will both go harpooning, or Queequeg won't." The two claims are truth-functionally equivalent.

V. The first significant work in analyzing and operating on claims with truth-functional logic is the work of translating them into symbolic form.

A. Ultimately there is no substitute for a careful examination of what the claims are saying.

1. Translating a compound claim into symbolic form means making its internal logical relations clear and precise.

2. Because ordinary language often gives us compounds with implied or submerged logical relations, we have to begin by making sure we know what they mean.

B. Especially with claims involving conditionals, a few rules speed up the process.

1. When "if" appears by itself, what follows is the antecedent of the conditional.

2. When "only if" appears as a phrase, what follows is the consequent of the conditional.

3. The placement of clauses in a sentence is not a reliable guide to their placement in a conditional. (Logical form often departs from grammatical form.)

4. Thus, "My car will run if you put gas in it" becomes (with "G" and "C" as our symbols) G → C.

5. "My car will run only if you put gas in it," on the other hand, translates as C → G.

6. "Provided," or "provided that," often introduces the antecedent of a conditional. "The car will run provided you put gas in it": G → C.

C. The expression "if and only if" goes peacefully into its logical form if we expand the claim it appears in, into a longer claim.

1. First, observe that "My car will run if and only if you put gas in it" may be rewritten, "My car will run if you put gas in it, and my car will run only if you put gas in it."

2. We have already symbolized those two compounds as G → C and C → G, respectively. It is child's play to link the parts with an ampersand and get (G → C) & (C → G).

D. Other sorts of conditional claims need to be inferred from the statement of **necessary** and **sufficient conditions.**

1. "Literacy is a necessary condition for college graduation" means that you must be literate to be graduated from college, though plenty of other things must be true as well.

2. We express this relationship by saying: If you are graduated from college, you are literate (G → L). Necessary conditions become the consequents of conditionals.

3. "Erudition is a sufficient condition for college graduation" means that if you have become erudite, you are guaranteed your graduation. That condition suffices.

4. We can say: If you are erudite, you will be graduated from college (E → G). Sufficient conditions become the antecedents of conditionals.

Deductive Arguments II: Truth-Functional Logic 133

E. The word "unless," for all its subtleties, translates as "v."

F. In other complex English claims, the location of words like "either" and "if" shows how to group logical relations, and hence where to place parentheses.

    1. "Either I will dance and sing or I will juggle" goes into logic as (D & S) v J, because the "either" and "or" tell you to put parentheses there.

    2. By comparison, "I will dance and either sing or juggle" becomes D & (S v J). Not the same thing at all.

    3. Along similar lines, "if" and "then" disambiguate claims that might otherwise be mistaken for one another. In "If I sing or yodel, then I'll get booed," we know to enclose the disjunction within parentheses: (S v Y) → B.

    4. Compare: "I'll sing, or else, if I yodel, I'll get booed." This is written S v (Y → B).

VI. Truth tables offer one method for testing an argument for validity. (We will also look at two others.)

A. This method builds from a single principle, the definition of validity.

    1. Recall that for an argument to be valid, it must have a true conclusion whenever all its premises are true.

    2. So, we enter all the premises of the argument, and its conclusion, in a truth table, and examine the rows in which all premises are true.

    3. If the conclusion is true in all such rows, the argument is valid. If even one row exists in which all premises are true and the conclusion is false, the argument is invalid.

    4. Sometimes all the premises of an argument cannot be true at once. (They contain a contradiction.) In that case the argument is still valid, for we have no rows in which all premises are true and the conclusion false.

B. When using this method, number the columns of your truth table and keep three sorts of columns distinct from one another.

    1. First, on the left, are the reference columns, headed by single-letter claim variables. You use those to calculate all truth values.

    2. Scattered among the other columns, you are likely to have columns for the parts of complex expressions. Do not confuse these with the premises and conclusions.

    3. The columns for premises and conclusions are the only ones that matter.

VII. A second method is known as the **short truth-table method.**

A. The short truth-table method is practically necessary.

    1. Complete truth tables are tedious to fill out.

2. Moreover, the number of calculations of truth values means greater opportunities for small errors that can lead to a wrong answer.

B. The short truth-table method is a kind of indirect proof.

   1. Rather than go directly to demonstrate an argument's validity, you work to see if it can possibly be invalid. If not, of course, it is valid.

   2. An argument is invalid in case any circumstance exists in which all its premises are true and its conclusion false.

   3. So the short method consists in trying to make the conclusion come out false and the premises true.

C. It is usually quickest to begin with the argument's conclusion, assigning the claim variables values that make that conclusion false and seeing what the values of the other variables must be.

   1. Here is an argument:

      ~A v B
      C → A
      ~B & D
      ~C

   2. For the conclusion to be false, C must be true. We begin:

      A B C D
               T

   3. We want all the premises to be true. If C is true, then the second premise can be true only if A is true; thus:

      A B C D
      T   T

   4. When A is true, naturally ~A is false. So the first premise can be true only on the assumption that B is true:

      A B C D
      T T T

   5. What about the third premise, ~B & D? We want it to be true. But no matter what truth value we give to D, ~B is false and makes the third premise false.

   6. We have failed to produce a set of circumstances that make the premises all true and the conclusion false; the argument is valid.

D. Some examples make it hard to use this method.

   1. There might be too many ways to make premises come out all true and the conclusion false. Sometimes we simply have to consider several possibilities.

2. At other times, it is easier to begin with one premise. Assume that the premise is true, and carry out the argument to make all the other premises true as well, and the conclusion false.

VIII. The method of **deduction** is the third and most sophisticated way of demonstrating an argument's validity.

    A. The method has disadvantages.

        1. It can be cumbersome as a test of invalidity, because failing to arrive at a conclusion from a set of premises can mean either that the argument is invalid, or that we have not found a good proof for a valid argument.

        2. Deduction also presupposes familiarity with a set of rules that guide you through the proof; these must be learned until they feel automatic.

    B. However, deduction possesses the great advantage of exposing the logical relations at work in an argument.

        1. Doing such a proof or derivation resembles thinking through an argument.

        2. You learn, through this process, not only that a conclusion is true when all the premises are, but why.

    C. Because deduction brings out the actual logical connections in an argument, it also makes excellent training in critical thinking.

        1. A truth table is a (very slow) computer program that delivers an answer for any argument you put in: a machine.

        2. Deduction, on the other hand, works like a tool and requires craft. So it leaves you more skilled than the truth tables can.

    D. In every deduction, certain basic principles apply.

        1. You begin with the set of premises and apply rules from Group I and Group II (see below) to them.

        2. If applying a rule produces the conclusion, the deduction is complete. If not, the result becomes another line in the proof, which you can use as you go as if it were a premise.

        3. When you produce a new line for the deduction, write (to the right of it) the lines you used in producing it, and the abbreviation for the rule you used. This is called the **annotation** for the deduction.

IX. **Elementary valid argument patterns** constitute the first set of rules you must learn before carrying out a deduction (Group I rules). These apply only to whole lines of a deduction, not to the individual parts of lines.

A. **Modus ponens** (MP; rule 1) says that, given a conditional claim in one line of a deduction, and the antecedent to that conditional in another line, you can deduce the consequent:

$A \rightarrow B$	$(A \mathrel{\&} B) \rightarrow C$	$\sim C \rightarrow (A \vee \sim B)$
$\underline{A}$	$\underline{A \mathrel{\&} B}$	$\underline{\sim C \hspace{3.5em}}$
B	C	$A \vee \sim B$

   1. Note, in the above examples, that either antecedent or consequent may be more complex.

B. **Modus tollens** (MT; rule 2) functions similarly. Given a conditional claim and the denial to its consequent, you can deduce the denial of the antecedent:

$A \rightarrow B$
$\underline{\sim B}$
$\sim A$

C. The **chain argument** (CA; rule 3), one of the easiest to remember, applies when the consequent of one conditional is the antecedent of another:

$A \rightarrow B$
$\underline{B \rightarrow C}$
$A \rightarrow C$

D. **Disjunctive arguments** (DA; rule 4) let you infer one of two disjuncts in a disjunction, when you are given the negation of the other disjunct:

$A \vee B$
$\underline{\sim A}$
B

   1. The motivating idea is simple: Given two alternatives, and the denial of one of them, you take the other alternative.

   2. Remember that an unnegated expression is itself the negation of the same expression with "$\sim$" in front of it. So, given $\sim(A \mathrel{\&} B) \vee C$, and $(A \mathrel{\&} B)$, you can conclude that C.

E. Because a conjunction asserts that both of its conjuncts are true, you can begin with any conjunction and derive either conjunct: This is **simplification** (SIM; rule 5).

$\underline{A \mathrel{\&} B}$
A (or B)

F. **Conjunction** (CONJ; rule 6), as its name implies, takes any two separate lines of a deduction and joins them:

A
$\underline{B}$
$A \mathrel{\&} B$

1. It is worth restating the obvious: The parts of this conjunction may be as complex as you like:

$A \rightarrow B$
$\underline{C \vee D}$
$(A \rightarrow B) \ \& \ (C \vee D)$

G. Superficially similar to these rules about conjunction is the rule of *addition* (ADD; rule 7). Given any line in a deduction, you may create a disjunction that contains that line as one of its elements, and anything at all as the other one:

$\underline{A}$ $\underline{A}$ $\underline{A}$
$A \vee B$ $A \vee (B \ \& \ C)$ $A \vee (C \rightarrow \sim B)$

H. The *constructive dilemma* (CD; rule 8) begins with two conditional claims and the disjunction of their antecedents, and moves to the disjunction of their consequents:

$A \rightarrow B$
$C \rightarrow D$
$\underline{A \vee C}$
$B \vee D$

1. If at least one of the antecedents is given, at least one of the consequents can be inferred. That's all the rule says.

2. This rule of course relies on modus ponens (rule 1).

I. In a *destructive dilemma* (DD; rule 9) we have two conditionals again, but the disjunction of the negations of their consequents; we derive the disjunction of the negations of the antecedents:

$A \rightarrow B$
$C \rightarrow D$
$\underline{\sim B \vee \sim D}$
$\sim A \vee \sim C$

1. As the constructive dilemma relied on modus ponens, the destructive dilemma relies on modus tollens (rule 2).

2. If at least one of the consequents is being denied, then at least one of the antecedents is being denied as well.

X. **Truth-functional equivalences** form the Group II set of rules (see definition (2)).

A. These rules work somewhat differently from the argument patterns that make up Group I rules.

1. Truth-functional equivalence means that two claims say exactly the same thing. We can therefore replace them with one another without changing the meaning of a claim.

2. Unlike Group I rules, which are rules of inference, rules of equivalence work equally well in both directions.

3. Also unlike those rules, which can only be applied to complete lines of a deduction, these let us replace any part of a line (part of a claim) with its equivalent.

4. Remember that you will still make annotations: Indicate the line you went to, and what you did to it.

B. *Double negation* (DN; rule 10) lets you remove two consecutive negation signs, or insert two such signs, anywhere:

A → ~~A

C. *Commutation* (COM; rule 11) applies to conjunctions and disjunctions. The order of their elements does not matter:

(A & B) ⟷ (B & A)
(A v B) ⟷ (B v A)

1. This should remind you of the commutative laws of addition and multiplication in arithmetic (7 + 5 = 5 + 7).

2. Just as those laws do not apply to subtraction or division, so commutation here does not apply to conditionals.

D. According to the rule called *implication* (IMPL; rule 12), conditionals can be turned into disjunctions, and vice versa:

(A → B) ⟷ (~A v B)

1. People sometimes find this one hard to remember, or even hard to believe. You may want to construct truth tables for A → B and ~A v B and see their equivalence.

2. Again, bear in mind that these equivalence rules work for more complicated expressions and for parts of claims:

A & (~B → C) ⟷ A & (B v C)
(A & ~B) → C ⟷ ~(A & ~B) v C

E. *Contraposition* (CONTR; rule 13) switches the antecedent and consequent of a conditional with the negations of one another:

A → B ⟷ ~B → ~A
~(A & B) → (C v ~D) ⟷ ~(C v ~D) → (A & B)

F. *DeMorgan's Laws* (DEM; rule 14) govern the negations of conjunctions and disjunctions:

~(A & B) ⟷ (~A v ~B)
~(A v B) ⟷ (~A & ~B)

1. Always remember to change the & to a v, or vice versa, when moving the ~ inside the parentheses.

G. One rule you might find hard to memorize, but that is worth keeping in mind, is *exportation* (EXP; rule 15):

$(A \rightarrow (B \rightarrow C)) \leftrightarrow ((A \& B) \rightarrow C)$

1. This is not as strange as it looks. When you say, "If I get invited to the party, then if it's on Friday night, I can go," you're naming two conditions that both must be met before you can go. You may as well say, "If I get invited to the party and it's on Friday night, I can go."

2. Note: This rule does not apply to a complex conditional of the form $(A \rightarrow B) \rightarrow C$.

H. *Association* (ASSOC; rule 16) tells you that strings of conjuncts or disjuncts may be grouped in any way:

$(A \& (B \& C)) \leftrightarrow ((A \& B) \& C)$
$(A \lor (B \lor C)) \leftrightarrow ((A \lor B) \lor C)$

1. Like commutation, this rule should remind you of the comparable rules of association in arithmetic.

2. All the signs must be the same for association to apply: You must have a string of letters all joined by & or v. (And it does not work for the conditional.)

I. The two versions of *distribution* (DIST; rule 17) let us handle combinations of conjunction and disjunction, as follows:

$(A \& (B \lor C)) \leftrightarrow ((A \& B) \lor (A \& C))$
$(A \lor (B \& C)) \leftrightarrow ((A \lor B) \& (A \lor C))$

1. Note the symmetry of the two rules. Once you have learned one, you can turn it into the other by replacing every & with a v, every v with an &.

2. Also note that the thing outside the parentheses, which has a sign next to it, keeps that sign next to itself.

J. Finally, trivially, and obviously, we have the rules of *tautology* (TAUT; rule 18). No comment is necessary:

$A \leftrightarrow (A \lor A)$
$A \leftrightarrow (A \& A)$

XI. Along with these rules of deduction, the method of **conditional proof** (CP) offers a strategy for showing the truth of conditional claims.

A. The idea behind the strategy is this: If a set of premises supports the moves from A to B, then those premises show the truth of $A \rightarrow B$.

1. The essence of the strategy is that A is not a premise given in the argument.

a. We add A as a hypothetical assumption.

    b.   Once we derive B (the consequent of the desired conditional) within the deduction, we may conclude that B follows from A, that is, that A → B.

2.   The complications of conditional proof follow from the fact that this additional premise is not really given. It must be used to derive the needed conditional claim and then eliminated, or *discharged.*

3.   Though the method may strike you as needlessly complex, it actually turns very hard arguments into manageable ones.

B.   The method of conditional proof consists of a few new steps:

   1.   We begin by writing down the assumed premise, the antecedent of the desired conditional.

      a.   We circle the number of that step.

      b.   The annotation reads, "CP Premise."

   2.   We continue through the deduction until we reach the consequent of the desired conditional.

   3.   In the next line, we state the conditional that unites the CP premise with the consequent.

      a.   We draw a line to the left, connecting the CP premise with the consequent.

      b.   The annotation lists all the steps bracketed by that line (e.g., "2–5"), and gives CP as the rule.

C.   In addition to the steps just listed, be sure to follow certain rules for conditional proofs:

   1.   They only prove the truth of a conditional claim.

   2.   If you use more than one CP premise to reach a single final conditional, discharge the premises in reverse order from their assumption. (Lines on the left don't cross.)

   3.   Once a premise has been discharged, none of the steps bracketed by the line may appear again in the deduction.

   4.   Discharge all CP premises.

KEY WORDS AND IDEAS

Annotation. In a deduction, a short note to the right of a line produced from the premises. The annotation consists of the numbers of the lines used in producing this new line, and the abbreviation for the rule used.

Antecedent. In a conditional claim, the subsidiary claim before the arrow, or immediately after the word "if."

Claim variable. A capital letter standing for a claim.

Conditional. A truth-functional relation, symbolized by the truth-functional "→" and usually translated "if-then." A conditional claim is false if and only if its antecedent is true and its consequent is false.

Conditional proof. A deductive method for deriving the truth of a conditional claim. If you can begin with a hypothetical claim and show that (given other lines of the deduction), another claim follows, you may state the conditional that has the hypothetical claim as its antecedent and the claim's implication as its consequent.

Conjunction. A truth-functional relation, symbolized by the truth-functional symbol "&" and usually translated "and." The conjunction of two claims is true if and only if both claims are true.

Consequent. In a conditional claim, the subsidiary claim after the arrow, or immediately after the word "then," or after the phrase "only if."

Deduction. The method of proving an argument to be valid. A deduction applies rules of Group I and Group II to the argument's premises until it arrives at the conclusion.

Disjunction. A truth-functional relation, symbolized by the truth-functional symbol "v" and usually translated "or." The disjunction of two claims is true if and only if at least one of the claims is true; it is false if and only if both are false.

Elementary valid argument pattern. In a deduction, a simple type of argument to be used as a rule in elucidating the steps of more complex arguments; a rule from Group I. These rules apply only to complete lines of a deduction, not to smaller parts of lines.

Necessary condition. A condition that must be the case in order for something else to follow. Oxygen is a necessary condition for human respiration (though you may have plenty of oxygen around and still not be able to breathe, as when being throttled). Necessary conditions become the consequents of conditionals.

Negation. A truth-functional operation, symbolized by the truth-functional symbol "~" and usually translated "not." The negation of a claim is true if and only if the claim is false.

Short truth-table method. An indirect proof of an argument's validity or invalidity. In using this method, we assume the conclusion to be false, and then try to assign truth values to the argument's premises to make them all come out true. If that is possible, the argument is invalid; if not, it is valid.

Sufficient condition. A condition that is enough (suffices) for something else to follow. Being born in the United States is a sufficient condition for citizenship (though you may also acquire citizenship through other means). Sufficient conditions become the antecedents of conditionals.

Truth-functional equivalence (1). The state or condition of having the same truth values under the same circumstances. Two or more claims are equivalent if and only if their columns in a truth table are identical.

Truth-functional equivalence (2). In a deduction, a statement of the identity of two forms of claims, which can be substituted for one another in carrying out a derivation; a rule from Group II. These rules can be applied to any part of a deduction's line.

Truth-functional logic. The branch of symbolic logic treating complete sentences and the relations among them; also called *propositional* or *sentential logic*.

Truth-functional symbol. A symbol for one of the operations that affect the truth value of expressions: "~," "&," "v," and "→."

Truth table. A table indicating all combinations of truth values of the component claims in a more complex expression or in an argument. It is used to test an argument for validity. We look for rows in which all the premises of the argument are true; then we check the truth values of the conclusion in those rows. If it is always true, the argument is valid; if false even once, invalid.

See the outline above for definitions of all specific rules (from Groups I and II) covered in Chapter 10.

REVIEW QUESTIONS

1. When is a conditional claim true?

2. Summarize the rules for symbolizing claims that contain the words "if," "only if," and "if and only if."

3. Explain the method for using a complete truth table to test an argument for validity.

4. Explain the fundamental principle behind the short truth-table method.

5. What are the differences between the ways of using Group I rules and Group II rules in logical deductions?

6. Explain the ideas behind simplification, destructive dilemma, and one of DeMorgan's Laws.

7. Sketch the justification for the strategy of conditional proof.

COMMONLY ASKED QUESTIONS

Why are there two kinds of logic? Does each have its own advantage, or is one clearly better than the other?

Much as a disagreement between two experts leaves us doubting both (Chapter 3), the existence of two kinds of logic can make us suspicious of logic in general. If the two work equally well, how can there be a logic? And if one is better than the other, why learn of the worse one, except as a historical curiosity?

Leave aside the historical questions of how each logic developed, and the technical questions of what theory justifies each one, matters beyond the scope of this course. What concerns us is the *practical* question of the work that each logic does and the advantage and disadvantage of each in evaluating arguments.

The principal difference comes down to the two logics' relationships to ordinary language. Categorical logic remains with the forms of natural sentences; truth-functional logic—like all modern logic, of which it is a part—departs from ordinary grammar. As a result, categorical logic makes for easier translation out of ordinary language.

However, categorical logic suffers from its attachment to grammatical form. First, it needs to specify in advance which sentences will work in arguments, namely those that can be put into forms beginning with "all" or "some." As a result, the logic of categorical statements only works with a limited number of sentence structures. Second, because we begin and end with recognizable grammatical forms, instead of with the logical forms that lie beneath them, the rules for testing an argument are often unwieldy. Categorical logic uses general statements about kinds of sentences instead of penetrating to the principles that make them work.

Formal logic presents a greater challenge at the beginning. Simply to translate a sentence into logic poses problems that do not arise in Aristotle's logic. Take "or." ("If-then" makes another example—see the next question.) The English "or" flexibly adapts to mean different things. "You are safe if your door is bolted or padlocked shut" gives an example of the inclusive "or": If you both bolt and padlock your door, you will be safe. Either alternative, or both, will do. But sometimes we use "or" to mean one or the other alternative but not both. If you tell a child, "You can have pie or pudding," you imply that the child cannot have both.

When clarity is essential to English, we make up for this flexibility by adding words. "Either" often is a way of emphasizing the exclusive "or": "You can have either pie or pudding." The inclusive "or" has no traditional linguistic markers, so people sometimes use "and/or" to indicate that they mean one or the other or both. Not felicitous English, but it does the job.

In formal logic we have no place for clarifying words, because the "v" already means one or the other or both. Because its meaning is fixed, some English sentences that use "or" do not go easily into logic. Let A be "You can have pie" and B be "You can have pudding." We can't render the sentence to the child as "A v B," for that leaves open the possibility of a pie-and-pudding treat. We write "(A v B) & ~(A & B)." A disappointment for the sweet-toothed youngster and a clumsy animal for the logician, but clear.

This departure from ordinary language makes our first use of truth-functional logic harder. But it creates one clear practical advantage: The rules are easier to learn. Despite the number of rules in Chapter 10, they can all be derived from simpler rules, each obvious once stated. You do not have to remember what a distributed term is, or which one is the middle term. Each sign carries a fixed meaning and can always be treated in a single way.

What exactly does the conditional mean, if not the usual "if-then"?

The conditional, like disjunction, is a logical connective that only approximately matches a grammatical one. No one objects to the conditional where the antecedent is true: If the consequent is true, then so is the whole statement, and if the consequent is false it likewise makes the whole thing false. But what about those pesky sentences with false antecedents?

It helps to bear in mind that we really care only about if-then statements whose antecedent turns out true. "If we find the map, we'll find the treasure." If the map is not found, what does it matter how we categorize the sentence? The conditional becomes irrelevant. It would make a better match with ordinary language if we assigned no truth value at all to conditionals with false antecedents. But logic will not permit such a move. Every connective must yield some constant truth value when the truth values of all its elements are known. We have to say something.

When the two component sentences of the if-then construction are both false, it makes more sense to call the conditional true than to call it false. Consider the sentence "If she's right, she's right." Surely that's true, even trivially true. But because she might be wrong in any given instance, the sentence could have a false antecedent and a false consequent. Nevertheless we have to call the compound true.

We are again asked to treat the conditional as true when it has a false antecedent and a true consequent. "If the reader of this study guide is an elephant, then the reader of this study guide is not an elephant." Logic calls the sentence true. Those who expect truth-functional logic to capture the nuances of natural language will rebel: Logic has turned raving nonsense—a sentence that sounds like a contradiction—into sturdy truth.

It is best to remember that we need the false-true combination to yield the same truth value in every case, whatever that value may be. We sacrifice flexibility to gain logical rigor and efficiency, somewhat as we sacrifice the pleasures of walking in order to get further, faster, in a car. The conditional should capture the core meaning of "if-then," even if subtleties fall by the wayside.

The crucial point is that calling such conditionals true makes more sense than calling them false. Logic gives one reason: If we call sentences of this form false, the truth table for "If A, then B" turns out identical to the one for "If B, then A." (Work them out and see.) But we want the two to mean different things. "If that's a hawk, it's a bird" can't mean "If that's a bird, it's a hawk."

A less technical reason arises out of our customary use of conditionals. What really matters to us in if-then claims? Above all, that we not find ourselves with a true antecedent and a false consequent. Those are the unreliable conditionals. The claim says, "If the car has gas in it, it will run"; you put gas into the tank, and still it does not run. It is essential to any use of the words "if" and "then" to call that a false conditional, and no other truth value of the conditional matters as much as that falsity. So we leave the other cases aside, by letting them stand as true, in order to focus on this one thing that a conditional shall not do.

One final comment about what the conditional means. The arrow is read "if-then," as in, "If A, then B." You might want the arrow to correspond to a word you say between the two letters; then you may read the sentence, "A only if B." But the arrow does not mean "if" by itself ("A if B"); and it does not mean "implies," which describes a logical relationship between two sentences.

TIPS ON APPLICATIONS

Because deductions in logic may remind you of math, you might expect them to be as hard as math problems. Absolutely false. Math problems and proofs call for intuitions about numbers and space that some people find more challenging than others. The great advantage of proofs in logic is that they depend only on intuitions about what makes sense; and every human adult already has these intuitions. Logic only makes them explicit.

There is no mystery about going forward with a proof when you have a strategy already in mind. But what if you don't? What if the premises and the desired conclusion sit there on the page, daring you to put them together, and you don't know where to begin?

Two things help at this point. They should not be taken as rules or strategies for logic, but as approaches that anyone can take when stuck.

1. Look for elements in the premises that are identical to, or remind you of, elements in the desired conclusion. If (C & D) is part of the conclusion and appears in one of the premises, start with that premise.

2. When all else fails, begin with the premises and do whatever you know how to do with them. If one premise is ~(A & B), use DeMorgan's Law to translate it into ~A v ~B. Will this help? It can't hurt. And it's likely that, after you have translated all the individual premises into other forms, something will spring to your eye. In the same spirit, if two premises seem to work together, derive their conclusion. For instance, if one premise is (B v C) → D, and another one is ~D, you know that together they produce ~(B v C), which becomes ~B & ~C. Will this help? Look at the other premises, and at the conclusion again, to see.

Finally, don't get discouraged. There is a finite number of things you can do to your premises, and to the consequences of your premises. Eventually, if the argument is valid, you will reach the conclusion.

This, by the way, is a known fact. *Every valid argument in propositional logic can be proved to be valid.* Another way of putting this is that a computer can be programmed to start with premises and reach a desired conclusion, if the argument is valid. The computer might be sloppy about it, trying every move in the book to get to its conclusion. But eventually the computer will reach its answer. And although computers are built to move much faster than human beings, they are more limited in their capacity to learn from experience. You will find that as you do more proofs, you will make fewer and fewer wrong moves, until doing proofs is as natural to you as tying your shoes (remember how hard that was!).

The point of mentioning computers is that programming them to do proofs is not particularly hard. Nothing about these proofs requires special insight. Again: Logic is not like math.

EXERCISES

Sample Exercises from the Book

10-2, 5. If Parsons objects then if Quincy turns the radio down Rachel will close her door.

P → (Q → R). Note the "then if" phrase. It tells you (1) that P will be set apart from everything that follows, and (2) that a conditional claim will come inside the parentheses.

10-4, 7. (P & R) → Q
$$\frac{\sim Q}{\sim P}$$

Invalid. Let's do this with the short truth-table method. Very quickly, a false conclusion and a true second premise give us P's truth and Q's falsity:

P	Q	R
T	F	

Looking up to the first premise, we see that its antecedent must be true to make the whole premise true (since Q is false). P is already true; R must be true as well. We get:

P	Q	R
T	F	T

No contradictions here; so the argument is invalid.

10-6, 5. (Q → T) → S
~S v ~P
$$\frac{R → P}{\sim(Q → T) \text{ v } \sim R}$$

Disjunctive dilemma. Note the negations of both consequents. Ignore the complexity of (Q → T). (In such cases, it helps to think of parentheses as a nutshell: You treat the nut as a single object, no matter how many bits may be rattling around inside.)

10-7, 10. 1. (T v M) → ~Q
2. (P → Q) & (R→ S)
3. T   /∴ ~P

Start by thinking strategically. The letter P will be in your conclusion, and premise 2 is the only line with a P in it, so you'll have to get the P from there. Premise 2 also contains an R and an S that you don't need; so use simplification to drop that whole part of the line. Now you have P → Q. How can you get ~P from that? Modus tollens will do it for you, if you can find a ~Q. But where can you get that? Your only choice is premise 1, which will give you a ~Q if you can only find a T v M. Premise 3 supplies the T. Now you can see what to do:

4. T v M   3, ADD
5. ~Q   1, 4, MP
6. P → Q   2, SIM
7. ~P   5, 6, MT

10-10, 7. 1. (M v R) & P
      2. ~S → ~P
      3. S → ~M   /∴ R

Two tricks here. First, looking at the conclusion, you realize that premise 1 will be vital to your deductive efforts. Second, you should be struck by the oddity of premise 2: both S and P negated, though they're not negated elsewhere. Use this as a clue that premise 2 will be more helpful with its negations gone—which means, if you take the contrapositive of it to produce P → S. Then, if you can get S out of that conditional, premise 3 gives you ~M.

    One more thing. You now see that both conjuncts in premise 1 will be necessary, the first because it contains the vital R that's in the conclusion, and the second because you've produced a conditional containing P. There's nothing wrong with going back to premise 1 twice and simplifying it both times, once to use P on your new conditional and the other time to use M v R to get you the desired conclusion. So:

      4. P → S   2, CONTR
      5. P   1, SIM
      6. S   4, 5, MP
      7. ~M   3, 6, MP

(Now we simplify premise 1 again:)

      8. M v R   1, SIM
      9. R   7, 8, DA

10-14, 4. 1. P → (Q v R)
      2. T → (S & ~R)   /∴ (P & T) → Q

It's obvious what your CP premise will be, namely P & T. But how will it lead to Q? The main strategy is to simplify that P & T once you've assumed it, and use the P and the T separately to get Q. Premise 1 will then do the trick; but premise 1 leaves you with a disjunction, which can't be simplified. That R needs to be eliminated with a ~R. Now you notice that premise 2's consequent contains a ~R that can be simplified out of the compound consequent. Now we begin:

      3. P & T   CP Premise
      4. P   3, SIM
      5. T   3, SIM
      6. Q v R   1, 4, MP

(The remaining work consists in also getting a ~R from the premises, which you'll then use in a disjunctive argument on step 6:)

      7. S & ~R   2, 5, MP
      8. ~R   7, SIM
      9. Q   6, 8, DA
     10. (P & T) → Q   3–9, CP

Additional Exercises

A. Express the following sentences in the vocabulary of truth-functional logic.

1. If either Xenia pounds out the dent or Yessenia paints the fender, then Zlatan will have his car by Thursday.

2. If Xenia pounds out the dent, then either Yessenia will paint the fender, or Zlatan will have his car by Thursday.

3. If Xenia pounds out the dent while Yessenia paints the fender, then Zlatan will have his car by Thursday unless Xenia doesn't pound out the dent.

4. Zlatan will have his car by Thursday if and only if Yessenia doesn't paint the fender while Xenia pounds out the dent.

5. Either Xenia will pound out the dent or Yessenia will paint the fender, but not both.

6. Yessenia will paint the fender only if Xenia doesn't pound out the dent, and if Xenia does pound out the dent Zlatan won't have his car by Thursday.

B. Put the following arguments into symbolic form and test for validity, by either the long or short truth-table method.

1. Andy and Charles are both going fishing. If Barbara goes rock climbing, Diane will run. If Diane runs, Andy won't go fishing. So Barbara isn't going rock climbing.

2. Barbara is going rock climbing if Charles goes fishing. Andy is going fishing if Diane doesn't run. Therefore, if Andy doesn't go fishing and Barbara doesn't go rock climbing, then either Charles isn't going fishing or Diane is running.

3. Diane will go running, but Andy won't go fishing. If Andy doesn't go fishing, neither will Charles. Andy goes fishing if Barbara doesn't go rock climbing. So if Charles goes fishing, Diane goes running.

4. Andy is going fishing unless Barbara goes rock climbing. Barbara won't go rock climbing if Charles and Andy go fishing. Only if Diane runs will Charles not go fishing. So Andy's going fishing.

5. Andy is going fishing unless Barbara goes rock climbing. Barbara won't go rock climbing if Charles goes fishing and Andy doesn't. Diane will run and Charles will go fishing. So Andy's going fishing.

6. Andy is going fishing if Charles is. If they both go fishing, then either Diane won't run or Barbara will go rock climbing. So if Barbara goes rock climbing and Charles doesn't go fishing, Diane will run.

C. Complete these deductions. Do not use conditional proofs.

1.   1. A → (~B → C)
     2. ~D
     3. (A v D) & (~B v D)   /∴ C

2. 1. (A v D) → (B & ~C)
    2. (B & ~C) → (C & D)
    3. A   /∴ C

3. 1. A → C
    2. (~B & D) v A
    3. (D v A) → ~C   /∴ ~B

4. 1. A & ~B
    2. (C & D) → ~A
    3. A → C
    4. (B & E) → D   /∴ A → ~(E & B)

5. 1. (M & N) & (~O → P)
    2. O → (M v ~N)
    3. ~M v P
    4. ~P v ~N   /∴ P

D. Complete these deductions, using conditional proofs.

1. 1. ~G v ~H
    2. I → G   /∴ H → (~I v J)

2. 1. A v B
    2. ~C → D
    3. ~B → ~(A & C)   /∴ ~B → (B v D)

3. 1. F & ~B
    2. D → (B v ~C)
    3. ~E v D   /∴ E → ~C

4. 1. P v (Q & R)
    2. (Q v S) → ~P
    3. ~S → (T → Q)   /∴ (~R & T) → Q

5. 1. E v D
    2. ~A v (C & ~D)
    3. (~C v E) → B   /∴ A → B

6. 1. P → (Q v R)
    2. (P v ~Q) & ~R
    3. (P v Q) → (~P v R)   /∴ (P & Q) → (~P & ~Q)

Answers to Additional Exercises

A. 1. (X v Y) → Z

    2. X → (Y v Z)

    3. (X & Y) → (Z v ~X)

4. $(Z \rightarrow (\sim Y \;\&\; X)) \;\&\; ((\sim Y \;\&\; X) \rightarrow Z)$

5. $(X \;v\; Y) \;\&\; \sim(X \;\&\; Y)$

6. $(Y \rightarrow \sim X) \;\&\; (X \rightarrow \sim Z)$

B. 1. A & C
   B → D
   <u>D → ~A</u>
   ~B
   Valid.

2. C → B
   <u>~D → A</u>
   (~A & ~B) → (~C v D)
   Valid.

3. D & ~A
   ~A → ~C
   <u>~B → A</u>
   C → D
   Valid.

4. A v B
   (C & A) → ~B
   <u>~C → D</u>
   A
   Invalid.

5. A v B
   (C & ~A) → ~B
   <u>D & C</u>
   A
   Valid.

6. C → A
   <u>(A & C) → (~D v B)</u>
   (B & ~C) → D
   Invalid.

C. 1. 1. A → (~B → C)
      2. ~D
      3. (A v D) & (~B v D)
      4. D v (A & ~B)   3, DIST
      5. A & ~B   2, 4, DA
      6. (A & ~B) → C   1, EXP
      7. C   5, 6 MP

2. 1. (A v D) → (B & ~C)
   2. (B & ~C) → (C & D)
   3. A
   4. (A v D) → (C & D)   1, 2, CA
   5. A v D   3, ADD
   6. C & D   4, 5, MP
   7. C   6, SIM

3. 1. A → C
   2. (~B & D) v A
   3. (D v A) → ~C
   4. (~B v A) & (D v A)   2, DIST
   5. D v A   4, SIM
   6. ~C   3, 5, MP
   7. ~A   1, 6, MT
   8. ~B & D   2, 7, DA
   9. ~B   8, SIM

4. 1. A & ~B
   2. (C & D) → ~A
   3. A → C
   4. (B & E) → D
   5. A   1, SIM
   6. ~(C & D)   2, 5, MT
   7. ~C v ~D   6, DEM
   8. ~A v ~(B & E)   3, 4, 7, DD
   9. A→ ~(B & E)   8, IMP
   10. A → ~(E & B)   9, COM

5. 1. (M & N) & (~O → P)
   2. O → (M v ~N)
   3. ~M v P
   4. ~P v ~N
   5. ~O → P   1, SIM
   6. N   1, SIM
   7. N & (~M v P)   3, 6, CONJ
   8. (N & ~M) v (N & P)   7, DIST
   9. (N & ~M) v ~(~N v ~P)   8, DEM
   10. N & ~M   4, 9, DA
   11. ~(M v ~N)   10, DEM
   12. ~O   2, 11, MT
   13. P   5, 12, MP

D. 1.
   1. ~G v ~H
   2. I → G
   3. H   CP Premise
   4. ~G   1, DA
   5. ~I   2, 4, MT
   6. ~I v J   5, ADD
   7. H → (~I v J)   3–6, CP

  2.
   1. A v B
   2. ~C → D
   3. ~B → ~(A & C)
   4. ~B   CP Premise
   5. ~(A & C)   3, 4, MP
   6. ~A v ~C   5, DEM
   7. ~A → B   1, IMP
   8. B v D   2, 6, 7, CD
   9. ~B → (B v D)   4–8, CP

  3.
   1. F & ~B
   2. D → (B v ~C)
   3. ~E v D
   4. E   CP Premise
   5. D   3, 4, DA
   6. B v ~C   2, 5, MP
   7. ~B   1, SIM
   8. ~C   6, 7, DA
   9. E → ~C   4–8, CP

  4.
   1. P v (Q & R)
   2. (Q v S) → ~P
   3. ~S → (T → Q)
   4. ~R   CP Premise
   5. (P v Q) & (P v R)   1, DIST
   6. P v R   6, SIM
   7. P   4, 6, DA
   8. ~(Q v S)   2, 7, MT
   9. ~Q & ~S   8, DEM
  10. ~S   9, SIM
  11. T → Q   3, 10, MP
  12. ~R → (T → Q)   4–11, CP
  13. (~R & T) → Q   12, EXP

5. 1. E v D
    2. ~A v (C & ~D)
    3. (~C v E) → B
    4. A   CP Premise
    5. C & ~D   2, 4, DA
    6. ~D   5, SIM
    7. E   1, 6, DA
    8. ~C v E   7, ADD
    9. B   3, 8, MP
    10. A → B   4–9, CP

6. 1. P → (Q v R)
    2. (P v ~Q) & ~R
    3. (P v Q) → (~P v R)
    4. P & Q   CP Premise
    5. P   4, SIM
    6. Q v R   1, 5, MP
    7. (P & ~R) v (~Q & ~R)   2, DIST
    8. (P & ~R) v ~(Q v R)   7, DEM
    9. P & ~R   6, 8, DA
    10. ~(~P v R)   9, DEM
    11. ~(P v Q)   3, 10, MT
    12. ~P & ~Q   11, DEM
    13. (P & Q) → (~P & ~Q)   4–12, CP

Answers to Review Questions

1. A conditional claim (like any other) is true when it is not false. A conditional claim is false when its antecedent is true and its consequent is false; so in all other cases it is true.

2. In general—because exceptions will arise—the clause that follows the word "if" is the antecedent of a conditional, while the clause that follows "only if" is the consequent of a conditional. Sentences containing the phrase "if and only if" between two claims are in reality two distinct conditionals, with the two individual sentences appearing in opposite orders: "A if and only if B" always becomes (A → B) & (B → A).

3. Set up the truth table with columns for all the argument's premises and its conclusion. (Keep those columns clearly labeled.) Calculate the truth values for the premises and conclusion. Find the rows in the truth table in which all premises are true; then look at those rows in the column for the conclusion. If every row has a "T" in it, the argument is valid; if the conclusion is false in even one of the rows, the argument is invalid. If no rows exist in which all premises are true, the argument is again valid.

4. The short truth-table method takes a shortcut to find rows in the completed truth table (if such rows exist) in which all premises are true and the conclusion is false. We usually begin with the conclusion and assume it to be false (although it also works to begin with a premise and assume it to be true). This assumption produces certain truth values for some

of the claim variables. Working from those truth values, and assuming all the premises to be true, we look for a consistent set of truth assignments that make the argument invalid. If no such set exists, the argument is valid.

5. One difference is that elementary argument patterns take you from one claim to another; they go somewhere; so you can only use them in one direction. Identity statements, however, may be applied to go in either direction (because if A is the same as B, B must also be the same as A). This also explains why identity statements may be applied to a single part of a complex expression, whereas the argument patterns only work when applied to the entire line of a deduction.

6. Simplification is an argument pattern that says that if you have both of the simpler claims in a conjunction, you have either one taken individually.

    Destructive dilemma, also an argument pattern, assumes modus tollens: A conditional plus the negation of its consequent implies the negation of the antecedent. So given two conditionals, and the disjunction of their negated consequents, you know that at least one of the consequents is being negated, hence that modus tollens will apply to at least one of the conditionals, hence that you can deny at least one of the two antecedents.

    DeMorgan's Laws, which are equivalences, work from intuitive ideas of negation. If two claims are not both true, at least one is false. But to say that at least one is false is to say: The first is false, or the second is false. Thus ~(A & B) means (~A v ~B). As for the other law, denying a disjunction means denying that at least one of the claims is true. That means that neither is true, that is, they're both false. So ~(A v B) means the same thing as (~A & ~B).

7. If you want to show that a conditional claim follows from a set of premises, it is enough to show that the antecedent of that conditional always leads to the consequent, given that set of premises. You show this by assuming the antecedent as a hypothetical premise and deriving the consequent from it, given the premises of the argument. If the consequent does follow, the premises of the argument support the move from the antecedent to the consequent, which means that the premises make the conditional claim true.

CHAPTER 11

INDUCTIVE ARGUMENTS

Good deductive arguments are not the only good arguments. Inductive arguments can produce reliable conclusions, too. They share some broad properties with deductive arguments, for both types ought to have reasonable premises that support their conclusions. But we do not evaluate inductive arguments as valid or invalid: We call them strong or weak. The next two chapters show what properties to look for in making those evaluations.

Chapter 11 takes up inductive generalizations and analogical arguments. Both of these types of inductive arguments use the properties shared by members of a group to establish the properties of something else: a larger group when we generalize inductively, an individual in cases of analogy. In both cases, we find that we must begin by looking at a large enough initial group (sample) that accurately represents the cases of the property we are interested in.

This chapter introduces some technical vocabulary from statistics, specific warnings about public-opinion polls, and the names of four fallacies that can derail inductive thinking. This material fills out the picture of how to judge the arguments that deductive logic does not call either valid or invalid.

CHAPTER SUMMARY

I. **Inductive arguments** try to show the likelihood of their conclusion.

   A. They differ from deductive arguments, which try to provide absolute support for their conclusion.

      1. As a result, the power of an inductive argument comes in degrees.

      2. There is no such thing as validity or invalidity in these cases.

   B. This chapter will focus on the degree of likelihood in the conclusion of a good generalization or a good analogy. Our discussion will depend on certain key concepts:

      1. The property under investigation is called the **property** or **feature in question**.

      2. The **sample** is a group of things already known or believed to possess the property in question.

      3. In the argument's conclusion, we attribute the property in question to a **target item,** whether that target is an individual or a larger group that contains the sample.

II. An **inductive generalization** applies what is true of a sample to a larger target class.

   A. The premise attributes the property in question to the sample, while the conclusion attributes the same property to the **target class.**

      1. The sample is a subset of the target class.

2. We reason inductively that if part of a class has a given property, the class as a whole has it, too.

B. Generalizations depend on the similarity between sample and target class.

1. The sample must **represent** the target class. It represents the target in so far as it possesses all the features of the target class that are relevant to the property in question and possesses those features in the way that the target class does.

2. If a sample contains too many unusual or idiosyncratic members of the target, it won't show us what the target class is like.

3. The less we can trust the sample's resemblance to the larger class, the less we can trust a generalization based on that sample.

4. If 20 percent of cats in the neighborhood never go outdoors, then before generalizing about all neighborhood cats we should choose a sample in which 20 percent never go out.

C. A **biased sample** is one that fails to represent the target class in some relevant fashion.

1. If we include too many free-roaming cats in our sample, that sample might lead us to false conclusions about the health of our neighborhood's cats (given that going outdoors exposes a cat to health risks).

2. The challenge in avoiding bias is that a sample should reflect all *relevant* features of the target class, but we don't always know in advance which features will prove to be relevant.

3. If 35 percent of neighborhood cats eat canned food, and we are studying a hacking cough that has turned up among them, we should probably make sure that 35 percent of our sample eats canned food as well. If 42 percent have been declawed, should 42 percent of the sample have been declawed? That probably isn't relevant.

4. We call a feature or property P relevant to another property Q if it is reasonable to suppose that the presence or absence of P could affect the presence or absence of Q.

D. When forming a sample in ignorance of which features of the sample are relevant, we can still preserve our confidence in the sample if:

1. The class is **homogeneous**. I don't have to drink the whole ocean to know that it's salty.

2. The class is **heterogeneous** but its sample is **random**.

   a. A randomly produced sample is most likely to represent its target class.

   b. In a random sample, every individual is as likely to be selected as every other one.

c.   A random sample may still fail if it is chosen from a nonrepresentative sub-group of the target class. If the target class is the neighborhood's cats, it may not do to take a random selection of cats from one street, especially (for instance) if buses run down that street and their fumes might exacerbate the cats' coughs.

III.   **Sample size**, **error margin**, and **confidence level** help us evaluate the accuracy of generalizations from random samples.

A.   **Random variation** can produce another kind of problem in the sample, which we express with an error margin.

1.   Randomly chosen samples are bound to differ from their target class to some degree, even though they are more or less like that class. One-tenth of all Americans may be left-handed, but a random selection of 500 Americans could well contain 40, 45, 55, or 60 lefties.

2.   Thus, the occurrence of some property in any random sample will be close to its occurrence in the target, plus or minus some percentage points.

3.   The error margin measures the range within which a generalization about the sample also describes the target—for example, 53 percent ±2.

B.   The closely related concept of confidence level measures the likelihood that an inductive generalization has produced a true conclusion.

1.   Confidence level indicates the percentage of all random samples in which the property in question occurs within the error margin.

2.   Suppose a study reports that 28 percent of Estonians have curly hair, with an error margin of ±3 percent and a confidence level of 88 percent. Assuming this study looked at a random sample of some given size, this result means that 88 percent of all random samples of the same size will contain between 25 and 31 percent curly-haired people.

3.   In most scientifically produced studies, confidence level is set at 95 percent.

C.   The confidence level and error margin both depend on the size of the sample.

1.   As the size increases, the error margin decreases, or the confidence level increases, or both.

2.   A poll of 50 people (within a sufficiently large target class) has an error margin of ±14 with a 95 percent confidence level. If the sample size doubles to 100, the error margin falls to ±10 with the same confidence level.

D.   These technical terms translate into a general guideline for everyday inductive arguments: The smaller the sample of a heterogeneous population, the more guarded the conclusion should be.

1.   In ordinary cases, we use imprecise terms instead of mathematical evaluations of error and confidence.

2. One way to make a conclusion more guarded is by using even less precise language.

3. Another way is by expressing a lower degree of probability that the conclusion is true.

IV. An **analogical argument,** also called an *inductive analogical argument* or *argument from analogy* applies what is true of a sample to another member of the population, the target item.

A. Analogical arguments make up the second important kind of inductive argument.

1. These arguments share the following pattern:

a. The members of a sample share some features with a target item. "Tom is a clown just like Dick and Harry."

b. The members of the sample also possess an additional feature, the feature or property in question. "Dick and Harry wear big shoes."

c. The target item also possesses the feature in question. Conclusion: "Tom must wear big shoes."

B. Analogical arguments resemble inductive generalizations.

1. Both forms of argument begin with a sample and identify a property or feature of the members of that sample.

2. Both conclude that the property in question is also shared by one or more items outside that sample.

3. The difference consists in the nature of that "outside item." In inductive generalizations it is a larger class that includes the sample, while in analogical arguments it is a single additional member (the target item) of that larger class.

4. Thus, we can easily restate an analogical argument as an inductive generalization by identifying the (usually unstated) larger class that the sample and the target item both belong to. We call this the **implied target class.**

5. We can then evaluate analogical arguments exactly as we evaluate inductive generalizations, considering sample size, representativeness, error margin, and confidence level.

V. Inductive arguments of both types tend to fail in one of four ways, which we may call fallacies of inductive reasoning.

A. Arguments that use too small a sample commit the fallacy of **hasty generalization**.

B. One kind of hasty generalization is the **appeal to anecdotal evidence**. In such appeals, one tells a story about one or two examples that is meant to demonstrate a general truth.

C. When we use an example, in anecdotal form or not, to reject a general proposition, the result is a **refutation via hasty generalization**.

D. A **biased generalization** uses a sample that may be large enough, yet does not represent the target class.

VI. Besides the general information about statistical generalizations, one should keep a few specific warnings in mind when evaluating public-opinion polls.

A. Polls are based on self-selected samples when the people whose opinions are measured put themselves into the sample.

1. A television call-in poll overrepresents people with strong enough feelings to call and register their opinions.

2. Although such polls may measure strength of feeling, they do not indicate what the general population believes.

B. Interviews in the street oversample people on foot and undersample people in a hurry.

C. Telephone surveys can produce bias because those without telephones or listed numbers get undersampled, those with more than one listed number oversampled.

D. Questionnaires can fail to get sound results because of the effort needed to fill out the questionnaire.

E. Advocacy groups might commission polls worded so as to produce a more favorable response.

1. This is a form of bias separate from the representativeness of the sample.

2. Sometimes nonargumentative persuasion (see Chapter 4) makes a question more appealing than it would be otherwise: "Should the city provide more emergency housing to those in need?" versus "Should more tax money be spent on public housing?"

3. At other times the order of questions skews the results.

4. Loaded questions (see Chapter 4) can pretend to solicit an opinion while suggesting a claim: "Do you favor reducing death and street crime by means of emergency housing?"

F. "Push-polling," not true polling at all, uses the disguise of a poll to shape public opinion.

1. For instance, if you have already indicated your stand on an issue, the questioner might ask, "Which of the following arguments for the other side do you consider most effective?" and then list them.

VII. The importance of large sample size in inductive arguments follows from a statistical principle, the **law of large numbers.**

A. When an event occurs at random, with predictable ratios of results, it will get closer to those predictable ratios the more often the event is repeated.

   1. Roll a dice 12 times and you might get a 3 twice, but maybe more times than that and maybe never.

   2. Roll the dice 12,000 times and it becomes more and more likely that 3 occurs one-sixth of the time.

B. The law of large numbers assures us that the individuals in large enough samples behave with the regularity that characterizes the target population.

C. Sometimes the law of large numbers is misinterpreted as the **gambler's fallacy.**

   1. That is the belief that past random occurrences influence the next one, that in order to reach the predictable ratios the next events have to catch up.

   2. The gambler's fallacy also occurs in nongambling contexts. For example, you may think: "We've had four boys. The next child is more likely to be a girl."

   3. Although large samples do tend to produce the numbers one expects, those numbers do not influence any particular event. Each time is a new flip of the coin.

KEY WORDS AND IDEAS

Analogical argument. Also *argument from analogy, inductive analogical argument:* an inductive argument that uses the properties of a group to establish the property of another thing that resembles the members of that group. The premises claim that one or more things have a property p, while the conclusion claims that the similar thing also has p.

Appeal to anecdotal evidence. A type of hasty generalization that presents a few familiar examples.

Biased generalization. An unjustified generalization based on an unrepresentative sample.

Biased sample. An unrepresentative sample.

Confidence level. A measurement of the likelihood that an inductive generalization will produce a true conclusion. Confidence level indicates the percentage of random samples in which the property in question occurs within the error margin.

(Note: Do *not* take confidence level in psychological terms, as a measure of how sure a person happens to feel about some generalization. It is a quantifiable measurement of a generalization's actual application to random samples.)

Error margin. A measurement of the range within which a generalization is an accurate claim. The error margin is stated in terms of plus or minus a number of percentage points.

Feature in question. Property in question.

Gambler's fallacy. The error of believing that future occurrences of a repeating random event will catch up with expected regularities. This is a misunderstanding of the law of large numbers.

Hasty generalization. An unjustified generalization based on an excessively small sample.

Heterogeneous class. A class or set of items that differ from one another.

Homogeneous class. A class of items that are identical to one another.

Implied target class. In analogical arguments, the class or set to which the sample and the target item both belong.

Inductive argument. An argument whose premise describes the property of a sample and whose conclusion extends that premise to a larger class containing that sample, or to an item outside the sample.

Inductive generalization. Also *generalization*; an inductive argument about a group that argues on the basis of a subset of that group for the existence of distribution of a property in the entire larger group. The premises claim that the sample has the property (or has it in some proportion), while the conclusion claims that the target also does.

Law of large numbers. A statistical principle about the properties of large numbers. "The larger the number of chance-determined repetitious events considered, the closer the alternatives will approach predictable ratios."

Property in question. The property being studied in an inductive argument. It is first identified in a sample, then claimed to exist in the target class or target item.

Random sample. A sample selected from a target class in such a way that every member of the target class stands the same chance of being selected.

Random variation. The difference (with respect to the property in question) that exists between random samples. The error margin expresses the likely degree of random variation.

Refutation via hasty generalization. A type of bad reasoning in which a few examples are alleged to bring down a general claim.

Represent. To resemble a larger class with respect to relevant properties. Samples are said either to represent or not to represent their target classes.

Sample. The group whose members are known to have the property in question. Inductive arguments begin with claims about a sample.

Sample size. The number of members in a sample. In all cases, larger samples make for more accurate conclusions. In the case of statistical generalizations, as the sample size increases, the error margin decreases, or the confidence level increases, or both.

Target class. The individual or group that may have the property in question. The conclusion of an inductive argument is a claim about its target class.

Target item. In analogical arguments, an individual outside the sample that is said to possess the property in question.

REVIEW QUESTIONS

1. Explain the premises of an analogical argument.

2. Explain confidence level.

3. Analogical arguments require relevant similarities between the sample and the target population. What corresponds to relevant similarity in the criteria for a good inductive generalization?

4. Name and explain three cautions to keep in mind about popular-opinion polls.

5. What is the law of large numbers? What is its relevance to inductive arguments?

COMMONLY ASKED QUESTIONS

Why are there so many similarities between analogical arguments and inductive generalizations, despite the big differences between them?

The question is how much the differences amount to. Certain concepts that we use in describing inductive arguments put the wrong spin on what is, from a theoretical point of view, a matter of emphasis or approach. You use the same processes of collecting and evaluating evidence in both cases.

The misleading concepts are "general" and "specific." At most, the distinction between specific and general lets us divide inductive arguments into two convenient categories: those that use observations to reach a conclusion about one item (or a few) and those that use them to establish a claim about a large number of items. These are, of course, analogical arguments and inductive generalizations, respectively.

The difference in the types of conclusions is the main feature that differentiates analogical arguments from inductive generalizations, so we should not be surprised to find the two kinds of inductive argument so similar to each other. Moreover, you may notice how easy it is to describe any analogical argument as a special case of an inductive generalization. Suppose that a number of things have properties *a*, *b*, and *c*—call them a+b+c things—and that all the a+b+c things you look at also have property *d*. You conclude (with more or less confidence, depending on sample size and so on) that "All a+b+c things are *d*." Now say you're looking at one specific a+b+c thing, X. You can further conclude, "X is *d*." This conclusion to an analogical argument also can be read as a consequence of the conclusion to your inductive generalization.

Why do these methods for testing inductive arguments look so completely different from the methods for testing deductive arguments?

If you had to distinguish quickly between deductive and inductive arguments, it would be hard to improve on David Hume's observation about the repetition of relevant experiences. If you apply logical principles to a deductive argument even once and see its validity, you will not grow more certain of your result by repeating the test. Maybe repeat once to check your work; then you have convinced yourself of the argument's validity. Repetition is irrelevant to logical truth, and is positively rejected by logical method.

But inductive arguments become more and more convincing the more observations you make in support of them. This is why, although we draw the premises of deductive arguments from experience as well, we more often speak of inductive arguments as having their basis in experience and observation. What we perceive, and how we perceive it, matters more directly to their effectiveness.

The methods outlined in Chapter 11 therefore focus on the quantity of our information, in a way that no deductive principles had to. Far more than anything else, this quantitative element in inductive argumentation produces its characteristic look.

Even the stress on similarity between sample and target class often turns out to mean something about sheer quantity. This is obviously true in inductive generalizations, where we can assume a large random sample to represent the target class—which means, we can assume it to *resemble* the target class.

Analogical arguments also use size to help ensure similarity. All things considered, a large enough random sample will probably be diverse with respect to any given property. Suppose you just bought your first toaster; you wonder if it might electrocute you under normal circumstances (no knives jabbed in, no baths during which you also make toast). You begin to ask people on the bus, in class, and at work whether they have ever been electrocuted by their toasters. While asking you realize that you've forgotten what brand of toaster you own. This is not necessarily a problem: Ask enough people, randomly enough, and the chances increase that some will own the same brand of toaster as yours, while others do not. If they all reply that no toaster of theirs ever shocked them, you will trust the answer, just because your large and random sample achieved diversity with respect to brand.

If sample size commonly helps to make the sample resemble its target, as well as being desirable in itself, it makes sense to call the sheer numbers of observations collected the single most important factor in establishing an inductive argument's conclusion. Here, again, lies the difference between deductive arguments and inductive arguments: The former pay no attention to numbers of claims, whereas the latter hardly pay attention to anything else.

TIPS ON APPLICATIONS

The philosophical problem of induction has had such a powerful influence that it is worth spending a moment on what the problem means, and what it does not imply about our examination of inductive arguments. For induction has posed more philosophical problems than deduction has. If David Hume bequeathed us a useful criterion for telling inductive arguments from deductive ones (see "Commonly Asked Questions"), he also stirred up trouble for induction by posing the question of its legitimacy.

The problem can be put simply: Inductive arguments are never valid. Suppose you want to argue that the sun will rise tomorrow. Hardly any conclusion could have more observations behind it: Think of the number of mornings on which you've known the sun to rise; then think of the uncountably greater number of mornings on which someone or other knew the sun to rise; consider the absence of any mornings without sun. Even this much evidence, Hume points out, produces no valid argument. To get a valid argument from the weight of past experience, you also need the premise that the future will resemble the past. Then you get:

> The sun has always risen on past mornings.
> The future will resemble the past.
> Therefore, the sun will rise tomorrow morning.

A valid argument. And sound? That depends on the grounds for the second premise. How do you know that the future will resemble the past? Well, every former future has turned out to resemble its preceding past. Today was the future yesterday; anyone who predicted yesterday that the future would resemble the past would have turned out to be correct.

But those are past futures. How can we rely on them to show that the future from our present point of view will continue to resemble what we now call the past? We again need the premise that the future will resemble the past. So inductive arguments always presuppose a non-deductive jump from established evidence to as-yet-unknown events.

There is no denying, after Hume, that inductive arguments are not deductive ones. It would follow that no inductive arguments can be good ones either, if tests of validity were the only ways of telling good arguments from bad. Induction would come off as a poor relation to deduction. But in fact, as Chapters 11 and 12 show, we possess many criteria for distinguishing good inductive arguments—that is, strong ones—from bad ones. Sample size and similarity to target are both reliable, from the point of view of guiding our judgment, and clearly applicable, from the point of view of practical assessments. Samples can be counted; people can reasonably discuss their resemblance to the target class. Arguing inductively does not leave us in the chaos of arbitrary experience just because it relies on *other than* deductive principles.

So keep the philosophical problem of induction separate from the practical problem of judging any particular inductive argument. Philosophers have continued to explore induction since Hume; some are still skeptics. But no global skepticism of this sort affects our response to inductive arguments.

Hence you may reply to an inductive argument in all sorts of ways, even challenge it in a number of ways, except by means of blanket doubt about induction. When you don't believe a new study about caffeine and pancreatic cancer, or about your mayor's unpopularity among the middle class, then by all means ask about the size of the sample studied, and its representativeness, and the questions the poll had asked, and the meaning of its error margin. Do not retort, "Studies don't mean anything," or "That's just a generalization."

EXERCISES

Sample Exercises from the Book

11-11, 2. Beatrice likes the representative from Tri-State Investments. He is polite, well informed, and kind. She decides, therefore, that he will not mislead her and agrees to purchase the life insurance policy he recommends.

Before rushing to give an answer here, try to stop yourself from thinking of items as individual people or objects. Beatrice is extending her observations of some of this man's personality traits to another. Once you see "items" this way, this becomes a standard analogical argument. Sample: the representative's manners, state of being informed, and degree of kindness. Target item: his reliability. Implied target class: his character traits. Property in question: goodness or praiseworthiness.

11-17, 4. According to the text, the largest number that he can safely bet hold the belief mentioned is _____ percent.

66. Table 11-1 shows that the error margin for a sample of 250 is ±6. So in 95 percent of all samples, 54–66 percent will hold the belief. Bear in mind that these error margins presuppose a large enough target population—10,000 or larger. In all the questions for 11–13, we have to assume that the student population at George's college is at least that big.

11-18, 7. Is the sample random?

No. Take a moment to recall the definition of a random sample. Every student in Professor Ludlum's courses must be as likely to turn up in the sample as every other student. In one way you might think the evaluation process preserves randomness, given that no one outside the group of students chose a few to submit their opinions. But that's not enough for randomness. Disaffected students, lazy students, and all those satisfied enough with their courses not to bother with evaluations drop out of the sample. They take themselves out, in the sense that no one prevents them from writing evaluations; but actually they are taken out, because the procedure presents an obstacle (it doesn't have to be a great obstacle) to the reports of evaluations by students without strong opinions.

11-19, 10. Overheard: "You're not going to take a course from Harris, are you? I know at least three people who say he's terrible. All three flunked his course, as a matter of fact."

Biased generalization; rather hasty, too. First, note why it is biased. We are not compelled to assume that the three people who call Harris terrible do so *because* they flunked his course (although that would explain a lot). It's plausible enough to think that they flunked because they considered him a terrible teacher, and so stopped coming to class and doing assignments. The students still form an unrepresentative sample, since we can expect those who fail a course to be in the small minority. As for hastiness, it is naturally possible that the speaker knows plenty of other people who took a course from Harris and didn't call him terrible: Can we leave our minds open about how hastily the speaker reasons? No. That only compounds the bias, since the speaker ignores the evidence against the "Harris is terrible" conclusion.

Additional Exercises

In each of the following examples, (a) identify the sample; (b) identify the target class or item; (c) name the type of argument (analogy or generalization); and (d) evaluate the strength of the conclusion, citing specific weaknesses (when they exist).

1. I'm scared to let Susan see me in this sweater. A couple of my other friends told me it makes me look like a child, and she's at least as critical as they are.

2. We approached women in malls, college campuses, office buildings, and airports, until we had interviewed a thousand. Sixty-two percent told us they don't feel disadvantaged by being women. Even accounting for the error margin, that gives a clear majority who feel this way.

3. You have to speak Sanskrit before you can say you know it. Would you believe someone who claimed to know Spanish or Russian and never spoke it? Sanskrit is a language just as they are.

4. A large proportion of people who read like to read something religious. Every day on the subway I count how many people are reading in my car; and a little over half of them have a Bible open in front of them, or the Koran, or some other religious publication.

5. A watch could not assemble itself, because it's too complex. The universe is at least as complex as a watch. So the universe could not have assembled itself either.

6. Senator Torriano walked down the street in Detroit asking people what they consider the most pressing issue in America. The first two said, "High taxes." When the third also complained about taxes, the Senator knew how to vote.

7. I'm painting our rooms green. When you go out into a field your eyes feel relaxed; that shows your eyes will feel relaxed in a green room, too.

8. Since the mid-1960s, most nominations to the Supreme Court have been clearly ideological, and the Senate approved or rejected them on ideological grounds. The President has to make a new nomination now, so we're probably in for a fight.

9. Overheard: "Sparrows have little heads and they're not very smart. Dolphins and elephants have big heads, and so do people, and they're smart. So pigeons must be smarter than sparrows."

10. It doesn't mean anything that a lot of people are opposed to same-sex marriages. People used to be opposed to interracial marriages, and now they're legal in every state.

11. Baseball is drama. You see new people each time in a new conflict; you never know what they'll do or how it will turn out; there's suspense.

12. New evidence that Americans want drastic reform of Social Security. A random telephone poll of 250 people asked, "Are you in favor of preserving Social Security from economic collapse through a reduction of benefits?" Fifty-four percent said yes.

13. How can you say that people act out of self-interest? Didn't you read the story about the airplane that skidded off the runway into the ocean? One man kept passing the life preservers to other people so they would live instead of him.

14. [Note: This is not an inductive argument but a criticism of one.] How can you say that people act out of self-interest? How many motives for human actions do you know about, including your own? A few thousand. There have been billions and billions of human actions since the beginning of human history. So your evidence doesn't reach very far.

Answers to Additional Exercises

1. (a) a couple of my friends; (b) Susan; (c) analogy; (d) fairly strong. Although the sample is small, it may be a good indication of what Susan will think, given her property of being at least as critical as they are.

2. (a) women interviewed in malls, campuses, and so on; (b) women; (c) generalization; (d) some strength, but not enough. Although the error margin (±3) does mean that we get a majority of at least 59 percent, the sample should not be taken as representative. This survey oversamples women with office jobs, educated women, and women who travel by airplane; thus it probably begins with a sample in a higher economic bracket than the average woman. That may influence opinions about disadvantage.

3. (a) Spanish and Russian; (b) Sanskrit; (c) analogy; (d) weak. The argument fails to establish relevant similarity, because Spanish and Russian are living languages, so the ability to speak them makes a more important difference.

4. (a) people who read on the subway; (b) people who read; (c) generalization; (d) weak: biased. Although the sample is large, it fails in two ways at being representative. First, people who ride the subway probably earn less money than people who don't and this bears on their religious attitudes; second, people who choose to read on the subway may differ from people who read but choose to do it elsewhere. People who read on the subway may work longer hours and can't find any other reading time. Or people willing to read in crowded and noisy conditions probably have a more committed attitude toward what they read.

5. (a) a watch; (b) the universe; (c) analogy; (d) weak. The tiny sample size leaves us with only manufactured objects to compare to the universe at large. We need to ask for more relevant similarities than complexity, such as signs of a purpose or function.

6. (a) three people on the street in Detroit; (b) Senator Torriano's voters (implied target); (c) generalization; (d) very weak. Hasty generalization. May be biased as well, but we don't have enough information to say.

7. (a) a field of grass; (b) the walls of the room; (c) analogy; (d) some strength. It is probably true that one reason for eyes' comfort in a field is the color of the grass; but other reasons include the open space, the natural light, and so on. These dissimilarities weaken the argument, though they do not destroy it altogether.

8. (a) nominations to the Supreme Court since the mid-1960s; (b) the President's new nomination; (c) analogy; (d) strong.

9. (a) sparrows, dolphins, and elephants; (b) pigeons; (c) analogy; (d) weak. There are too many dissimilarities between mammals like dolphins and elephants and birds like sparrows and pigeons.

10. (a) people's sentiments about interracial marriages; (b) people's sentiments about same-sex marriages; (c) analogy; (d) a tricky call. The argument's strength depends on the similarity between race and sexual orientation. Work on the problem by finding resemblances and differences between the two.

11. (a) theatrical performances (implicit sample); (b) baseball; (c) analogy; (d) weak. The similarities—human participants, conflict, suspense—don't outweigh the dissimilarities: baseball has no story, dialogue, and so on.

12. (a) 250 American people; (b) Americans; (c) generalization; (d) weak. Assuming a confidence level of 95 percent, the error margin for a sample of 250 is ±6; we might have only 48 percent favoring the change. Moreover, the question is loaded.

13. (a) a man in an airplane accident; (b) human beings; (c) generalization; (d) weak. Anecdotal evidence; and the speaker doesn't claim to know much about that anecdote.

14. The speaker in this example is criticizing a generalization on the grounds of sample size. The criticism has some merit against a narrow claim—"People always act out of self-interest"—since even one good counterexample would defeat that claim. Against a broader claim—"People typically [or almost always] act out of self-interest"—it runs counter to what we can predict about error margins. A sample of a few thousand gives an error margin of less than ±2 with high confidence level. So generalizing is not inappropriate.

Answers to Review Questions

1. The premises make three claims: first, that the sample items possess certain distinguishing properties; second, that the target item possesses those same properties; third, that the sample possesses some additional property (the property in question). For example: "I have a healthy heart. I'm a marathon runner, and they have healthy hearts." The first premise is the claim that certain other people are marathon runners. The second premise is that the speaker is a marathon runner as well, and hence resembles them. Third, those people have healthy hearts (the property in question). Conclusion: The speaker has a healthy heart.

2. The confidence level gives a mathematical measurement of the likelihood that an inductive generalization will hold true regardless of the sample chosen. A certain percentage of random samples of the same size as the one examined will possess the property in question to the same degree as the original sample, within the error margin. If one random sample of 1,000 Texans reveals 37 percent to be smokers, and the error margin with a confidence level of 95 percent is ±3, that means that in 95 percent of all random samples of 1,000 Texans, the percentage who smoke will lie between 34 percent and 40 percent.

3. In generalizations, the comparable criterion is representativeness of the sample. The representative sample has relevant similarity to the target population in containing the same proportions of relevant groups as the target.

4. Here are five. The sample may be biased in a number of ways: by interviewing a self-selected group, by interviewing in the street or by telephone, or by mailing out questionnaires. In each instance, one group may be oversampled. For instance, interviews in the street oversample people who frequent that given neighborhood and people who get about on foot. The poll itself may contain other misleading features, such as questions designed to elicit one response rather than another, or question ordering that paves the way for one response rather than another.

5. The law of large numbers states that a predictable ratio of occurrences in a repeated random event is more and more exactly reached as the number of repetitions increases. For instance, the number of times a coin comes up heads will approach 50 percent as the number of times the coin is flipped increases. The law of large numbers underscores the importance of sample size in making reliable inductive arguments, because it means that a random sample becomes more representative the larger it gets.

CHAPTER 12

CAUSAL ARGUMENTS

Inductive arguments, in the broad sense of that phrase, try to reach conclusions about regular relationships among things. Causal arguments are inductive arguments that aim at one kind of conclusion about regularity, namely the regularity of a causal relationship. In daily life we most often think about causation as it applies to specific events, but causation can also be a matter of trends or patterns among populations.

The two kinds of causal relationships call for different argumentative methods and different standards of evaluation. This chapter outlines the reasoning proper to each causation, as well as the most common errors in each. Causation in population requires us to draw distinctions among types of causal studies, and also to master enough mathematical statistics to tell how reliable a study's results are.

CHAPTER SUMMARY

I.   A **causal claim** says that one thing causes another; a **causal argument** offers support for a causal claim.

II.   **Causation among specific events** is established in one of two ways.

A.   Causation among specific events occurs when one event has brought about another event.

B.   One type of argument for such causation identifies an event X as the *only relevant difference* (or simply **difference**) that has brought about the effect Y.

1.   More precisely, we say that one item has a feature that other items lack (the feature in question), and that only one relevant difference (the difference in question) distinguishes the item with the feature from the items without the feature; the difference in question then causes the feature in question.

2.   To make such an argument, we need to know about at least two circumstances or facts, one in which Y occurs and one in which it does not. If X is present along with Y and absent when Y is, then X might cause Y.

3.   For example: "I ate my usual breakfast today, but with bacon instead of my usual sausage, and now I feel thirsty. Bacon tastes saltier than sausage, so I think the bacon made me thirsty."

a.   The bacon with breakfast is being put forward as the only occurring difference.

b.   Also notice that the speaker is claiming some relevance to this difference. Bacon tastes saltier than sausage, and we know that salty foods can make us thirsty.

4. Arguments from an only relevant difference can be as conclusive as any kinds of reasoning we know.

    a. If you walk into a room, flip a switch beside the door, and see the lights go on, you conclude that you found the light switch on the basis of an only-relevant-difference argument. Only the facile skeptic would remain unconvinced.

    b. Even less indubitable arguments about the only relevant difference can provide as much certainty as ordinary experience ever gives us, as long as the difference in question is truly relevant.

    c. A difference is relevant if one is not unreasonable in supposing that it brought some effect about.

    d. Background information often helps us tell which differences are relevant, as it did in the example of bacon and thirst.

C. In another type of argument, we link a cause to the feature in question on the grounds that it is the *only relevant common thread* (or simply the **common thread**) among possible causes of Y.

    1. In such an argument, we begin by noticing that the feature in question (Y) occurs more than once, and that some common thread X is present on every occasion. If X is absent when Y is, we conclude that X causes Y.

    2. Such reasoning requires that we know of more than one circumstance in which Y occurs.

    3. If more than one other factor is present in every case of Y's presence, we find ourselves considering more than one possible cause of Y. Like differences in the last type of argument, the common threads must all be relevant.

D. The two forms of argument are not equivalent. Reasoning from a common thread works better when forming hypotheses that one later tests with reference to a difference.

    1. In cases of a common thread, the separate occurrences of Y might have separate and unrelated causes—that is, the appearance of any common thread at all could be a coincidence.

    2. When Y occurs on a number of occasions, it is quite possible that all those occasions are linked by more than one common thread.

    3. In the former case, a test for an only relevant difference helps us see if the common thread could have caused it. In the latter case, a test looking for a difference will help us choose from among the rival candidates.

III. Arguments for causation among specific events most often go wrong by overlooking other possible explanations.

A. Arguments on the basis of an only relevant difference face four kinds of challenges.

  1. Is the difference relevant?

  2. Is the difference unique (the only possible relevant difference)? In ordinary life, with its buzz of varied events, this can be the hardest question to answer.

  3. Can we have **reversed causation**? In such instances we have indeed discovered a cause and an effect, but we confused them with each other.

     a. "Whenever I go to bed I feel sleepy. The bed must make me sleepy." It's more likely that feeling sleepy sends you to bed.

     b. This error is a partial success in that both cause and effect have been discovered; they've only been mislabeled.

  4. Have we **ignored a possible common cause**? In these cases we call X the cause of Y when in fact something else, W, caused both X and Y.

     a. "After the leaves fell off the tree, the tree blew over. So the loss of leaves weakened the tree." More likely a disease that made the tree lose its leaves also left the tree trunk brittle.

     b. Such arguments correctly spot a link between X and Y. They go wrong in not looking for underlying causes of both.

B. Arguments from a common thread face six different challenges, many of them like the challenges to arguments from a difference.

  1. Is the common thread relevant to the effect?

  2. Is the common thread the only relevant common thread?

  3. Is the common thread ever present when the effect or feature in question is not? That would make the common thread only part of the causal story.

  4. Can we have reversed causation?

  5. Have we ignored a possible common cause?

  6. Could the common thread amount to mere coincidence?

     a. This is a possibility peculiar to arguments from a common thread.

     b. Multiple occurrences of some single effect might have multiple causes.

     c. Sometimes a lot of airplanes crash in one month, and people jump to the conclusion that some particular factor is responsible. Then investigations reveal completely different causes at work in the accidents.

C. Uncritical reasoning about causation can lead to the fallacy called *post hoc, ergo propter hoc*.

1. That Latin phrase means "After that, therefore because of that."

2. The mere appearance of Y after X makes us call X the cause of Y. "My car stopped running after I filled the tank with gas; therefore, the gasoline stopped the engine."

3. This mistaken reasoning gets its plausibility from a resemblance to good arguments about X as the difference that caused Y. It goes wrong by not making sure to establish that X is the only relevant difference.

4. To escape this error, avoid arguments that are based on nothing more than the mere appearance of Y after X.

D. On other occasions, arguments for causation have simply overlooked the possibility of coincidence.

1. Two events might be completely unrelated to each other.

2. In common-thread cases, we might take one common thread to be significant when in fact it is only present by coincidence, and some other common thread does the explanatory work.

3. In yet other common-thread cases, multiple occurrences of some event derive from multiple causes; then there is no point looking for any common thread.

IV. **Causation in populations** differs significantly from causation among specific events and needs other arguments.

A. Most general causal claims do not mean that a causal link will exist between two particular events.

1. Running makes for a healthier heart. Yet Jim's running might not improve Jim's heart.

2. It does not even have to follow that running causes health of the heart in the majority of people who run.

B. A claim of causation between C and E in a population P means that C is one factor producing E.

1. More exactly: There will be more E in P when C is present (in every member of P) than when C is absent (from every member of P).

2. This reasoning might remind you of the argument about differences. But notice one shift: In the case of specific events, we need X to be *the* difference that produces Y; in populations, we only expect X to be *a* difference.

C. Three kinds of empirical studies yield support for claims of causation in populations.

V. **Controlled cause-to-effect experiments** try to show directly that the presence and absence of C among all members of a population yield different frequencies of E.

A. Such experiments separate an experimental group from a control group and expose the first, but not the second, to a suspected causal factor.

1. We use the abbreviation **C** to denote the suspected causal agent, and **E** to denote the effect we're trying to find a cause for.

2. The **experimental group** is the sample of the target population whose members are exposed to C.

3. The **control group** is that sample of the target population whose members are *not* exposed to C.

4. In all other respects, the experimenters treat the control group and the experimental group alike.

5. We use **d** to signify the difference between the frequency of E in the control group and its frequency in the experimental group.

B. When d is large enough not to have resulted from chance, we conclude that C causes E.

   1. We calculate d by first calculating the **frequency of effect,** E, in both groups.

      a. The frequency is the percentage of members of a group who exhibit the effect.

      b. The difference between these percentages is d.

   2. Like error margin (see Chapter 11), **statistical significance** distinguishes between a real difference and one that could be the result of chance.

   3. Again like error margin, statistical significance depends on the sample size and the expected confidence level.

      a. Table 12-1 shows some minimal values of d to establish statistical significance with a confidence level of 95 percent.

      b. This means that there is only a 5 percent chance of d's random occurrence.

      c. Larger samples and lower confidence levels will mean smaller values of d before we call a result statistically significant.

C. When evaluating reports of experimental findings, there are several points to keep in mind.

   1. A sample might not be large enough to guarantee significance; so even a large value for d carries no weight.

   2. A sample may be large and still not make d significant, if d is small.

   3. Applying the results of a controlled experiment often means reasoning by analogy from one population to another.

      a. Controlled experiments typically involve animals, but their results matter most to humans. So one is reasoning by analogy that what affects rats or flies also affects humans.

    b. As with all analogical arguments (Chapter 11), consider the relevant similarities and dissimilarities between the groups.

4. As with inductive generalizations, the samples (control group and experimental group) must be representative of the target population.

    a. Both groups should be randomly selected.

    b. In the case of reliable scientific experiments, you can assume random selection of groups.

VI. A **nonexperimental cause-to-effect study** also tries to establish causation in populations, but with different methods and standards.

A. Such studies most often involve human beings and causal factors that may greatly affect health or well-being.

1. The members of the experimental group are exposed to C, but not by the investigators (for obvious ethical reasons).

2. So, instead of creating the experimental conditions, they use a group that has already been exposed to C.

3. As in experiments, the control and experimental groups are identical except for their exposure to C.

4. The members of both groups also must not have shown evidence of the effect E.

5. After both groups are watched for E, results are evaluated by calculating the frequencies of E and the difference d, as in controlled experiments.

B. More cautions are needed when evaluating these results.

1. As in the experimental case, watch for analogical arguments that extend the results to other populations.

2. Watch for possible bias in the samples (see Chapter 11 on representative samples for inductive generalizations).

C. Bias can enter good nonexperimental studies when a possible factor C is accompanied by other factors.

1. Controlled experiments begin with random samples and then administer C, and only C, to the experimental group.

2. The experimental group in a nonexperimental study may still be composed of randomly selected individuals who have still been exposed to C (or say they were), but they might differ from the target population in some other respect.

    a. A study of the effects of knuckle-cracking on arthritis will randomly select people who crack their knuckles, but they may not represent the target.

    b.   If men crack their knuckles more than women, the experimental group will be disproportionately male; and men and women have different chances of developing arthritis.

  3. Studies try to control for these factors by choosing a control group that resembles the experimental group.

    a.   Thus, if 61 percent of all knuckle-crackers are men, and the experimental group reflects that distribution, the control group should also be 61 percent male.

    b.   A good study will begin by trying to imagine all relevant factors of this sort and adjusting the control group accordingly.

  4. Because we do not know which factors might bear on a given effect, we cannot control for all of them. So all nonexperimental studies yield weaker results than experimental ones.

  5. When evaluating a nonexperimental study, ask whether other factors could have biased the samples.

VII. A third type of study for causation in populations is called a **nonexperimental effect-to-cause study.**

  A. This type of study reasons backwards from an existing effect to its possible cause (or to one causal factor).

    1. This time investigators begin with a given effect, E; they select an experimental group that exhibits E and a control group not exhibiting E.

    2. Members of both groups are inspected for exposure to C, the suspected cause.

    3. If the frequency of C in the experimental group significantly exceeds the frequency in C, we call C a cause of E in the target population.

  B. The cautions about nonexperimental cause-to-effect studies also apply here.

    1. As before, the members of the experimental group may differ relevantly from the rest of the target population.

    2. If we begin by studying people with arthritis, we must first recall that they will be older than an average member of the population.

    3. Again, we adjust the control group to resemble the experimental group.

    4. Again, if you can think of other factors that could have influenced C, make sure the control group was adjusted to reflect them.

  C. One final alert about effect-to-cause studies: They are less useful in making causal predictions about the population.

    1. Effect-to-cause studies show only the probable frequency of the cause in cases of a given effect, not the probable frequency of the effect in cases of a given cause.

2. Therefore, they don't permit us to say what percentage of the target population would display E if everyone were exposed to C.

3. Ideally, we would follow such a study with a cause-to-effect study, watching people with C over a long period to see if they develop E.

VIII. The meaning of "causal factor" shows why appeals to anecdotal evidence do not belong in discussions of causation in populations.

A. If such causation meant that C always causes E, then one or two examples to the contrary would indeed bring down the conclusion.

1. It would be striking if someone went without food or drink for two months and lived.

B. But when C is a causal factor, we mean only that exposure to C by the whole population will produce more examples of E than if C were absent.

1. This claim is entirely consistent with the existence of counterexamples and is not weakened by them.

2. Indeed, the claim predicts such cases: If 69 percent of those exposed to C develop E, we have reason to believe that 31 percent will not.

KEY WORDS AND IDEAS

Assuming a common cause. An error in causal reasoning that claims a link between two effects where none exists; a bad form of reasoning on the basis of a common thread.

C. In studies of causation in a population, an abbreviation for the suspected causal factor.

Causal argument. An argument that offers support for a causal claim. The form of such arguments depends on whether the causation concerns specific events or populations.

Causal claim. A claim that one thing causes another.

Causation among specific events. A link between one event and another, such that the first brought the second about. We usually establish such causation on the grounds of a difference or a common thread.

Causation in populations. A kind of causal effect relevant to a population. To say that C causes E in a population P is to say that C is one factor producing P. Such causation is determined through a controlled cause-to-effect experiment, a nonexperimental cause-to-effect study, or a nonexperimental effect-to-cause study.

Common thread. In arguments about specific events, a reason for seeing X as the cause of Y. X must be the only factor common to more than one example of Y; and the examples of Y should not be linked by chance.

Control group. In studies of causation in a population, a sample of the target class whose members are not exposed to C (or known not to display E). In all other respects, the members of the control group are treated exactly like the members of the experimental group.

Controlled cause-to-effect experiment. A study intended to demonstrate causation in populations, by means of the exposure of an experimental group, but not a control group, to a suspected causal agent C.

d. In studies of causation in a population, an abbreviation for the difference between frequency of effect (or cause) in the experimental group and frequency of effect (or cause) in the control group.

Difference. In arguments about specific events, a reason for seeing X as the cause of Y. X must be the only relevant difference between a situation in which Y occurs and situations in which Y does not occur.

E. In studies of causation in a population, an abbreviation for the given or suspected effect.

Experimental group. In studies of causation in a population, a sample of the target population whose members are exposed to C (or known to display E).

Frequency of effect. The portion of the experimental or control group (measured as a percentage) that displays E.

Ignoring a possible common cause. An error in causal reasoning that makes X the cause of Y, when some other event W might have caused both X and Y.

Nonexperimental cause-to-effect study. A study intended to demonstrate causation in a population, by means of an experimental group that has already been exposed to suspected causal agent C, and a control group that has not.

Nonexperimental effect-to-cause study. A study intended to demonstrate causation in a population, by means of an experimental group that has already displayed effect E, and a control group that has not.

Post hoc, ergo propter hoc. An error in causal reasoning that makes the mere appearance of Y after X a reason for calling X the cause of Y.

Reversing causation. An error in causal reasoning that correctly attributes a causal link to two events, but calls X the cause of Y when really Y has caused X.

Statistical significance. The sign that a measure of d could not have arisen by chance. We speak of d's being statistically significant given a certain confidence level; so if the level is 95 percent, to call d statistically significant is to say there is only a 5 percent chance that d could have been a random result.

REVIEW QUESTIONS

1. Explain the uses and pitfalls of looking for an only relevant common thread among events.

2. Compare and contrast the errors of ignoring a possible common cause and reversing causation.

3. Which group do we use in a controlled cause-to-effect experiment to determine whether its results are statistically significant?

4. Why do we ever do nonexperimental studies? What are their limitations?

5. Compare what is needed for an argument from difference and an argument from a common thread. Name the evidence each requires and the cautions it calls for.

COMMONLY ASKED QUESTIONS

Is there a method for knowing which criticisms to employ against arguments about causation among specific events?

The best first thing to do is see whether the speaker has made an argument about causation, and, if so, which sort of argument it is. This technique will guide you to three of the four main criticisms.

If the causal claim has no argument behind it but the mere order of events, a safe answer is *post hoc, ergo propter hoc.* Cause and effect do not work so simply that one observation announces the relevant causal connection. (Do keep in mind, though, that a casual observation of this sort can provide a hint as to where to look next; but then it becomes legitimate only if the person does look again, and more closely.)

But while *post hoc* is often a safe answer, it does not illuminate a causal argument as well as other criticisms can. It can tell that reasoning has gone wrong but says little about how it went wrong. To put it another way, this criticism has only negative value, showing up the weakness of a causal claim without adding to our knowledge about the causal link (if any) in question. The other criticisms have more substance.

If the speaker made an argument on the grounds of a difference between situations in which Y occurred and situations in which Y did not occur, the best criticism to try is that he or she ignored a possible common cause. This criticism works best when one of the effects of the possible common cause precedes the other. Then the first effect more often looks like a cause of the second. Some kinds of flu begin with vomiting and develop into a longer period of fatigue. It might look natural to call the vomiting the cause of the fatigue (no food; hence people look tired), but both follow from the viral infection.

Watch out for one thing: When accusing someone else of having ignored a possible common cause, you ought to be able to suggest some such possibility. Not that you need to prove or even argue at length for the other possibility; but it would help at least to describe it. "My cat Dee-Dee chewed up a magazine for the first time yesterday, and today she had no appetite. The magazine must have satisfied her." You will not get far just saying, "Maybe something else caused her to eat the magazine and then not eat her food." If you get more specific you will have made progress: "Maybe she's come down with something that makes her chew paper and not want food."

In some cases the suggested common cause needs more support than that. See the box titled "Cigarettes, Cancer, and the Genetic Factors Argument." The tobacco industry has claimed that a genetic factor causes both a tendency toward smoking and susceptibility to cancer. Researchers' inability to discover such a factor makes the argument weak: When the original causal claim has evidence behind it, the alternative needs not only a name but evidence of its own.

Suppose the argument was based on a common thread. The speaker may again have ignored a possible common cause; but this might also be a case of assuming a common cause where none exists. You will probably find this an unsatisfying criticism to make, because it denies the exceedingly worthwhile human practice of looking for unifying explanations behind our observations. Still, not all events have common causes, even apparently similar events. A good test is plausibility: The proposed cause of two or more events ought to possess significantly more plausibility than a chance connection. This is only common sense. If you get two phone calls in one day that are wrong numbers, you will not think about it. Wrong numbers happen, and two in a day don't make enough of a coincidence to wonder about. But four in the same day, or several a day for a week, will make you think there's a reason: A new business has opened with a number close to yours; or someone with a new number gave it out erroneously, so that dozens of people now have the wrong one; or you are being hounded by spies (but don't jump to this conclusion). Whatever the cause, you have a sense of how many wrong numbers will happen randomly, and you won't start looking for explanations until other explanations make more sense than chance does.

The kind of causal argument given will not help you much when the problem is reversing causation. Reversed causal claims can come up under any circumstances. People tend not to think of this criticism, mainly because most causal claims don't work well in reverse. Sophie's cold may or may not have made her grouchy, but it's a safe bet her grouchiness did not bring on the cold. Here, too, start by considering plausibility. If someone claims that X caused Y, how plausible is it that Y could have caused X? In the case of the magazine-chewing cat, we may have a reversal of causation: Because she hates the taste of this cat food, Dee-Dee goes hungry and therefore chews whatever she sees. The mere existence of this alternative does not settle the argument, but it suggests an obvious test. Try another cat food, and see what changes occur in her eating and chewing.

What are the most successful lines of criticism against arguments about causation in populations?

The simplest criticisms to use here are, sad to say, not the most useful ones. The simplest criticisms focus on the size of the samples and the size of d, to argue that d cannot be statistically significant with a sample of that size. Although the mathematics may look like an obstacle, you will find that you need no real math to apply this line of reasoning. Simply consult a table like 12-1 to see whether a given result, at a given confidence level, must have arisen from some cause other than chance.

(While we're on this subject: Watch out for confidence level. Acceptable levels of d for statistical significance are much lower with lower confidence levels. But when the confidence level gets too low, it means less to say that a level of d is statistically significant. Some figure for d may be statistically significant at a confidence level of 60 percent; but then all you know is that there is a 60 percent chance that these significant results did not arise by chance.)

Most large-scale studies, including quite unreliable and even unscrupulous ones, respect the rules of statistically significant findings and confidence levels. So unless you are dealing with a small local study, or an informal job, you will not be able to marshal such considerations against the proposed result. Remember that this is not the end of the story. Even quite prestigious studies may prove vulnerable to two other lines of criticism: problems in the analogical extension of the result and bias in the sample.

We are all familiar with analogical arguments that apply what has been discovered about rats and other laboratory animals to human beings. When a study concerns complex phenomena we should be suspicious: Monogamy in rats, or rats' ability to learn new information, will probably not tell us much about the corresponding phenomena in human beings, as our mating habits and learning abilities develop under more elaborate conditions than a laboratory survey could ever mimic.

But this line of argument does not work as well against medical findings. Rats especially have been seen to develop cancers under conditions very much like the ones that cause cancer in humans. This is a premise that supports the analogical extension: X causes Y in rats; rats have been seen to resemble humans in their history of Y; therefore X probably causes Y in humans. When researchers reason that some medical finding about nonhumans may apply to us as well, they probably have some such justification for the analogy. When they don't, they say so. For instance, one of the complications in laboratory experiments on HIV is that the virus does not seem to give chimpanzees AIDS. They are susceptible instead to SIV, the Simian Immunodeficiency Virus, which resembles HIV in many but not all respects.

Criticisms of the analogical extension work better when one unusual human population is studied for insights about all human beings. Say a village in another country contains a high percentage of people more than 100 years old. Investigators may try to run an effect-to-cause study in that village, controlling for families with and without very old members; still, we suspect that too many other differences exist between urban U.S. culture and the culture of that village for us to know what all the relevant factors are. Watch out for studies of populations that differ in too many relevant ways from your own.

Biased samples take even more work to talk about. The more technical the finding, the more background knowledge you will need before even suspecting that some causal factor has not been controlled for. When the effect in question is a matter of health or happiness, and the suspected causal agent belongs in people's ways of life—exercise, diet, place of residence, occupation, access to medical care—some background knowledge will alert you to the number of causal factors that can occur together. For example, people who exercise regularly into and past middle age will probably be people who also watch what they eat and enjoy a higher level of education (and hence, maybe, less work-related anxiety). Most studies of exercise will control for these factors. But if these are also people who go more often to their doctors and take prescribed medications more carefully, they may live longer regardless of their exercise.

Even so, medical results are easier to evaluate than claims about social and psychological phenomena such as crime and intelligence. It pays to be especially open-minded about factors that can bias the samples in such studies. Just for starters, all generalizations about criminal activity begin with data about reported crimes. Most murders get reported; but one's likelihood to report rape, robbery, and assault depends on a number of other social factors. So researchers have a harder time assembling representative samples. Studies of convicted criminals face other obstacles: They oversample those who have been caught (through carelessness, inexperience, or excessive aggressiveness) and those arrested for more vigorously prosecuted crimes.

Keep your eyes peeled for biases in the sample that could skew the study's result in one direction or another.

Intelligence makes a still more difficult matter, because more people disagree about how to measure intelligence than about how to measure crime. *The Bell Curve,* by Murray and Herrnstein, tried to show a causal connection between race and intelligence; responses to that book, most notably Gould's review in the *New Yorker,* have taken up the issues of bias in the samples and the book's failure to control for other factors. Although neither the book nor the review is easy to read, Gould's argument is a classic example of how to criticize a claim of causation in populations.

TIPS ON APPLICATIONS

The strength of good causal arguments, and their power to help us learn about the world, show the value of observation, especially when we collect observations carefully, evaluating their significance with the techniques described in this chapter.

But this stress on observation makes it easy to fall into an error about causation—not a fatal mistake when we're evaluating someone else's causal arguments, but certainly a misleading picture of human knowledge, and often enough an obstacle to the investigation of nature. *We think of ourselves as a passive audience recording whatever regularities occur in front of us.*

In many cases this assumption does no harm. Take one of the first links established between cancer and an environmental cause: In the late nineteenth century, London doctors observed a steep increase in cases of cancer of the scrotum. So many of the patients were chimney sweeps as to suggest an obvious connection between the men's cancer and the soot they were constantly exposed to. Hardly a leap, when anyone seeing all the same patients would have had the same idea.

But things are rarely so straightforward, especially when we look for causation in populations. The time, trouble, and expense of running a responsible study mean that we can't go fishing for causal links without a clear, plausible, and justified hypothesis. Nature won't give an answer until we ask a question.

Where do these hypotheses come from? Suppose you want to study intelligence, as measured by IQ tests, to discover its causes. Where do you begin? Not with people's heights, because you have good reason not to expect intelligence to depend on height. What about parents' relative ages? Could it be that when two people are closer together in age, their children may score better on IQ tests than when the parents' ages are further apart? Maybe. A large and careful study will either confirm or refute the possibility. But where did the question come from? Someone has to think it up.

The plain fact is that effects don't come with possible causes written on them. Suppose fewer women in Guatemala have osteoporosis than U.S. women do. You start looking at the two groups' dietary calcium. But what if that hypothesis does not pan out? A wide range of cultural differences between the two countries gives you more possible causes than one researcher could hope to track down. You don't throw up your hands and call the matter inscrutable—such differences are bound to come from somewhere. But where do you find your questions?

Background information helps, and if you were a medical researcher you'd possess more and better background information. You would not set up studies of the two groups' different clothing or language, or of the forms of government they live under. You might look more generally at diet (i.e., more broadly than just with an eye to calcium), at childbearing patterns in the two countries, at the minerals that find their way into drinking water, or at the physical exertion typical of the cultures. Then, if you noticed anything unusual, you might formulate a hypothesis and then construct an effect-to-cause study.

So the questions are not stabs in the dark. But neither are they the results of just looking at the world. The questions that start off a causal investigation are made by the investigators, not found nestling among the evidence.

In one way this does not matter; in two ways it does. The contingency of the original questions—the fact that someone has to think them up; the fact that different people will think up different ones—does *not* diminish the truth or reliability of our causal conclusions. Sample size, attention to alternative causes, and so on, ensure that we can trust a statistically significant result. From the point of view of truth, it doesn't matter if someone dreamed the hypothesis, as long as evidence supports it.

However, you have to remain alert to the origins of causal hypotheses when you are engaged in looking for a cause. If you expect possible causes to shout at you from a mass of observations, you will be disappointed, and probably unsuccessful at finding a cause.

Additionally, the invention of hypotheses permits one kind of criticism that, while not denying the truth of the conclusion, does question the bias behind it. Take the number of studies linking pregnant women's smoking, drinking, and use of drugs to low birth weight and other medical problems in their children. Without denying the reliability of those studies in themselves, we might ask why there have been so few studies of men. What happens when a man has been smoking, drinking alcohol or coffee, or using drugs immediately before his child's conception? There may be more of a connection than we know; but the role of women has been studied far more extensively than that of men. You may well accuse investigators of bias in asking one sort of question and not the other.

EXERCISES

Sample Exercises from the Book

12-9, 4. The only time in my entire life that I've had a backache was right after I tried lifting weights. I'll never do that again!

a. Lifting weights caused the backache. (Take care to ignore the speaker's announced conclusion, "I'll never do that again," since that is not a causal claim.) b. X is the difference: "the only time." c. In the interests of looking for relevance, you might ask exactly what exercises were done, as well as whether anything else sets the time in question apart. d. There is no obvious alternative. e. No fallacies. f. Fine argument. Notice, in these cases, the degree to which your background information influences both your questions and your evaluation.

12-9, 14. The recent volcanic eruptions in Hawaii were preceded by earthquakes around the Pacific Rim. Evidently, therefore, the earthquakes caused the eruptions.

Earthquakes are the common thread. So your first question should raise the possibility that an earthquake was a difference between one eruption and another. If some eruption came without a previous earthquake, the causal claim has been weakened. But to criticize this claim most effectively, try out both the charge of ignoring a common cause *and* that of assuming a common cause. If the speaker in this case assumes a common cause where there is none, that's because the connection between earthquakes and eruptions was coincidental. (Chance is always a possible, though not always plausible, alternative explanation.) If the speaker ignores a common cause, there may be geological events that caused both the earthquakes and the eruptions. Since a regular link between earthquakes and eruptions probably rules out coincidence, you can accuse the speaker of ignoring a common cause. Bear this in mind: One is most likely to ignore a common cause when one of its effects precedes the other.

12-14, 17. According to two reports in the *New England Journal of Medicine,* oil from fish can prevent heart disease.

(b) causal factors in populations. Watch out for a phrase like "heart disease," which is stated in the singular. In such instances a singular noun indicates a group. (See Chapter 2 on grouping ambiguity.)

12-19, 5. What is the frequency of the effect in the experimental and control groups, including size?

First, make sure you've identified the effect. Since we can assume that the point of a vaccine is to prevent infection, rather than cause it, we call the effect "remaining uninfected." One hundred percent of the experimental group enjoyed this effect. As for the control group, infection in 39 of the 446 children means that 407 remained uninfected; divide this number by 446 to get about .91, which means 91 percent. Then d, incidentally, is 9. We round the experimental group size up to 500 (for simplicity's sake) and learn from Table 12-1 that this d exceeds the figure of 6 demanded by the group size. So the result is statistically significant.

12-21, 12. "A new study shows that the incidence of cancer tumors in rats exposed to high doses of X-rays dropped dramatically when the food intake of the rats was cut by more than half. Dr. Ludwik Gross . . . noted that this study is the first to demonstrate that radiation-induced tumors can be prevented by restricting diet.

"The experimenters exposed a strain of laboratory rats to a dose of X-rays that produced tumors in 100 percent of the rats allowed to eat their fill—about five or six pellets of rat food a day.

"When the same dose of X-rays was given to rats limited to two pellets of food a day, only nine of 29 females and one of 15 males developed tumors, the researchers reported. . . ." (Paul Raeburn, *Sacramento Bee*)

The book's answers to most of the questions here are self-explanatory. But a few are worth commenting on. First, although the answer to b. is "rats," do not use the subjects of such studies as a way of dismissing their results. Rats resemble human beings closely in their development of cancer and responses to treatments. All things being equal, we have good reason to expect a result about rats to apply to humans.

c. Controlled cause-to-effect experiment. This one is easy as soon as you notice that a study was conducted experimentally. Any experiment must be cause-to-effect.

e. As above, the desired effect is not having a tumor. This effect exists in none of the control group. While we don't know the size of that group, we do know it has a 0 percent frequency of effect. In the experimental group, 10 rats developed tumors, so 34 did not. Dividing that number by 44, we get about .77, or 77 percent.

f. Assume that the control group is roughly the size of the experimental group, that is, near 50. Then d must exceed 19 to be significant. Since d = 77, we have no problem with statistical significance.

Additional Exercises

A. Causation among specific events. What type of reasoning is at work in these examples? Is there any problem?

1.   Every time it snows, the weather's warmer. Somehow the snow must warm up the air.

2.   Students who plan to go on to graduate or professional schools are more likely to complete four years of college. So advisers should talk to their students about law school right away; it's doing them a favor.

3.   It's a jinx to be elected or reelected president in a year that ends with a 0. The presidents voted in in 1840, 1860, 1880, 1900, 1920, 1940, and 1960 all died in office.

4.   Look at the people who ride the early morning bus: tired, depressed. Riding the bus must be bad for you.

5.   Admissions director: Our study shows that incoming first-year students who send a picture of themselves for the handbook are more likely to remain in college for the full four years.

     Professor: Then why don't we take every new student's picture and keep them all here?

6.   Susan woke up Monday with a headache; she took an aspirin and it went away. On Friday she woke up with a headache again, took a garlic supplement, and couldn't get rid of her headache. She concluded that aspirin got rid of her headache.

7.   Since 1945, at least one nation in the world has possessed nuclear weapons. Also since 1945, most colonial nations have achieved their independence. So nuclear weapons have promoted decolonialization.

8. Since 1945, at least one nation in the world has possessed nuclear weapons. Also since 1945, the world has seen no full-scale war between major powers. So nuclear weapons have prevented warfare.

9. Three people at the party learned that they shared the birthday of March 15; interestingly, they had all been born by cesarian section. Now, March 15 was the day that Caesar was killed, and they say he was born by cesarian section. There's something about being born on that day.

10. I woke up today and my arthritic fingers suddenly felt limber and comfortable. Funny, I was expecting a bad day, because yesterday I got stung all over my hands by a swarm of bees. Instead, they must have relieved my arthritis.

11. For my science experiment I put twenty ants into a shoe box and taped it shut. I wanted to see the effect of darkness on animal motion. Three weeks later I took the box out of the closet and it was empty. I guess darkness makes ants disappear.

12. Most cocaine users have, at some point, smoked marijuana regularly. Therefore, marijuana use causes cocaine use.

B. Causation in populations. What type of investigation produces causal claims in these examples? What is the causal claim? Is there any problem with the argument?

1. Dr. Ian Wilmut fused 277 sheep-udder cells with an equal number of sheep eggs. Twenty-nine of the eggs developed into embryos, which Dr. Wilmut implanted into other sheep (surrogate mothers). Thirteen became pregnant; of these, one carried the pregnancy to term and gave birth to a live lamb, Dolly. So cloning does produce new lambs. But since pregnant animals usually proceed to live birth in two-thirds of all cases (once embryos have been implanted in the uterus), the last step of this process seems to be plagued by an as yet undetermined impediment.

2. Our study looked at 310 residents of Roanoke, Virginia. About 70 percent favored the use of the death penalty in at least some cases; the other 30 percent opposed its use under any circumstances. Among women who had undergone an abortion, only 5 percent opposed the death penalty in all cases, whereas 23 percent of women who had not had an abortion opposed it. So either women who value life less in the first place are more likely to have abortions, or women who have abortions come to value life less as a result of the experience.

3. Before birth, the fetus hears the mother's heartbeat at a volume of about 95 decibels. Do newborns feel comforted by a comparably loud heartbeat in the hospital nursery? To test this hypothesis, researchers at a hospital near New York's LaGuardia airport played a heartbeat at 85 decibels, and found that the infants cried less and gained more weight when the heartbeat was played than when it was not. (Lee Salk, *Scientific American* 1973)

4. "Macfarlane tested whether a newborn would discriminate between, on the one hand, the smell of his mother and her milk, and, on the other hand, the smell of another mother and her milk. The smells came from gauze pads that the mothers had kept

within their brassieres to absorb any milk seeping out. Along one side of the baby's face, Macfarlane draped a pad from the baby's mother; along the other side he draped a pad from another mother. Thirty-two two-day-olds showed no sign of discriminating one pad from the other: roughly half of them turned toward each pad. However, more than two-thirds of the six-day-olds he tested turned toward their mother's pad, as did more than three-fourths of the eight- to ten-day-olds. Young babies prefer the familiar to the unfamiliar: here they recognized their mother's odor, and turned toward it." (Daphne Maurer and Charles Maurer, *The World of the Newborn*)

Answers to Additional Exercises

A. 1. Common thread. The claim probably reverses causation: It's more likely that warmer weather permits precipitation than that snow on the ground warms the weather.

2. Common thread. The claim ignores the common cause of motivation that makes students both seek further education and complete four years of college.

3. Common thread. Assumes a common cause. (This old cliche quickly disappeared after Ronald Reagan, first elected in 1980, completed both terms in the presidency.)

4. Common thread. Ignores a possible common cause: People who ride the morning bus have to get up early for their jobs.

5. The causal claim is based on common-thread reasoning. The professor's suggestion is *post hoc, ergo propter hoc* and ignores a possible common cause (that students motivated enough to send a picture will be more motivated to stay in school).

6. Difference. Good argument.

7. Common thread. Assumes a common cause.

8. Common thread. More plausible than the last conclusion; but note that the time involved, just over fifty years, is too short by historical standards to support a completely reliable conclusion.

9. Common thread. Assumes a common cause. Cesarian sections are just not rare enough any more to make this anything but coincidence.

10. Difference. We need to know more about what happened the preceding day, as well as how often the arthritic fingers suddenly loosened up anyway. So this may be *post hoc, ergo propter hoc.*

11. Difference. *Post hoc, ergo propter hoc.*

12. Common thread. Ignores a possible common cause (the desire to try drug experience; problems with social adjustment).

B. 1. Controlled cause-to-effect experiment. We assume a control group of all the sheep not fertilized by cloning. Causal claim: The implantation of cloned embryos is not as likely to result in live birth as the implantation of embryos by other means. Note the size of the relevant experimental group: 13 sheep with implanted embryos. One out of 13, or

8 percent, gave birth to a live lamb, as opposed to 67 percent of sheep fertilized through other means. This does produce a d within the realm of statistical significance; but you shouldn't bank too heavily on the results.

2. Nonexperimental effect-to-cause study. Causal claim: Women with abortions are less likely to oppose the death penalty unconditionally. To evaluate this result, think about what the numbers might mean (since we're missing so much information). How many of the Roanoke residents studied are women? Say half, or 155. How many of them would have had an abortion? No more than 20 percent, or 31. To get a statistically significant result, we must have a figure of d around 25; but here d = 18.

3. Controlled cause-to-effect experiment. Causal claim: Newborns feel comforted by a heartbeat sound as loud as the heartbeat they had heard before birth. The control group here is also the experimental group, on the (probably safe) assumption that, because all the newborns had already heard their mothers' hearts, the effect of the sound would matter only while they were hearing it. This example leaves out the numbers involved, but we can still identify a relevant additional factor: Being near the airport, the hospital picked up the loud sound of landing airplanes. Any sound that drowned the airplanes out would be likely to comfort the babies.

4. Cause-to-effect experiment. Causal claim: Newborns can tell the difference between a familiar smell and an unfamiliar one. Assume as a control that newborns not exposed to these milk pads would turn to one side half the time. Then the frequency of E in the control is 50 percent. For six-day-olds, the frequency is about 67 percent, so d = 17. For eight- to ten-day-olds, the frequency is more than 75 percent, so d = 25. Only this last result is statistically significant with a confidence level of 95 percent.

Answers to Review Questions

1. Looking for a common thread is typically more reliable than looking for a difference, because greater regularities will more often signal a cause of some event. It goes wrong mainly when the common thread binds together events that don't belong together: Then this is a case of assuming a common cause where there is none. Anyway, what a common thread reveals to us almost always needs to be verified or tested by another method (usually an argument from the only relevant difference). Because a group of objects or situations are likely to share more than one trait, each of their shared properties needs to be looked at separately before we can identify a cause. We ask of each property, "Does this distinguish between a case where the feature in question is present and a case in which it is absent?" That is, we look for an only relevant difference.

2. In both cases, one spots a true connection between two events. In both cases, one gets the specifics of the connection wrong, by taking an effect to be a cause. The difference is that ignoring a possible common cause leaves the true cause undiscovered, whereas reversing causation misidentifies the cause as the effect.

3. We use the size of the experimental group, assuming that the control group is roughly the same size. The size of the experimental group gives us the size that d must be in order to ensure statistically significant results.

4. We do nonexperimental studies most often because experiments would be unethical. Thus they tend to be studies of human beings and their health or well-being. Nonexperimental studies are inherently weaker than experiments, because they cannot isolate a single causal factor. It is impossible to know in advance what all the relevant factors might be, and we can fall into the trap of ignoring a possible common cause. In practical terms, nonexperimental studies require more stringent selection of groups and adjustment for possible bias.

5. The two kinds of argument require similar evidence: more than one example of situations relevant to the feature in question. They differ in that the argument from difference has to start with a situation in which Y is present and a situation in which Y is absent; the argument from a common thread needs more than one situation in which Y is present. As for cautions, both arguments need to be made with attention to the possibility that other relevant causes will fit the criterion (of difference or common thread). But the argument from common thread must also consider the possibility that the occurrences of Y have separate, unrelated causes.

CHAPTER 13

MORAL, LEGAL, AND AESTHETIC REASONING

Although you can put critical thinking to work in any discussion on any subject, some matters call for the especially conscious, especially focused application of the skills and methods found in this book. Those tend to be matters concerning essentially unclear or essentially disputable ideas. Of course a disagreement in biology or history can take years to settle; and we can debate the best way to sole a shoe, scramble eggs, or tile a floor, with plenty of opportunities for vagueness and miscommunication. But these kinds of disputes, however heated or protracted, don't have the air of impossibility that surround conversations about moral, legal, or aesthetic issues.

Chapter 13 will therefore tackle the arguments that most often arise around such issues, covering essential vocabulary and the main general positions proper to each domain. The section on moral reasoning defines prescriptive claims and identifies the role of facts in moral arguments. Several frameworks show the varieties of justification we can make for a given view, or the varieties of criticism we can use against it.

In our treatment of legal reasoning, we first set it apart from moral reasoning, then examine philosophical attempts to justify laws, and practical attempts to clarify and apply those same laws.

Discussions of art raise a different assortment of issues. For one thing, reasonable arguments aim at showing something about art as much as at persuading. For another thing, aesthetic arguments take more diverse forms than moral and legal ones; those forms need to be differentiated from one another, so that we know when one argument is relevant to another.

You should treat this chapter as the beginning of what comes after a course in critical thinking. The specific examples here will call on skills covered in Chapters 1–12. The individual skills are already in place; what's left is seeing which to use where.

CHAPTER SUMMARY

I.   **Moral reasoning** is any reasoning we do in response to a **moral issue.**

   A. Moral issues arise when we wonder what we should do, what someone else should do, or whether a situation is right or fair. Examples include:

      1.   "Should I call for an ambulance about that man asleep on the sidewalk?"

      2.   "Should my boss criticize us in front of each other?"

      3.   "Is it appropriate to let adult bookstores operate in any commercial area they choose?"

B. Moral reasoning includes, but is not limited to, arguments for the claim that a person should do something. It amounts to all reasoning of morally relevant matters.

   1. You may consider what possibilities for action are open to the person: "I can call for the ambulance, but the nearest phone takes me two blocks out of my way; or I can do nothing and hope that someone else calls."

   2. You may weigh the consequences of one action rather than another: "Criticizing us in front of each other makes us all more eager to work well; but it also spoils the mood of the workplace."

   3. You may describe a situation as right or wrong without reaching a decision about action: "Having adult bookstores on every corner is the sign of a sick society."

   4. Finally, you may reason your way to a decision: "I ought to call our neighbor and admit that I broke her window."

C. Even people who believe the general claim that morality comes down to matters of pure opinion employ one or more of these forms of reasoning at one time or other.

II. The conclusions of moral arguments about action are **prescriptive claims;** for this reason, such arguments must contain prescriptive claims among their premises too.

A. Prescriptive claims make the essential difference between moral reasoning and other sorts of reasoning.

   1. A prescriptive claim (value judgment) praises or condemns a person, action, or situation; it prescribes an action to take, a goal to seek, a kind of person to become.

      a. "You should stay quiet when Mom's on the phone."

      b. "The purpose of all public policy should be the maximization of personal liberty."

      c. "She's very brave to speak her mind at our meetings without worrying about getting fired."

   2. Prescriptive claims stand opposed to **descriptive claims,** which assert what is taken to be a fact without passing judgment on its value.

      a. "He's quiet when Mom's on the phone."

      b. "The purpose of all public policy is decided by the legislative branch."

      c. "She speaks her mind at our meetings without worrying about getting fired."

   3. Claims may be prescriptive and not moral. Any evaluation counts as a prescriptive claim.

      a. "That bus exhaust is disgusting."

      b. "*Middlemarch* is the perfect English novel." This is an aesthetic judgment.

B. Note that while prescriptive claims typically contain certain words, those words don't necessarily make a claim prescriptive.

   1. The words include "good," "bad," "right," "wrong," "ought," "should."

   2. "The taxi should be here any minute": no prescription.

   3. "Running from home to third base is a wrong move": again, nothing prescriptive about that claim.

C. A valid argument with a prescriptive conclusion must have at least one prescriptive premise. No claim with a moral "ought" follows from claims with only "is."

   1. Although this principle is still controversial, it makes a good guide to forming moral arguments.

   2. The **naturalistic fallacy** consists in assuming some facts to imply a prescriptive claim.

   3. For example: "Your stereo is so loud that the downstairs neighbors are getting stomachaches. You ought to turn it down." This is an invalid argument.

      a. It becomes valid with the addition of a premise: "You shouldn't enjoy music at a volume that gives other people stomachaches."

      b. That additional premise must be prescriptive.

   4. This added premise may seem obvious. But that only explains why we normally don't say it. We still *assume* such a premise when making a good moral argument.

   5. Making such premises explicit often helps us evaluate moral arguments.

   6. "Your mother begged you to go to medical school. So you should go." Another invalid argument.

      a. It becomes valid when we add the premise "You should do whatever your mother begs you to do."

      b. Now you see the operative principle at work and may want to contest it.

III. **Inconsistency** is a fault in moral reasoning, regardless of which moral framework one uses.

A. In one form of moral inconsistency, we treat one member of a group differently from another.

   1. For example: You distribute Halloween candy to most children who come to your door, but not to ones you take a sudden and unexplained disliking to.

   2. Moral inconsistency resembles logical inconsistency, in that we implicitly say "All X are Y" but "Some X are not Y."

   3. This form of moral inconsistency is clearly unfair.

4. Equally unfair, though not exactly inconsistent, is a practice that treats different cases as if they were alike: paying equal wages to employees who arrive promptly every day and to those who take many unexcused days off.

B. Another form of inconsistency consists in judging similar moral situations differently.

1. You may disapprove of gambling but not of Bingo.

2. This does not amount to unfairness, because no human being is necessarily being mistreated.

3. Whether or not it is true inconsistency is often hard to settle in practice.

4. The burden of proof lies with the person who appears to hold inconsistent views, to show that the situations are in fact different from each other.

IV. Moral reasoning does not typically rest on such straightforward principles; rather, people use a framework or perspective to ground their arguments.

A. **Relativism** holds that right and wrong depend on the beliefs of one's culture.

1. People sometimes act as if relativism followed from the fact that different groups have different moral beliefs.

2. But the mere fact of such disagreement might just as easily mean that one group is wrong.

a. It is one thing to assert that other people, or other nationalities, think differently from us. No one could deny that claim.

b. There is a huge leap, however, from that claim to the claim that the others are right when they think differently from us.

3. Taken to its extreme, relativism becomes subjectivism, which makes right and wrong matters of individual opinion. (See Chapter 5 on the subjectivist fallacy.)

4. Such views provide no guidance in settling moral issues. When two groups or persons disagree about right and wrong, we are left calling a single action both right and wrong.

B. **Utilitarianism** evaluates all actions in terms of the happiness they produce.

1. Utilitarianism (like other approaches to moral reasoning) considers only the consequences of actions.

2. It narrows down those consequences to happiness, so its rule becomes: Maximize happiness and minimize unhappiness.

3. In practice, you apply utilitarianism by trying to predict how much happiness each available option will lead to:

a. How many people will be affected by each action you might take?

b. How strongly will they be affected? (Two people's extreme delight normally outweighs the mild satisfaction of four.)

c. How certain are you of each prediction? (The more reliable a prediction, the more weight its outcome gets. A bird in the hand.)

d. Have you counted each person as equally open to happiness? (Of course, the better you know people, the surer you are of what will please them; and you are surest of all about what will please you.)

4. Other people's joy being a fine goal to pursue, utilitarianism has an obvious appeal.

5. But in many specific cases, it yields unsatisfying or false results.

6. Utilitarianism pays no attention to intrinsic human rights, or to moral duties that make no difference to happiness.

7. It also pays no attention to people's motives when evaluating their actions. Consequences make an action right or wrong, regardless of what the person meant to do.

C. Kant's **duty theory** can be thought of as the denial of utilitarianism on each weak point. It bases morality on duty.

1. Whereas utilitarianism neglects human rights and intrinsically binding duties and downplays the relevance of motive, duty theory bases all rightness on duty and makes rights inviolable, and calls motive the only relevant issue.

2. Kant distinguishes between hypothetical and categorical imperatives, calling only the latter moral commands.

a. An imperative is any claim about what we should do.

b. Hypothetical imperatives tell what we ought to do in order to reach some desired end.

c. "You should fulfill contractual obligations if you want to get more clients."

d. Categorical imperatives have an unconditional quality, commanding certain behavior regardless of its consequences, only because it is right.

3. For this reason, the only moral acts are those that follow a categorical imperative with no motive but the act's rightness.

a. Specifically, you must act from the motive of moral duty.

b. It even helps to have no other motives that would incline you to perform the action.

4. We determine the content of duty by applying the test of universalization. Can you want the principle you're acting from to be a universal moral law?

5. You consider lying in some situation. You ask yourself, "Can I want to make the acceptability of lying a universal principle?" No, because making a lie universally permissible means making reliable communication impossible—in which case lying (which presupposes a general adherence to the truth) stops bringing any benefits.

6. In other words, a moral system that smiled on lies would be a system under which lies accomplish nothing: You'd be asking for a system in which your contemplated selfish lie wouldn't help you be selfish.

7. Kant's analysis tries to show what is logically wrong with making yourself an exception to moral rules.

8. The differences between duty theory and utilitarianism go beyond theory: The two disagree on the rightness of certain specific actions.

   a. For example: With no one around, you promise to scatter a dying friend's ashes in the ocean. Do you have to? Duty theory says yes; utilitarianism can't see why.

   b. Living in a police state, you find a revolutionary friend coming to hide in your house; then the police knock and ask if you know where she is. Do you lie? Utilitarianism says yes; duty theory won't let you.

9. Kant gives another test for moral duties: Never treat other people merely as means to an end. (Don't use people.)

   a. Kant calls this test equivalent to the universalization test.

   b. Seeing people as ends in themselves supports a view of inalienable rights.

D. **Divine command theory** traces the rightness of actions to God's commands.

   1. It is a type of general command duty theory, the view that moral duties are determined by an authority's orders.

   2. One problem with applying divine command theory is the problem of knowing just what God commands.

      a. Even if you accept a book (Bible, Koran) as God's word, it often needs to be interpreted.

      b. Then we have to agree on who interprets the book.

   3. A more philosophical problem concerns cause and effect: Is what is right right because God commands it, or does God command it because it is right?

      a. On the first alternative, God's commands look arbitrary: Drug dealing could be as splendid as volunteer work in hospitals, if God chose to will it.

      b. On the second alternative, moral principles have their value whether or not God commands them, as if they stood above God.

E. Unlike all the preceding theories, **virtue ethics** focuses not on (right and wrong) acts, but on (good and bad) character.

　　1. The goal of life is not to do certain things, but to be a certain kind of person.

　　2. Virtue ethics was the dominant mode of moral reasoning in ancient Greece.

　　3. Good action follows from a balanced and moderate character that knows how to respond to any situation.

　　4. Aristotle identifies and analyzes the virtues that make up a good life.

　　　　a. Wisdom, self-control, and generosity appear on his list, along with many others.

　　　　b. Each virtue is an appropriately moderate response standing somewhere between two extremes or vices: Generosity avoids both stinginess and wastefulness.

　　　　c. Virtue is also a solid and reliable character trait, that is, a habit.

　　5. Virtue theory gets its appeal from our common wish to be good people, and our frequent practice of approaching problems with the thought, "What would X do?"

　　6. Its main failing is that such a question does not always help us think through an ethical predicament.

V. Moral deliberation uses the insights of these various perspectives to clarify the ethical meaning of an act or situation.

A. People tend not to realize how much moral reasoning they use.

　　1. Real-world deliberation incorporates elements of several perspectives: We think about making people happy, about universal principles, about what admirable people would do.

　　2. The flaws in moral thinking also recall errors we have studied: logical slips, fallacies, unfounded causal claims.

B. We make progress in moral reasoning by first identifying the perspective at work in an argument.

　　1. If we see that our reasoning rests on divine command theory, for instance, we should ask whether we want that theory to settle all moral issues.

　　2. When more than one moral theory delivers the same answer, keeping the theories distinct helps us clarify which details of a case are the morally relevant ones.

C. Ultimately, each of these frameworks can be defended and attacked on abstract grounds, with theoretical arguments. Much of philosophical ethics is about discovering the best framework for moral reasoning.

VI. **Legal reasoning** addresses itself both to the foundation of all law in general and to the interpretation of specific laws.

   A. In some respects, but not all, legal reasoning resembles moral reasoning.

   1. Both are prescriptive, though the commands of law come with clear social enforcement behind them.

   2. The content of moral and legal claims overlaps.

      a. Most laws square with morality, outlawing practices we consider immoral: theft, assault, rape, fraud, and so on.

      b. But some immoral actions are not illegal, such as breaking a promise (other than a promise in a contract) or making fun of the way someone talks.

      c. And some laws concern nonmoral matters, such as laws about what businesses you can operate in a certain neighborhood.

   B. One main question within legal studies, the more philosophical question, asks what the law should be, how it should be formed, and what principles it should rest on. There are four central lines of argument:

   1. **Legal moralism** is the position that the law should prohibit anything immoral.

      a. On these grounds, prostitution should be illegal because it is morally wrong.

      b. The legal moralist could also argue against legal access to divorce.

   2. According to the **harm principle,** the law should only prohibit activities that harm others.

      a. Here prostitution would be outlawed only because those engaging in it could spread diseases to their unwary sexual partners.

      b. In most ways, the harm principle leads to the smallest number of laws, and the greatest limitation on their scope.

   3. **Legal paternalism** goes beyond the harm principle in also justifying laws that keep people from harming themselves.

      a. Because prostitution can bring harm to both the prostitutes and their customers, paternalism would argue for its prohibition.

      b. Laws that limit the hours in which bars may open (e.g., on Sunday mornings) also get their justification through paternalistic considerations.

      c. This is the principle that we stop people from behaving a certain way for their own good.

   4. Partly overlapping with legal moralism, the **offense principle** gives a society the right to ban activities that are generally found offensive.

a. Again there are grounds for outlawing prostitution, since one could argue that most people find its practice offensive.

b. One would argue against the right of members of the Nazi party to march in a public demonstration on these grounds.

C. The other main question within legal studies, the more practical one, asks what the law says and how it should be interpreted.

1. Such questions inevitably arise, partly because any law must be stated in broad terms, and partly because no human legislator can predict all the situations that might arise.

   a. For example, fraud is defined in terms of what a reasonable person would believe on the basis of someone's claim; we sometimes have to decide whether an actual person's belief is reasonable.

   b. Legal interpretation thus addresses itself to issues of vagueness (see Chapter 2).

2. Arguments about the application of a law may be, like other arguments, deductive or inductive, valid or invalid in the former case and strong or weak in the latter.

3. Many important legal arguments involve an **appeal to precedent,** in which one uses an established judicial decision to interpret a new case.

4. Appeals to precedent are based on the desire for consistency, the similar treatment of similar situations.

5. The claim that two cases are similar rests on an analogical argument (see Chapter 11), in which the settled case is the sample and the new case the target.

VII. We use **aesthetic reasoning** to defend or criticize judgments about art, usually with one of the following eight aesthetic principles.

A. Objects are aesthetically valuable if they have a meaning or teach something true.

1. This principle identifies value in art with its ability to fulfill cultural or social functions.

2. Typically, this view finds a teaching in art that nonart cannot provide.

3. For example: "This soap opera makes you think about what you'd do in this situation, without having to live through it."

B. Objects are aesthetically valuable if they express the values of the cultures they arise in, or the artists who make them.

1. This principle also identifies value with art's ability to fulfill cultural or social functions.

2. Note that you don't have to believe what the object says, or take it to have argued for that value.

3. "The *Iliad* makes a warrior's values vivid."

C. Objects are aesthetically valuable if they can lead to social change.

1. This is the third principle that identifies value with art's ability to fulfill cultural or social functions.

2. In this case, you need to believe that the social change is an improvement.

3. "*The Jungle* led to reform of meat-packing laws."

D. Objects are aesthetically valuable if they give their audience pleasure.

1. This principle connects aesthetic value to a thing's ability to produce a type of psychological experience.

2. We can put this a little more broadly by saying that the art object contributes to our happiness.

3. "*Four Weddings and a Funeral* brings pure delight."

E. Objects are aesthetically valuable if they give their audience certain emotions.

1. This principle, like the last one, connects value to a thing's ability to produce a type of psychological experience.

2. We may not want to have those emotions aroused in daily life, but we still value art for awakening them.

3. "*The Blair Witch Project* keeps you on the edge of your seat with terror."

F. Objects are aesthetically valuable if they produce a special experience that comes only from art, such as the willing suspension of disbelief.

1. Again, aesthetic value comes down to the production of a certain subjective state.

2. You may think of the state as nonemotional, or as a special art-emotion.

3. "*Lolita* is so perfectly constructed that it made me feel as though I were writing it."

4. Like all the other principles described so far, this one connects aesthetic value to a function that art has.

G. Objects are aesthetically valuable if they possess a special aesthetic (formal) property.

1. No explicit reference to function comes into this principle, though it may enter when one defines aesthetic form.

2. In its simplest form, this principle identifies the aesthetic property with beauty; more complex versions speak of artistic unity and organization.

3. *"Harlem Airshaft* begins with a simple melody, breaks it down into its elements, and reorganizes them in a surprising new form: Every part gets beautifully reinterpreted."

H. Objects are aesthetically valuable because of features that no reasons can determine, and that no argument can establish.

　　1. This principle corresponds to moral subjectivism: There's nothing to say in reasoned discourse about tastes.

　　2. Roughly, this is the view that an object is aesthetically valuable if someone values it.

VIII. Aesthetic reasoning employs one or more of those eight principles in the attempt to produce reliable grounds for an aesthetic judgment.

A. We can sometimes appeal to more than one principle in a single argument, but not always.

　　1. It is easy to unite the first and the third principles, and believe that an object gets its value both from teaching something important about morality and from (thereby) influencing us to become better people.

　　2. Other principles contradict each other at the theoretical level, as when the special nonemotional experience of the sixth principle conflicts with the claim of ordinary emotional experience in the fifth.

　　3. Two principles may agree theoretically, but lead to disagreements in particular cases. You can value both social change and pleasure; but an enjoyably fluffy television show becomes good on the second criterion and bad on the first.

B. Objects are evaluated positively according to a given criterion if they satisfy its requirements, negatively if they don't.

C. A good argument supports an aesthetic judgment by describing features of a work, as long as they are both relevant and true.

　　1. The relevance of a feature depends on the aesthetic principles one believes.

　　2. Features must also have descriptive truth: You can't say, "This movie gets its socially educational value by depicting every stratum of U.S. society," if the film only has three characters—a married couple and their child.

IX. Aesthetic principles may not have the foundation that moral or legal principles do, but they nevertheless contribute to aesthetic experience.

A. On some views, aesthetic principles try to capture the definition (see Chapter 2) of aesthetic value.

　　1. These principles effectively teach the language of art.

　　2. But we must recognize that innovation in art can lead us to expand our definitions of its value.

B. On another view, aesthetic principles are inductive generalizations (see Chapter 11) of the features of objects we have called good art.

   1. In that case, applying such principles to new objects amounts to making an analogical argument, with accepted works of art as our sample and the new ones our target.

   2. Because art does change, however, we can find ourselves making analogies among dissimilar things.

C. Even if these two accounts work together, the changes in art may make general principles seem inadequate to the process of evaluation.

D. We may agree that aesthetic principles are not true claims and still use them to guide our experience.

   1. In that case, aesthetic arguments have emotive force.

   2. The argument directs our attention to certain features of a work in order to influence our reaction to it.

   3. Even without being true, claims can be worded more or less successfully, depending on their clarity, relevance, and so on.

E. What matters more than aesthetic principles, then, are the features of a given work that the principles draw our attention to.

   1. So we can use the principles to focus our reaction to a given work, noticing features we might not have looked for.

   2. We can then incorporate those features into an argument that effectively recommends to other people that they focus their own reactions in a similar way.

KEY WORDS AND IDEAS

Aesthetic reasoning. Any reasoning that aims at defending or criticizing a judgment about art.

Appeal to precedent. In legal reasoning, the use of an established court case to argue for an interpretation of the law in a similar case. Appeals to precedent entail analogical arguments.

Descriptive claim. As opposed to a prescriptive claim, an assertion about a clear matter of fact.

Divine command theory. A moral theory or framework according to which actions are right or wrong because of God's commands. Stealing is wrong because the Ten Commandments prohibit it.

Duty theory. A moral theory or framework, especially connected with Kant, according to which actions are right or wrong because of their inherent content, and the motive (namely duty) from which they are done. Stealing is wrong principally because we can't make taking property a universal law.

Harm principle. A justification for laws against some action: The action must harm other people. We are right to ban false advertising, not because it is a lie, but because it can mislead people to their detriment.

Inconsistency. In moral matters, the treatment of some people differently from others for no relevant reason, or the belief that one action or situation is morally permissible while a similar one is not.

Legal moralism. A justification for laws against some action: The action must be immoral. We are right to limit private sexual behavior, because certain behaviors are wrong.

Legal paternalism. A justification for laws against some action: The action harms the person who does it. We are right to forbid drug use, because it degrades and incapacitates the user.

Legal reasoning. Argumentation about either the foundation of all law or the interpretation of specific laws.

Moral issue. Any issue concerning how one ought to behave, how others ought to behave, or whether a situation is proper or improper.

Moral reasoning. Any reasoning about a moral issue. Moral reasoning includes arguments about what one should or shouldn't do, but also considerations of available options, and all similar deliberation about morally relevant matters.

Naturalistic fallacy. In moral reasoning, the mistake of assuming a set of descriptive claims to imply a prescriptive claim.

Offense principle. A justification for laws against some action: The action offends most people. This principle overlaps in practice with legal moralism. We are right to ban the public display of blasphemous art, because most people find it offensive.

Prescriptive claim. A claim that prescribes action or otherwise evaluates a person, action, or situation; a value judgment. "You should find that bike's rightful owner and return it." We distinguish prescriptive claims from descriptive ones.

Relativism. A moral theory or framework according to which actions are right or wrong because of the beliefs of one's culture or group. Stealing is wrong because our culture doesn't like it.

Utilitarianism. A moral theory or framework, especially connected with Mill, according to which actions are right or wrong because of the total happiness they bring about. Stealing is wrong because it makes more people more unhappy than a rule against stealing does.

Virtue ethics. A moral theory or framework, especially connected with Aristotle, according to which ethical value inheres in people's virtues. Virtue ethics focuses not on actions but on good and bad character. Stealing is wrong because the person of balanced character would not give in to the temptation to steal.

1. According to Kant, how do you test an action to see if you have a duty to do it?

2. What questions would you ask yourself when evaluating an action on utilitarian grounds?

3. What would legal moralism, legal paternalism, and the harm principle say about laws banning cigarette advertising on television?

4. What two broad categories do most aesthetic principles fall into?

5. Describe and defend a function for aesthetic arguments other than persuading someone of an aesthetic judgment.

COMMONLY ASKED QUESTIONS

What's wrong with using tolerance as an ethical principle, and then not having to go through the process of moral reasoning?

No one can deny the beauty of tolerance, nor the pinched and unfree quality of life in intolerant societies. But even beautiful virtues have their limits, and making tolerance our single dominant virtue will leave us without answers to important questions.

Everyone acknowledges that tolerating actions has its limits: We don't sit back condoning crime just because someone else chooses to value it. Instead, you might say, we permit whatever does not hurt someone else. Why this distinction? Where do we get the ethical principle that hurting other people is wrong, but nothing else is? Well, no one wants to be hurt. But plenty of people also don't want to see what offends or annoys them; how do you keep the principle of not hurting without adopting the principle of not offending?

Theorists on all sides have proposed answers to that question. The point is that toleration *needs* defending, that it does not reveal its truth to all onlookers. And even as a social virtue, tolerance does not settle all matters. If intolerance means simply *calling* someone's actions wrong (as opposed to arresting or striking the person), why shouldn't that act of moral judgment be tolerated as well? How can toleration justify its own standing as an ethical principle, as long as intolerance doesn't hurt anyone?

Then the greater problem. We tend to think of ethics as a way of judging other people's actions. And no wonder, when most public discussions of morality condemn sexual practices, music, medical decisions, and so on. But we also rely on ethical reasoning to make decisions about what we should do. And here toleration is vacuous: It can't help you make a decision when you're genuinely perplexed about what you ought to do. Consider these questions:

> Should I visit my friend's terminally ill mother?
> Should I commit adultery, just this once, when no one will know about it?
> Should I keep this envelope full of money that I found in a phone booth?

When someone you know tries to reach answers to these questions, you may decide to accept whatever conclusion that person comes to: In this respect tolerance gives an answer, if not always a good answer. When the questions are your own, toleration leads you nowhere. At most you may reassure yourself that whatever you decide is right; but when you're in an ethical quandary that answer will not satisfy you.

What's the point of having principles that justify the law, when the law already exists and has binding force?

Since laws already exist, it may seem beside the point to find theories that justify them. We still have to obey unjustified laws; why waste time talking?

Here we should note an important difference between moral and legal frameworks: Moral frameworks agree with one another to a much greater degree when we get to specific cases.

Sometimes duty theory and utilitarianism, for instance, conflict dramatically. Utilitarians see no consequences to breaking a secret promise, while duty theorists refuse to allow it. But all these frameworks are sophisticated enough, in their completed versions, to agree with most of our existing intuitions about right and wrong. After all, we don't go to a moral theory for surprising results, but for an explanation of what we already believe.

Principles of legal justification, on the other hand, point to very different conceptions of society, and so yield very different answers to particular cases. Should we require drivers to wear seat belts? Paternalism says yes, the harm principle says no, and moralism says nothing. Should cocaine have the legal status of alcohol? The harm principle may say yes; moralism and paternalism give an unequivocal no.

Speaking roughly, we might say that legal moralism envisions a society that reinforces moral principles; that the harm principle wants society to keep us from hurting each other, but otherwise to leave us alone; that legal paternalism is working toward a society that takes care of its citizens; and that the offense principle adds to other considerations the dream of a society in which no one has to suffer offense. Leaving aside this last case, we find ourselves with three distinct visions of what government should do and be.

Two things follow. First, we use these legal principles in deciding whether to vote for a proposed law (or whether to vote for a candidate who wants to pass that law). As the different principles lead to quite different conclusions, it matters which one we adopt.

Second, each of these principles—insofar as it implies a view of what society should be—is embedded within a more general political philosophy, a picture of what makes government legitimate, what purposes a government ought to serve. Every responsible citizen should participate in public life: voting, of course, but also joining in open debate, serving on juries, writing to elected officials, and so on. And participating responsibly means acting on the basis of political principles. So thinking about what justifies a given law is part of a larger process of taking part in the public life of one's society.

How do I know which aesthetic principles to use in a given situation, or in general?

A serious answer to this question could only begin with a course on aesthetics. Especially since the eighteenth century, but also for thousands of years before that, philosophers have debated the meaning of art and the right criteria for evaluating it. But before taking that plunge, you may use two methods for choosing among aesthetic principles that you can then apply to particular works.

We have already encountered a reason for the first method: Aesthetic principles sometimes conflict with one another. The social and ethical effects of a work of art either matter to an aesthetic judgment or do not. We can't adopt all these principles. So as a first step you should identify those principles that cannot be held simultaneously, and choose among them. Does aesthetic judgment come down to an experience that no one can reason about? Then don't use any of the other principles.

You have now narrowed down your list of aesthetic principles, but probably not by much. The second step (assuming, again, that you want to put off the commitment of a course on aesthetics, or an armload of books) begins with those works of art that you can use as definite test cases. Compile a list of those objects whose value as works of art you consider undeniable. (No one's perfect, and someday you may quickly deny what you now deem undeniable; but this is a place to start.) Ask which aesthetic principles best fit the value of those works. If you find your list packed with art you find emotionally stirring, you probably have an allegiance to (5). If you gravitate toward works that seem to teach something deep, then (1) has worked as one of your guiding ideas. You are reasoning backwards from your most solid aesthetic commitments to principles that you can then apply in less certain cases.

Of course, there is more to aesthetic judgment than adhering consciously to ideas that have been guiding you vaguely. But at least this way of clarifying your own assumptions will keep you from falling into immediate and blatant inconsistency. You won't get caught praising a movie for its intrinsic significant form, when all the other movies you've called great owe their merit to their social conscience.

TIPS ON APPLICATIONS

It is hard to give advice about applications for this chapter. Applications are its whole purpose. Chapter 13 has failed if you are left curious about where in daily life to apply it.

Still, think about one thing. You have no doubt noticed—maybe with frustration—that Chapter 13 has a different tone and texture from that of all the preceding chapters. At every turn the methods we use (e.g., the critique of a moral position as inconsistent) are acknowledged to be hard to apply, open to further debate, far from the last word on the subject. And though we have frameworks for organizing our moral, legal, or aesthetic reasoning, each framework appears alongside several others that contradict it. How can a moral perspective simplify our deliberations if we then have to deliberate about which framework to adopt?

There's no mystery here. Chapters 1–12 have isolated certain elements of critical thinking to make them easier to see. Each chapter's exercises give real-world examples of the points they illustrate; still, those examples are artificially simplified to fit into a given chapter. You now return to the buzzing confusion of daily life's critical thinking, in which examples arrive unaccompanied by hints about which methods to apply to them.

The right question is not whether a critical question leads you to decisive answers about any of these cases, but whether it lets you make progress on them. After all, you will probably never run a mile in less than four and a half minutes. But you will get closer to that elusive goal if you keep it as your ideal and if you train with a regimen designed to approach four and a half minutes. It is wise to expect as much from critical thinking: By showing what a complete and precise answer can be, it gets you as close to those answers as we can normally come, even if it does not reach them.

EXERCISES

Sample Exercises from the Book

13-1, 1. Marina's car runs terribly; she should get it tuned up.

Prescriptive claim. Note that this sentence in fact contains two prescriptive claims, signaled by the words "terribly" and "should." The first evaluates the running of the car, and the second recommends one line of action for Marina. Also notice that morality does not appear in either claim: It is prescriptive without concerning itself with ethics.

13-3, 2. When Sarah bought the lawn mower from Jean, she promised to pay another fifty dollars on the first of the month. Since it is now the first, Sarah should pay Jean the money.

People ought to keep their promises. This is a good point at which to observe something about prescriptive premises. You don't want to make them either too narrow or too broad. In this example, an excessively narrow premise would say, "People ought to keep their promises about paying for lawn mowers"; true enough, but not a general principle we carry around with us, and hence not a justification we can reach for in moral argumentation. An excessively broad premise would say, "People ought to do whatever they say they will." Such premises have the advantage of more clearly prescribing one course of action rather than another, but the disadvantage of being less likely to be true.

13-5, 3. Criticize affirmative action from a Kantian perspective.

As the hint suggests, the Kantian test to use here is the treatment of people only as means to an end, rather than also as ends in themselves. The critic of affirmative action can say that it denies some people's equal opportunity to get a job in the interests of promoting the social good of racial or gender equality; since that is an end to which we sacrifice the individual autonomy of some, it fails the test.

Note a couple of things. First, duty theory runs into the most trouble when two people's rights conflict with each other. A case like this one pits fairness toward one applicant against fairness toward another (since the point of affirmative action is to make sure that no one loses a job because of discrimination). When one of them will be treated merely as a means no matter what, we have no further test that will tell us what to do.

Second, you could work out a Kantian defense of affirmative action, depending on how you conceive that program. If affirmative action is designed to equalize opportunity, the emphasis on women and minority job candidates works against a built-in bias against them. Then the point is not to hire more women or minority candidates, but to give them the same chance everyone else has.

13-11, 4.   a.   Laurence Olivier's film production of *Hamlet* has merit because he allows us to experience the impact of the incestuous love that a son can feel for his mother.

       b.   Nevertheless, Olivier's *Hamlet* is flawed because it introduces a dimension inconceivable to an Elizabethan playwright.

(a) relies on principle 5, which you can arrive at as follows: The phrase "allows us to experience" shows that the audience's psychological reaction is the crucial element, so we choose from 4, 5, and 6. We eliminate principle 4 on the grounds that the impact of incestuous love is not a source of pleasure in healthy audiences; we eliminate principle 6 because "special non-emotional experiences" does not capture what (a) is saying.

(b) relies on principle 2, as the phrase "Elizabethan playwright" gives away. Only principle 2 clearly refers to what the artist feels or believes.

As for compatibility, the two principles may both be true. Indeed, they have very little to do with each other (and therefore have few chances to contradict each other). Principle 5 bases aesthetic judgment only on what happens to the audience, whereas principle 2 looks away from the audience to the artist alone. For this reason, the principles don't bump up against each other.

Additional Exercises

A. Moral reasoning: consistency. Are the views described in the following cases consistent or inconsistent? Explain.

     1.   Shem is morally opposed to hunting, whether he or anyone else does it. But he doesn't see any problem with fishing.

     2.   Helen is morally opposed to hunting, whether she or anyone else does it. But she doesn't see anything wrong with eating meat.

     3.   Shawn is morally opposed to wearing furs; but he eats meat.

     4.   Barbara thinks smoking marijuana is morally wrong. She doesn't see any moral issue surrounding alcohol consumption.

     5.   "Smokers with lung cancer get what they deserve," Alex said. "It's completely different when people driving their cars get into an accident. They're not necessarily to blame, and they should be treated with sympathy."

     6.   Erin says: "Sexism is wrong. Widespread, too, because all men are sexist."

B. Moral reasoning: frameworks. Use two or more moral theories (frameworks) to derive answers to the following questions. Be on the lookout especiallly for cases in which two theories produce contradictory answers.

     1.   Should I commit adultery just this once, if no one will ever find out?

     2.   Should doctors help their terminally ill patients commit suicide by prescribing lethal doses of pain medication?

3. I really want to get pregnant, but my husband's against the idea. Should I stop using contraception and not tell him?

4. Should I give money to beggars?

5. Should I quit school and work part-time as a bartender? I'll make a lot less money and leave my talents undeveloped, but it'll give me a lot more free time.

C. Legal reasoning. For each of the following types of law, find one of the four grounds discussed in the text to justify it. If possible, find another ground for arguing against the law; or state that no such ground exists. Explain your reasoning where the answer is not obvious.

1. Laws against false advertising.

2. Laws limiting the amount you can collect in a liability suit (e.g., against a company that makes a defective product).

3. Laws against marrying your first cousin.

4. Laws against begging on a bus or subway.

5. Laws requiring all public transportation to be wheelchair-accessible. (Such laws would not permit, for instance, the alternative of special cars or vans to chauffeur people in wheelchairs wherever they want to go.)

6. Laws requiring all cigarette packages to come with warnings about the dangers of smoking.

D. Aesthetic reasoning. For each of the following types of objects, first (a) classify it as clearly a work of art, clearly not a work of art, or possibly one or the other. Then (b) find an aesthetic principle according to which the object might have aesthetic value.

1. a television drama

2. a television commercial

3. a subway car

4. a pair of jeans

5. a piano sonata

6. a landscaped piece of real estate

7. a urinal, turned upside down and signed, and entered in an art exhibition

8. the socks you are now wearing

9. a stack of Brillo boxes that look exactly like the commercially made boxes that Brillo actually comes in, but produced by an artist

10. your student ID card

11. the Pacific Ocean

Answers to Additional Exercises

(NOTE: The "answers" here will be less definitive than they were in any other chapter. Use them as guides to the methods you should be using.)

A. 1. Consistent, if what Shem objects to is not the killing of animals, but the pain that killing causes them. He will then have to argue that hunted animals have either a greater capacity to feel pain than fish, or a greater understanding of what is happening to them.

 2. Consistent, if what Helen objects to is not the killing of animals, but killing them for pleasure.

 3. Consistent, if what Shawn finds objectionable in wearing furs is that it is not necessary. But then he will have to argue that eating meat is necessary, or at least not as easily substituted for as fur coats are.

 4. Consistent, if part of Barbara's reason is that marijuana is illegal, and we have a moral reason to obey laws. Otherwise, she will have to argue that smoking marijuana has effects that drinking alcoholic beverages does not.

 5. Consistent, if Alex believes that driving a car is necessary in a way that smoking cigarettes is not. It won't do for him to say that smokers engage in the harmful action themselves, while drivers don't set out to do harm; for smokers also don't set out to harm themselves.

 6. Probably inconsistent; but it depends on what sexism is. If "sexism" means a belief that the two sexes are unequal in some way relevant to moral standing, this is probably sexist, since it makes all men morally worse than women in an important way. Note: Sexism must amount to more than any claim about differences between the sexes. (The average man is taller and heavier than the average woman; the average woman has a higher voice than the average man; and so on.)

B. 1. Simple utilitarianism would probably not condemn this action, unless a secret act of adultery could turn out to have harmful effects. Duty theory prohibits it: If you tried to universalize the principle, you'd be saying that there should be no such thing as marriage, which in turn would make the adultery impossible. Divine command theory appeals to the Ten Commandments to prohibit adultery. Virtue theory does not especially lend itself to an answer, as Aristotle says. (Adultery, according to him, can't be right regardless of the character of the person committing it, or the way in which one goes about it.)

 2. Utilitarianism would call this a right action, since it maximizes happiness. Duty theory can be interpreted to either condemn or condone it; likewise virtue ethics. It is hard to make a case for doctor-assisted suicide with a divine command theory.

 3. In developing a utilitarian answer, include considerations of the pleasure of existence that will come to the probable child. Duty theory would rule against this action as a case of lying, while virtue ethics would probably also rule against it as not an action

that an admirable person would take. The answer from divine command theory would entail complex interpretation of one's holy book.

4. Probably all four frameworks answer yes to this: utilitarianism because the money will make other people happier than its absence would hurt you; duty theory because you are treating others as ends in themselves and because the action passes the test of universalization; divine command theory most clearly, because most religions require giving to beggars; virtue theory, too, on the grounds that such giving displays generosity, a crucial virtue.

Notice one thing: Of the four frameworks, the last three support *some* amount of giving to beggars, but not an indefinitely large amount. Utilitarianism calls for you to give in large quantities, until you reach the point at which you become more unhappy than the beggars become happy.

5. This is probably the trickiest case. Duty theory would probably ban this decision, on the grounds that self-development is a universal duty; but the argument gets shaky. Utilitarianism more clearly would criticize the decision, since you are likely to improve the society around you by developing your talents to a degree that outweighs the pleasure a more idle life brings. Virtue theory very clearly criticizes it: Virtuous people make the most of their capacities. Finally, divine command theory might argue that one should always develop legitimate talents to their utmost.

C. 1. Justified by legal moralism (since lying is immoral), the harm principle (since false advertising can hurt the unwary), and legal paternalism (since people should be sheltered from unscrupulous types). No clear ground for arguing against the law.

2. Justified by legal moralism (if wanting an excessive settlement is greedy). The offense principle and legal paternalism are silent. The harm principle would weigh the benefits to companies being sued against the greater social good that might come of having companies worry more about lawsuits.

3. Justified by legal moralism (because this usually counts as incest) and perhaps by the offense principle (because the sight of such marriages may deeply offend others). Legal paternalism says nothing clear. Since the popular belief that such marriages produce disabled children has little truth behind it, the harm principle would work against this law.

4. Justified by the offense principle, on the grounds that people may be repelled by the sight of beggars. For similar reasons—for example, beggars produce an unsafe environment—the harm principle might also justify such laws. Both of the other frameworks are silent.

5. Justified most strongly by legal moralism. Equal access to public transportation contributes to one's sense of belonging in a community and so has moral justification. The only other framework that gives an answer is the harm principle, and its answer has to be worked out in detail. How much more are taxpayers hurt by the cost of changing all trains and buses than they would be by the cost of individual vans, cars, and drivers?

6. Justified clearly by legal moralism and legal paternalism. The harm principle would argue against such a law, on the grounds that everyone already knows what cigarettes do, and mandatory warnings amount to a penalty on cigarette manufacturers.

D. (Only (b) is answered here.)

1. May have aesthetic value according to principles 1, 2, 3, 4, 5, and 6. Principle 7 is hardest to justify in this case; principle 8 always lets something have aesthetic value.

2. May have aesthetic value according to principles 1, 2, 3 (maybe), 4, 5, and 8. Not 6, because advertising works against the suspension of disbelief and related experiences; probably not 7 either.

3. May have aesthetic value according to principle 2, if the layout of the car reflects democratic ideals; also principles 4 and 8.

4. May have aesthetic value according to principle 2, again if the jeans reflect ideals of work and human equality; maybe 7; and, of course, 8.

5. May have aesthetic value according to principles 4, 5, 6, 7, and 8. 1–3 are hardest to apply to pure music.

6. May have aesthetic value according to principles 1, 2, 4, 7, or 8.

7. May have aesthetic value according to principles 4, 7, or 8.

8. Principle 4 might work here; otherwise, only principle 8.

9. May have aesthetic value according to principles 1, 2, and 3 (since the Brillo boxes might express and teach something about modern technological life); also 4 and 8.

10. Only principles 4 and 8 would work here, neither of them perfectly.

11. Principles 1, 3, 4, and 5 could all work in arguments for the ocean's aesthetic value.

Answers to Review Questions

1. Kant offers two tests. The main test, universalization, requires that you observe the principle you're acting on in some situation (the "maxim," he calls it) and ask whether you could consistently want to make that a universal law of morality. The other test, which Kant considers identical, consists in asking whether you are treating other people merely as means to an end, or also as ends in themselves.

2. How many people would benefit from this action, as opposed to some available alternative? How much would they benefit in each case? How certain am I of the happiness that results in each instance? Am I counting each person as equal?

3. As it is not immoral to smoke, advertising that encourages smoking would also not be immoral, unless it aims at persuading children to begin the practice. So legal moralism would endorse such bans in limited fashion. Legal paternalism would strongly endorse such bans, since they help to protect people from their own tendency to smoke. The harm

principle, on the other hand, would work against these bans, since they do not outlaw any activity that directly harms others.

4. Most aesthetic principles fall into either (1) the category of principles that praise art for its social or ethical content or effect, or (2) the category of principles that praise art for its emotional effect on its audience.

5. Aesthetic arguments may lead someone to see a work of art in a new and valuable way. A persuasive, reasoned argument can alert its audience to features in a work that they may not have noticed. Because we tend to value the aesthetic experience, such arguments are significant even if they do not communicate and support an objectively true claim; if they enlarge or educate someone's taste, they are justified within the aesthetic realm.